MW01289475

MAGNET
ASS

AND THE STONE-COLD
TRUCK HUNTERS

*The story of Vietnam's
most impossible flight.*

A MEMOIR BY WILL CUNNINGHAM.
WITH PAUL PASTOR

ISBN-13: 978-1722194512
ISBN-10: 1722194510

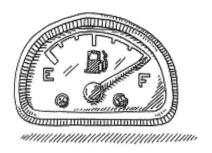

DEDICATION

In the pantheon of words unique to the military, one exists that catches the ear in a way the others don't, for it speaks of home and beckons the airman back across the fence to his warm bed in the barracks. The word is, "Bingo," and it means, "We have just enough gas to make it home."

This story is dedicated to Al and the truck hunters, and to the 1,353,000 children of God who perished in Vietnam between November 1, 1955 and April 30, 1975.

It was a war that resisted ending, barely defined by words.

CONTENTS

FOREWORD

Ask your children how long the Vietnam War lasted, and they will peer at you like codfish from a grocer's freezer. Ask yourself the same question, and your answer will have the effect of boiling water on a blood stain. Ask your parents, and you'll understand the power of secrecy.

So, it falls on me to tell you some secrets.

To begin, *Magnet Ass* is a very different memoir than you may have read in the past. It is a war story, but it is also *not* a war story. It has everything to do with a white-hot mission over the Plain of Jars in 1970, for which ten men earned one of history's most coveted aviation trophies. At the same time, it has *nothing* to do with any of that at all. It is gritty, and it is holy, sometimes full of shit and shrapnel – other times as demure as a duck flying over a pond in the dead of winter. It burst my gut to write it. Drew things out of me I wished had remained hidden. Bankrupted me nearly. Broke me entirely. It sings and it cries.

Secondly, you will struggle with this book if you are used to memoirs where the author remains out of sight. Early in the interview process, I realized Al's story intertwined eerily with mine. Thus, "I" am all over this memoir, something I'm told is never done in *normal* memoirs. In a very real sense, this is a "me-moir", a combination of the *auto* and *bio*graphical records of two men, who came to know and love each other deeply. Hopefully, it will be a "you-moir" by the time you're finished reading. Then, Magnet Ass will be your story, too.

But to be clear, this is still Magnet Ass Milacek's story, and he is *still* front and center, standing before the troops like the leader he has always been and always will be. He will hate me for saying this, but he remains the "hero" until the very last page.

Magnet Ass is wild and free, as are the characters who wrote the story with their lives back in 1970. When they weren't loading ammo in Magnet Ass's cannons, the truck hunters spent most of their time hanging out the cargo door of their AC–119K gunship by an inch-thick tether, watching for incoming artillery fire. Let me rephrase that last statement. Their *whole* job was shooting trucks while dodging bullets!

Let us speak no more of occupational hazards.

HISTORICAL PROLOGUE

Between the winter of 1968 and the spring of 1972, the United States military conducted a covert campaign against North Vietnamese forces along the key supply corridor known as the Ho Chi Minh trail. Vital to the success of the North Vietnamese Army, the trail, running from North Vietnam to South Vietnam through a small section of Laos, provided a daunting challenge to air forces tasked with preventing deadly resources from making it to their destination. Responding to a creative, adaptable foe, the US Air Force developed a series of slow, side-firing, fixed-wing gunships, lethally equipped for one specific task: hunting an endless convoy of trucks in the jungle, and the men who drove them in the dark.

   None of these planes made it back to US soil.

PART ONE

"OVER THE FENCE."

23:36 / 7 MAY / 1970

A battalion of sweat beads formed on the airman's neck and began a slow march down his spine. Down it rolled, over tight trapezoids, between scapula, past thoracic outposts, pushing to the smooth, umber plain of the lumbar region, until at last, the sweat reached the band of Ed Lopez's boxers, where it halted and reorganized itself as a clammy sop. It was the hot season in Laos. 104 degrees, sometimes. Even at night, even in the air, the heat was stifling.

A little shiver woke Lopez from thoughts of whiskey. The droning engines of Stinger 883 sounded far away; their vibration could be coming from under the jungle. He wiped the small of his back, then wondered where to wipe his hand.

They'd done this ninety-nine times before, but that didn't make it easier. Out of nervous habit, he checked his flares for the umpteenth time. Then the illuminator for good measure. Withering wind howled through the gunship's open doors, and in whistled the smells of flight. Lopez looked around. Jones pressed his headset against his ears, trying to douse the noise. Moisture beaded on everything, making the slick deck shine in the light of a ten-percent moon. Across the plane, Firestone was still fidgeting with his chest-pack parachute. *Damn the wonks who thought this model would be good for gunners to wear! All it does is get in the way.* He took the pack off and pitched it on top of the ammo racks with Wilson and Cofer's chutes, where any sudden maneuver by Al up behind the yoke could send them all (men and packs alike) fluttering out into the stars.

Mother Moon peeked through the door to scold the boys for not taking better care of themselves. Her pale and pumpkin features threw an eerie glow in the plane's coffin-shaped cabin, suspended several thousand feet above the tangled floor of the world.

The gunship flew on. Damp turned to wet. Within half an hour, 883 acquired Route 7. Below them in the dark, the Plain of Jars began to stretch away. Al worked his way further northeast in a random search pattern. As they approached Ban Ban, Jones' NOS spotted a convoy. Five trucks. They moved like red ants along the trail, just west of the intersection with Route 6.

"I've got a mover."

"Roger that," concurred Russell. "Magnet Ass, you're cleared to engage."

With a squeeze of his index finger, Al sent a hail of crimson earthward, waggled his wings to expand his target area, and waited for the usual explosion from the road below the tracers. Blackness.

He fired again. Nothing.

"Something's up, Clance," said Magnet Ass, through his head-set. Roger Clancy checked the computers, to see if they were synchronized with Al's 20mm guns.

Lopez, listening, licked his lips. God, he was thirsty.

"Hold tight, boss," said Clancy. "I'll try to adjust the offset. Could be the bore sights are screwy. We can go with FLIR tonight, if that'll help. You good with that, Jones?"

"I'll have to be," said Jones, hopping mad at tonight's unchar-acteristic impotence. He knew Clancy was right, though. Compared to his NOS, Russell's infrared was less affected by bright light. And the fires already erupting in the jungle below were certainly bright. Still, he was pissed. *They're in plain sight,* he thought. *And so are we. We better shoot them before they start shooting us.*

"We got a twenty out of ammo!" called Cofer, suddenly.

What else could go wrong? thought Jones. He looked at Wilson, who was spotting AAA at the adjacent doorway. With a jerk of his head he ordered his pal to reload. Wilson grabbed two ammo cans and turned toward the guns on the port side of the deck.

His fingers, slick with moisture, weren't moving fast enough. Every man on deck held his breath, knowing at any moment the ground could spit fire back at them.

Al circled, drawing perpendicular to the convoy again. "You got bullets for me, boys?" he asked.

"Number-two 'twenty' online, sir," said Firestone, breathing hard.

"Any luck with the computer, Clance?"

"One more tweak, Al."

"We're dawdling, men – I don't care for dawdling."

"He's at your ten," said Obie.

"I know, I know."

"Cleared to fire!" said Clancy.

With a flick of his finger, Al destroyed the lead truck. The crew let out a war whoop. They were back in the saddle. Continuing his pylon turn, Al gave the same business to the last truck in the column, bookending the three remaining vehicles with smoke and flame. One more burst of red metal, and a third truck disintegrated. Al zeroed in on the fourth truck.

But as the sights lined up, Mother Moon looked down and shook her head.

In the moment just before the blast, Al was thinking of home. He remembered the wheat field to the south of his house in Waukomis, bulging gold and begging to be harvested. The heads rustled in the sun, dry with the color of Vietnam moonlight. Pat and the girls hung laundry on the line. Pat laughed, but there was something hollow and missing in her voice. A buttery sun melted on the horizon. Across the road, a meadowlark whistled in that way they often do:

Come further! Come further!
I'm here, across the lane!
Come – come – come – come!
Further on and find me!

The whole crew was lost with Al in a brief flicker of images ... the newspaper Jones had read that afternoon ... Firestone's cheery boat ride from the Siri Udorn hotel to the base ... farmers driving cartloads of sugar cane ... cute Thai girls carrying Don Ganh baskets, waving at Lopez as if they knew him ... silk, saki, the smell of roasting pork ... Buddhist priests in saffron robes, rivaled by flowers sold on crowded sidewalks ... a dozen remnants of beauty that hung for a moment outside of time ... then were suddenly torn by ripping gunfire from the ground.

Bullets from below hailed around ten men dressed in drab Nomex.

Then began the shouting, and the clenched teeth, and the muttered prayers, and the real sweating, and Al's arms straining against the yoke. Then, though they'd been in the air for hours, their real flight started, one that would land them in the historic annals of a war that most would never seem to notice.

Then, from somewhere under the jungle canopy, the infinite dead who had gone before those ten airmen in Stinger 883 chanted up in unison:

Are you coming down tonight?
Come – come – come – come!
Further down and find us!

Then, Mother Moon looked down and whispered to the shuddering plane, "Much of war is unremarkable, darlings ... but not all of it."

There was one more flash of silver metal. With a mighty ripping blast, Stinger 883's right wing tore off....

... and went hurtling into space.

CHAPTER ONE

INTRODUCTIONS

Nowhere on God's good earth does the sky look bigger than in Oklahoma.

It is an ocean above the earth, scudding with white clouds, darkening with thunderheads, flashing ghostly green in the sickening of the storms. It is the farmer's friend and enemy. It brings the gentle rain and the punishing hail. It releases both the honeybee and the locust. It is a place of omens, both kind and menacing. In the day, the sun smiles from it, calling up the crops. In the night, the stars and moon keep time, a tapestry of light that sinks to the horizon, the constellations dancing in the wheat fields. The birds fly and fly, leading the eye up from the earth, past crops and phone lines, to the endless horizon. And through it all, through passing seasons and generations, the Oklahoma sky has beckoned to every farm kid who ever perched on an earthen tractor:

Touch me. I dare you.

I was fifty-six and unemployed when a friend approached me to write the story of Lt. Colonel Alan "Magnet Ass" Milacek, "the man who flew his plane on one wing" in Vietnam. Not wanting to commit too soon, I consulted Google to see how big a deal that was. Google told me such a feat was possible, but only if the plane had the thrust of, say, an F–18. By comparison, Milacek's AC–119K Gunship had been a colossal toad, a converted garbage hauler pressed into wartime service, and bloated with a ten-man crew and their equipment. It was lucky to get off the ground with two healthy wings, let alone stay aloft with one shot off.

An image flickered across my screen, apparently scanned from an old newspaper clipping. I clicked. A group of ten men – most in uniform, one in a Seventies-era suit – gathered around a trophy as big as a birdbath. Behind them, the stars of the American flag were barely visible, like a peek of the night sky through a closing window. And to the right of the trophy, their captain, Al Milacek, smiling with a kindness that was tangible even across the decades. There was something in Milacek's eyes, something good and strong, but that I couldn't quite place....

My curiosity was piqued. I said "yes" to the initial interviews with the mysterious pilot.

I also made it very clear to everyone involved that I was *not* committing to anything beyond that. Having previously written five books, I knew firsthand why writers like me are called "starving artists." Besides, I had two job offers in the wings, and expected I'd be much too busy to follow through on writing the story of another man's life, even if he was a war hero.

I prepared for a first meeting, scheduled at Lt. Col. Milacek's home in Waukomis, Oklahoma – a flattening drive east from my Colorado home. My plan was to get to know the man, record interview material, and tenuously feel out what the story here was, exactly. As I began my research in earnest, the fall leaves were beginning to crisp in the dry air from the mountains. The news cycles of 2014 were an unbroken litany of violence, tension, and despair. Somehow, assembling the facts of a few wartime hours in 1970 felt cathartic, calming. *There was something in those eyes.*

The impossible had happened in the sky over Laos, and Milacek and his crew gave me hope for our world. When they won the Mackay trophy in 1970 for the most meritorious flight of the year, the entire crew of that flight joined Air Force legend. They, in the eyes of the service, stood with the likes of Eddie Rickenbacker, Chuck Yeager, and an unbroken line of other airmen clear back to 1912. As I studied their famous mission, I scratched my head in wonder, certainly at the harrowing details of that dark, May night, but even more so at the unlikely camaraderie the crew had developed through hardship. By every indication, they were mismatched misfits, seemingly brought together by nothing more than mutual mayhem. They were a 'flying America': six whites, one black, an Irishman, and a Mexican – each so fond of their fun-loving, Czechoslovakian farm-boy-of-a-pilot, that when their plane was hit by artillery over the Ho Chi Minh Trail and Milacek ordered them to bail out, they disobeyed him instantly, ignoring his commands in an attempt to stay together and save their pilot's life. They loved their boss too much to leave him, even in the face of imminent death. I was eager to interview a man who could inspire such sacrificial action. I'd soon have the opportunity.

Waukomis is a tiny farming town – 1200 people, and a whole bundle of wheat. To get there from my place in Colorado, you drive and drive and drive down from the mountains, smack dab into the desolate middle of Kansas. Then you take a long right.

My initial road trip there was an act of faith. Unemployed as I was, I had no income for the first time in the thirty-three years of my marriage, and there was no guarantee this project would even produce a workable story, let alone a contract. My wife was a rock through it all, working hard to make ends meet, while we waited for my next gig. But even still, there was something in me that felt disturbing as, day-after-day, I watched Cindy drive off to her part-time job at a local school.

Meanwhile, the inner compass spun as I cut the grass and fed the birds and checked my email as much from habit as expectation. What did my wife think of me, now that I wasn't producing? More hauntingly, what did *I* think of me? Having never been depressed before, I was shocked to find myself in a tailspin. Then one day ... as if dropped out of the sky ... Milacek's story had come along like a parachute, bright and billowy.

Driving from Denver to Waukomis gave me time to ponder the project. With more thought came a squadron of doubts. Who was I to write a book about Vietnam? All I really knew of the war was that its popularity in America – decades after its end – rivaled that of a root canal. I was ten during the "summer of love," eleven the year Milacek flew his one hundred and fifty missions. I vaguely recalled glimpses of brave, young men on the nightly news, slogging through steaming jungles, their heads wrapped in bloody bandages, M—16s ever-present on their shoulders. Had my father been present, I imagine he would have put his hand around my shoulder ... said something strong and memorable, like ... "Son, don't let these things bother you too much. Sometimes a man just has to fight. And those times usually sneak up on him when everything is going great, and it catches him off guard. But he can survive if he keeps his head about him ... if he remembers pain and trouble are nothing to fear. So don't fret, son, those boys on the TV will be okay. And you'll have what it takes when that 'fighting time' comes your way, too. I just know it. I believe in you."

That conversation, however, never happened, and it lives only in the imagination of a boy whose father was kind as May, but absent as April. Bill Cunningham was, after all, an ophthalmologist, busy giving sight to the blind – a terribly respectable endeavor. So, I sat alone in the den, lured by images of the unspeakable, tortured by Walter Cronkite's commentary on something called 'the draft', until my mother changed the channel, or called me to set the dinner table.

To be fair to my father, I should mention he eventually quit surgery and left a great deal of money on the table, so he could keep a lighter schedule, have a normal life, (whatever that is), and get to know the four small humans who shared a house with my mother and him. Whether my three sisters were affected by our father's absenteeism is a matter I may never know; A man can only be certain of his own wounds. But I'm sure he did his best to make up for lost time. Unfortunately, by the time my father set his surgical practice aside to be a family man, I was turning twelve ... all grown up and ready to explore the world.

Anyway, my own military experience was limited to the Cub Scouts of America, where I had been highly decorated with the coveted Wolf and Bear badges, and had learned a few things that would be conceivably handy in combat, including how to tie a square knot, identify the North Star, and make a damn good balsa wood car.

I mention these things so the reader can understand why I nearly flipped a U-turn at the Oklahoma state line and headed back for Colorado.

I wheeled off Highway 81 into the sun, and listened to the soft *chunkety-chunk* of loose gravel against the undercarriage of my Buick. To my right, miles of red Oklahoma dirt sprawled northward to Kansas, etched with the newly plowed lines of some proud farmer. To the left was the exact same dirt, splendid in its redundancy. My brain whirred with questions, some of them legitimate, most of them ridiculous. I felt nervous, and silly to be feeling so.

What does a war hero look like? Does he live in a bunker with an old German shepherd, and a cot for a bed? Should I greet him with a handshake or a salute? What will he serve me for dinner? Hard tack with sardines? Old, moldy rations, left over from 'Nam? What if we spend the evening pouring over dusty topo maps and don't eat anything at all?

What makes a hero a hero?

Chunkety-chunkety-chunkety-chunk. The gravel was noisy, but my racing heart was noisier. The man's name was "Magnet Ass," for heaven's sake! Why was I showing up at his house?

By the time I arrived at his mailbox, I had settled on a two-fingered salute – casual, yet (I thought) fitting for the context. I turned my car into the Milacek family's hard-packed driveway.

Key turned and out of the ignition. I opened the door. I stepped onto the gravel drive of a typical Oklahoma farm. Neatly mowed Bermuda grass. A line of native cedars. Cowbirds on every wire in sight. Fuel and feed tanks stood next to the barn. A southwest-facing porch gazed at the horizon, as if the house was watching for someone to fly back over it. Hay rounds lined the east side of a red brick house, standing guard against nothing. And everywhere one looked, miles and miles of red flatness stretched under the autumn clouds. What memories that rich dirt held, I could not see.

The back door snapped open and – I swear I'm not making any of this up – I glanced at my tennis shoes to see if they were shined. Bracing for inspection, I looked back up at the person who had appeared on the porch, and I smiled at my oversight. In my rush to meet a war hero, I had imagined him a monk.

"Hello, Will," said Pat Milacek, her voice like a meadowlark's, full of wind and wheat. "Alan and I are so glad you're here." I walked over. "We've been waiting such a long time for this," she continued. I held out my hand to shake, but Pat ducked in for a hug. Her strong embrace spoke of hard work with hay bales.

"Pleased to meet you, Pat," I said, watching the screen door. Something shadowy moved behind the gauzy mesh.

"You'll have to excuse Alan's pace," said Pat, standing back and sizing me up. "He should be along any minute now. Don't be surprised if he doesn't look you in the eye. A cow got him down a few years back, and he still has a time holding his head up. Please don't think he doesn't like or respect you. It's just hard on his neck to keep eye contact. Anyway ... "She paused and gazed at the field. "You take the weeds with the wheat."

Pat's greeting had calmed me down. If this was Al's copilot, I wasn't so afraid to meet the man. On the porch, the handle of the door turned, and the screen swung open. But I was unprepared for what came through it.

Slowly, a set of metal legs with plastic wheels emerged, followed by a tray, and then a second pair of metal legs shod with tennis balls. They seemed to feel around like the legs of a half-blind insect. Next, a set of human legs stepped out, hesitant and pale, wearing shorts, white socks, and Reeboks. Attached to the legs was a nondescript, dark-shirted torso. And finally the only part of the man that was just as I had imagined them to be – his blue eyes, calm and commanding.

"Hello, Will," said the Colonel.

"Will Cunningham reporting for duty, sir!" I said, snapping to attention as I had rehearsed in my mind on the drive down. I think I saluted with two fingers, but some extras might have found their way in there. "'Al will do," he replied, smiling. He crept forward with his walker, side-stepped it, and gave me the same hug his wife had given me. "We don't shake hands around here," he added.

"Yessir – Al – sir," I replied, awkwardly. I was shocked by the shape he was in. I had expected a grizzled warrior, ready to put me in my place. Al was grizzled, but looked like he was flying on one wing himself. We filed into the house. Al's slow trajectory led us through the laundry room, accompanied by Pat's pleasant tour guide commentary. She pointed happily. "Here's pictures of our two daughters when they were babies," she said. "Here's the shower. You can get cleaned up whenever you have a mind to. Over here's the washer and dryer. Don't pay attention to the mess – I've been trying to overseed that bare spot by the back door with fescue, and there's nothing like Oklahoma dirt to give your washer fits." On she chirped, delightfully, and I was loving every minute of it. Ahead of us, Al moved with the slowness of a glacier. When we got to the kitchen, he excused himself and headed to the bathroom. Pat used his absence to fill me in on his health.

"He was diagnosed with esophageal cancer five-years and twenty-three-trips-to-Mayo ago."

"Twenty-three trips," I whispered. "Is he ... I mean, will he be...."

"Will he be up to interviewing?" said Pat, finishing my sentence. I nodded, even though what I meant to say was, "Will he even be *alive* by the time I finish a book's first draft?"

"He wouldn't miss this for the world," continued Pat. "Like I said on the porch, we've been waiting for someone to tell Alan's story for a long, long time."

Since the Colonel was slow in the bathroom, Pat went on to describe an eleven-hour surgery to remove a section of Al's esophagus (longer than the average open-heart procedure), plus the nearly two dozen journeys to Mayo for checks ups, many of them over the snow-packed roads of Minnesota. They still had more trips ahead of them.

"Sometimes our daughters do the driving. Sometimes it's one of our son-in-laws. We've got a whole team of people looking out for Magnet Ass."

At the sound of the Colonel's nickname, I must have looked startled to Pat, because she touched my hand reassuringly.

"Ol' Magnet Ass," she repeated, as plain as if she was taking roll at the Drummond Salem Methodist Sunday School Class. "You *have* heard that name before, haven't you?"

"Of course I have," I said. I just hadn't heard it from the mouth of a lady, with wind and wheat behind it, and bits of sunlight that made one wonder, *How do war and beauty live together*? In time, I would learn that Pat was just as tough as Ol' Magnet Ass.

"It's what his crew used to call him, on account of the triple-A he drew every time he flew a mission," continued Pat. "Sometimes another crew would be short a gunner or a navigator, and one of Al's crew would have to fly with them. So each of his men had opportunities to fly with other pilots during their tour in Vietnam. But they always wondered why *nobody* got shot at as much as Al. Flying with Al was like flying with a magnet. That's why they gave him the nickname. He couldn't help but attract fire; it's what leaders do. Anyway, I think it's cute."

Who wouldn't? I thought. "So, you're saying Alan's a sucker for trouble?"

"You have no idea," said Pat.

The sound of plastic wheels coming across the carpet signaled it was time to change the subject, and for my inner-health-care-professional to kick into gear. This has happened all my life, particularly when the pain of the sufferer touches upon my inability to ease it. I have often used the "I'm-not-a-doctor-but-I-played-one-on-television" routine, just to mask my dread of human misery—as if by transcending pain, I could avoid descending into it.

"Do you need anything?" I asked Al. "Water maybe? A sandwich?" *How about a brand new esophagus*? I thought.

Al shook his head, and sat down in a chair—obviously *his* chair—by the big picture window. In time, Pat would assure me there was no *topic non grata* as far as Al was concerned, and that if I was going to write his story, I had better learn to relax in his presence. He wasn't going to shatter. He had become as comfortable with sickness as he had been with health. There was a beautiful pattern in this family—resilience, no matter what fire was coming up from below—and I was beginning to understand it.

Over a supper of Swiss steak, potatoes, carrots, and salad, Al began to open up. "I suppose you should know that Pat and I slept together before we were married," he said, matter-of-factly, between bites of meat.

My own bite fell off my fork and onto my plate with a noticeable 'thud,' where I pushed it around for the better part of an awkward minute, feeling like a twelve-year-old who just walked in on his mother in the bath. Finally, I forced myself to look at Pat. There was a sparkle in her eye.

"Alan loves to tell stories on me," she said. "When he finds a good one, he tells it right into the ground. You'll see."

I looked at Al, but his neck kept him from looking back at me. But even with his head bent toward his plate, I could tell he was hiding a laugh.

"What he doesn't like to do is tell the *rest* of the story," Pat continued. "You see, Alan and I go *way* back."

"Childhood sweethearts?" I asked.

"Nope—infant lovers. Alan was a cradle-robber. One night, his parents and my parents got together to socialize, and my mother thought it would be a fine idea to place us side-by-side on the bed while they played cards in the other room. Ten minutes into their canasta game, I was wailing like a cat, and Mother had to come and rescue me. Alan's been telling the world about our premarital rendezvous ever since. As you can see, he's happy to let *me* do the explaining."

This time when I looked at Al, he lifted his head ever so slightly from his plate. I could definitely detect a smile.

After sponge cake and strawberries, I asked if they were up for an interview. Al said he normally went to bed around nine, but he was "probably good 'til ten tonight." Pat said she would join us after she finished the dishes. "You and the Colonel need some time alone together," she insisted, as she stacked several plates and headed off to the kitchen. I turned to see Al struggling to get up from his chair. Not knowing whether to help him or not, I watched as he made several attempts to reach his walker, which was two feet at most from his place at the table. He made one attempt, then sat back down abruptly. A second attempt, and I saw his tired knees buckle. Again, he sat down. After his third try, I set aside my fear of appearing condescending and walked around to Magnet Ass's side of the table.

"May I help?" I asked. Al's answer caught me off guard.

"It would be an honor," he replied.

He latched onto my extended forearm, and I felt for the first time the strength that must have grasped the yoke that night over the Plain of Jars. His legs may have failed him, but he was still farmer-strong from the waist up.

After he was settled in his favorite chair, we small-talked for a while, and then I finally decided it was time for the question I'd driven so many miles to ask.

"So...," I began, "You flew a plane on one wing?"

In spite of his neck, Al looked up and to the right. A faint grin came to his lips. "It wasn't exactly the *whole* wing that was shot off. They say it was seventeen feet off the leading edge, I think. Something like that."

"It was seventeen-and-a-half feet, to be exact!" shouted Pat from the kitchen. "The experts say there's no way in the world your plane was flyable in the condition it was in! Even *they* said it was a miracle. You're always downplaying things, Sugar."

I shut off the tape recorder. "Do you want us to hold the interview for you?" I called to Pat.

"No. Don't worry about me. You and Alan go ahead with your conversation. I'll just chime in when Al's being too modest."

That happened about a half-dozen more times before Pat joined us in the living room. We had almost completed one side of a ninety-minute tape, and Al's voice had dwindled down to nothing.

"We left a lot of UXOS over there," he whispered.

"Excuse me?" I said, acting as if I hadn't heard him. The fact is I had no idea what Al was talking about.

"Unexploded ordnance," supplied Pat.

"Right," I said.

"Bombs that didn't blow up," explained Al, discerning my ignorance, but being ever so patient with me. "They weren't supposed to be dropped on the Plain of Jars. It was a religious place. The rules were supposed to protect it."

"Rules?" I said.

"Geneva," said Pat. "1954. The laws of neutrality – all that stuff. You went to high school. You know about it."

"Right," I said again. Wanting to create at least a thin veneer of competency, I made the mistake of using more words. "So – um – you and your crew were *bombardiers*?"

"Heavens, no," said Pat. "Alan's plane was a *gunship*."

"My plane just shot bullets," said Al. Then he drew in a sharp breath, closed his eyes, and exhaled slowly. For a long time, he sat in silence, and I began to wonder if the interview had come to its natural conclusion. But then something reanimated Magnet Ass. "We told ourselves we were just shooting trucks," he said. "But whenever I was alone, in between missions with time to think about it all, I ... I realized..."

I waited as Al searched for the words.

He sighed. "We left a lot of broken things behind when we pulled out of Vietnam. I think a lot about the children still – the ones whose parents were truck drivers."

With the added strain of these few sentences, Al was nearly spent. But there seemed to be one more thing he wanted to say. I scooted the recorder closer to his chair, so as not to miss a word.

Isolated in thought, Al gazed at the painting that hung above his fireplace. It was an oil done by a man in Lake City, Colorado, to commemorate the famous mission I was there to hear about. Dark and foreboding, the painting showed a night sky over a landscape from hell, tumefied with artillery nests, ablaze with horrid, streaking eruptions of gunfire. Above it, a heavy plane, painted for war, hung in an eternal moment of weightlessness. All around it, bursts of red and orange lit the underbellies of clouds. A great portion of the right wing was hurtling away into space. I was lost in the painting, I could hear the rending of the metal, almost smell the caustic spurts of fuel, the dry prickling odor of infinite gunpowder.

Al's hands were trembling in his lap. I watched him struggle to swallow.

"When I was a boy, I had a dream about a plane that wouldn't fly straight," he murmured.

The hairs on my neck went up.

"I had that dream almost every night," he whispered.

"Were you the one flying it?" I asked.

"I was trying," said Al.

Except for the cadence of the grandfather clock, the living room was quiet for a long time. But behind everything, I felt I could almost hear the hum of overtaxed engines, hear the bitter wind shrieking alarm on the edges of a ragged wing. For a moment I felt that I was in another man's dream, a near-nightmare which had begun before I was even born.

A perceptible tremor appeared at the corner of Al's left eye, as if beneath his skin a tiny seismograph was vibrating. After a while, he stirred and reached for the walker. Like a flight engineer giving his plane a once-over before takeoff, he fiddled with the tennis balls, jiggled the tray, pressed against the legs to make sure they would support his weight. Then, as if to say, "I have a lot more flight left in this old plane than anybody thinks I have," he hoisted himself up from his chair with surprising energy and took command of his machine.

"It's late," he announced in a voice like a captain's. "I better call it a night." He offered multiple apologies for quitting on me; I rejected each one. He had answered too many questions, and I couldn't blame him for throwing in the towel. After Pat put some drops in Al's eyes, he turned and gave me another strong hug.

"I love you so much, Will," he said.

I was astonished to hear these words from a virtual stranger. Then he shuffled across the room, and was gone for the night. I looked back at the painting, thinking about the feeling of weightlessness one has before falling, falling.

"He has had that dream all his life, Will," whispered Pat. "Always the same. A plane that won't fly straight. Then he wakes up, soaked with sweat as if we were sleeping in the jungle." The grandfather clock seemed to be preparing to strike. "You'd think that somewhere in his life, he'd stop having that dream. Wouldn't you?" She looked at me with pleading eyes.

"I'm so sorry," I said, but the words sounded hollow.

The clock struck, and Pat stood up to remove the apron that was still tied around her waist. "Well, I'd better turn out the lights and lock up the house now," she said. "See you in the morning."

Then she was off to perform the duties that Colonel "Magnet Ass" Milacek had surely performed every day of his marriage, when he was feeling better, and he wasn't off flying in some far-removed province. These days, it seemed he was doing well if he could get himself out of his easy chair. I hoped like crazy he would get a good night's rest. We had a lot to talk about.

Back in my bedroom, I searched "esophageal cancer" online to see what Al was fighting. The results were not encouraging.

"*Esophageal cancer is cancer that occurs in the esophagus – a long, hollow tube that runs from your throat to your stomach*," the Mayo Clinic's website explained. "*Your esophagus carries food you swallow to your stomach to be digested...*"

It was like explaining war at a child's level of comprehension.

As I lay there, reading about symptoms, and causes, and risk factors, and complications, I suddenly realized that in the face of a new enemy, my interest in Al's story must feel like a lifeline for him, the chance for his life's defining moment to be held, to be known by many. For his voice to transcend a ragged and cut-away throat. This thought of helping bring hope to an old war pilot brought a huge smile to my face, which grew into hopeful, muffled laughter, which gave way to unexpected tears, which dissolved into stifled sobbing, which never, ever happens to me. When I realized I didn't have a tissue handy, I wiped my eyes with the polka-dot bed sheets and laid back in the soft lambency of my glowing computer. *Where did that come from*? I wondered.

Tomorrow, I would ask Magnet Ass about the truck hunters. I closed the computer.

Tomorrow, I would start my education in the bulging language of the military, with all its acronyms, and idioms, and hilariously vulgar vernacular. I lay back on the unfamiliar pillow.

Tomorrow, I would begin to read, too – researching the Mackay Trophy, and the planes, and the trucks, and the guns, and the flights suits, and the tiger cages, and the bamboo torture, and the Ho Chi Minh Trail, and the enemy, and....

I began to drift up in the night air. The Oklahoma sky was calling, welcoming, freckled with stars. My body grew heavy, but still lifted through the clouds. Coyotes watched me from below, moaning like forgotten ghosts.

Tomorrow....
Tomorrow....
Tomorrooooooooow....

Somewhere, between the black sky and the blue, I slept, and dreamed. And I saw a plane, at one moment as solid as steel, but the next only painted in brusque oils on the canvas of the night. I tossed and sweated and flew until nearly morning, straining at the yoke.

For in my dream, the plane would not fly straight.

CHAPTER TWO

PHANTOMS IN THE DARK

"We were all pretty young when we went truck hunting on the Ho Chi Minh Trail," said Al as we began the next morning's interview. He sat no straighter in his chair, but there was an energy to him that encouraged me for our day's work.

He had slept well, and agreed heartily when I said I was famished for the tasty things Pat was fixing in the kitchen. The smell of fresh eggs and bacon made my mouth water and my concentration dull. Last night was fuller of dreams than rest for me, and I felt a bit like a wreck, especially before the coffee was ready. *What did I dream*? *Something about a plane, I think*. I leaned closer to Al's chair, working to listen. The batteries to my tape recorder had died the night before, and I was stranded with my notepad.

"I was thirty in 1970. And several of the crew were close to my age," said Al, rubbing his forehead. "If my memory serves me correctly, only Lopez and Wilson were older. But to Cofer and Firestone ... Ha! I must have been an old man," he added. A look of longing and humor flickered across his face, which I interpreted as, *Wonder what they'd think now*?

I wrote this down in my notebook, followed by a pop slogan from the Sixties: "Never trust anyone over thirty." I suppressed a grin, and imagined that line of thought flying right out the cargo door the first time the "old man" pulled an evasive maneuver under artillery fire. Al was their *pilot*, for crying out loud.

"I was the lowest ranking officer of the sixteen Stinger pilots in the squadron at Udorn," Al continued. "So, all the other pilots got first pick of the men. I got the ones who were left."

Like getting picked last for kickball. "Did you resent it?" I asked.

"What do you mean?" Al asked.

I suddenly felt like I'd crossed some line I hadn't known was there. "Well ... I mean ... did you feel as if you had been given the rejects?"

Al's grey brows knit in defense. "There was nothing second-rate about my crew," he declared. "My men were the best in the bunch, hand-picked by God!"

"Of course, they were," I said, quickly. "I wouldn't doubt it for a minute."

It was the first time I had seen Al bristle. For a moment, the veil of age and atrophy had lifted ever so slightly, giving me a glimpse of the young pilot who lived on the other side of it. Then the veil dropped again, and Al changed the topic.

"I remember a recon mission one afternoon at Udorn," said Al, suddenly the most lucid I had seen him so far. "It was a Phantom scheduled to check out a line of communication in northwestern Laos, not long before our Mackay mission."

I wrote down the phrases, "phantom" and "line of communication," with a star next to them.

"Anyway," said Al. "The mission was assigned to a couple of pilots I had heard about; I think 'John' and 'Joe' were their names. I can't remember their call sign. They took off around thirteen-hundred hours, heading for their target on the other side of the Mekong."

"River," I interjected, for no other reason than to sound as if I had paid attention in geography class.

"Hmm?" asked Al, looking over.

"Nothing," I replied.

Al lifted his head, staring again at the painting over his fireplace. "They were probably moving at five-hundred knots or so with at least five miles of visibility. They were in a big, right climb-out, heading back to Udorn. Then they got hit. Neither pilot remembered any ground fire before they started to climb. But when Joe looked out the window, he saw a—"

Al paused for a moment, as if what he was seeing in his mind's eye had transported him from his easy chair to a completely different kind of chair, one that made him young and vigorous again. He sat up in the puffy La-Z-Boy, vigilant. In the kitchen, Pat's bacon crackled in the pan like gunfire.

"What did he see, Al?" I asked.

Al stirred and looked at me. "He saw a six-inch hole in the right wing by the spoiler ... and a light on his dash that said his hydraulics had failed."

A plate clinked from the other room.

I sat forward. Such simple words, from an old veteran in the living room of a little American farmhouse.

Al looked back at the painting. "John made the call to Ethan Control, and EC sent out a plane to assess damage and to check on controllability of the Phantom."

"John was the pilot?" I asked, writing.

"Yes," said Al. "And Joe was the navigator behind him in the cockpit."

"Okay," I said. "Sorry."

Al waved off my apology with his left hand, while his right seized his walker with a grip that whitened his knuckles. "The second plane intercepted the first one about 20 miles east of Udorn. The F–4's UHS was out, too, so that presented new problems."

"UHS ... I'm sorry, Al. I just—"

"Utility Hydraulic System," said Al. He, too, was having to adjust to our communication dance. "Anyway, in spite of the UHS problem, the men decided the F–4 was controllable. They would attempt to lower its hook and gear."

I started to open my mouth, but Al beat me to it.

"*Arresting* hook and *landing* gear," he said smiling, as if the explanation to new ears was doing as much for him as Mayo had. I made note of the healing power of my stupidity.

"The hook and gear were lowered," said Al. "They cleared the plane for a no-flap landing on runway 30, a strip I had landed on many times in my days at Udorn. John positioned the Phantom for final at a hundred and eighty-five knots. From where I stood on the ground, I remember everything looking straight and controlled."

Al paused.

I saw the knuckles of his right hand nearly bursting through his translucent skin as he gripped the walker. He had lost sixty pounds since the onset of cancer. Pat had confided yesterday that the slightest exertion was enough to tire him out for an afternoon.

"You all right, sir ... I mean, Al?" I asked.

Again, Al waved me off, as if he was shooing away a bird. "About a half-mile out, the Phantom just sort of rolled to the right," he continued. He closed his eyes and released his hands from the walker, spreading them out like wings.

"The pilot fights to counter the roll with full left stick and rudder," said Al, speaking now in present tense. I could tell he was no longer in Waukomis. He was in Laos, a young man, fighting to keep John and Joe's plane from spraying itself from the jungle to kingdom come. I put my pen down and watched like an observer at the edge of a runway.

"The controls have no effect on the aircraft," said Al, the corners of his eyes twitching. "The plane rolls, drifts to the right. It has a mind of its own, like a bad cow. The pilot tries a go-around. But the right roll is unstoppable." He closed his eyes, lifting his head farther than I thought was easy for him. "The plane is still moving at more than a hundred and seventy-five knots."

Suddenly, Al dipped his right arm, and his left rose at a corresponding angle, the man becoming a plane long destroyed. His voice took on a timbre I had not heard him use before, as if he were calling to John and Joe across the long decades that separated his La-Z-Boy from their cockpit.

"You're sixty degrees of bank, sir! Nose high attitude! Get her under control boys ... get her under control!"

The hair on my arms prickled. At the feeder beyond Al's picture window, the finches pecked up sunflower seeds, unaware of John and Joe careening through the air, through the years, toward the sudden earth. The ground is a floor to most of us. It only takes a few feet, a few degrees of orientation to make it a deadly wall.

I was vaguely aware of Pat standing at my shoulder, holding a tray of breakfast.

Al's voice trailed away. He opened his eyes. His chest rose and fell behind his thin, short-sleeved shirt, and his brow glistened. He gave a short, involuntary cough. "I think it's time for breakfast," he said, leaving the F–4 suspended in the sky. I looked at Pat and she shook her head, as if to say this was a story that should be left dangling. This was not how I pictured the interview would go. I felt that something meaningful was happening, but it was visceral – the work of harsh and immediate memory. It was beyond my control. Maybe beyond Al's.

What he had seen in his memory was not the moment of fate for the Phantom and her pilots, but the moment of decision.

We ate our eggs and bacon in relative silence. Al consuming the blander parts of the breakfast, following doctor-ordered, dietary restrictions – and me gobbling up all the things he wished he could eat. Pat came to our rescue once with news of the Pumpkin Festival in Waukomis, and her plans to enter a sweet potato pie in this year's contest. Al smiled at that announcement, and said Pat's pies were his favorite thing to eat. As for me, I was happy for the rumors of quiet life in Mayberry, but what I really wanted was the conclusion to the F–4 story. As soon as was polite, I excused myself to "use the bathroom." I ducked down the hallway to my bedroom and closed the door behind me. Sitting on the bed, I flipped open my laptop.

F–4 *Phantom crash at Udorn in* 1970, I typed, as soon as the wheel of death stopped turning. (I have a very old computer.) I clicked the second link near the top of the page: (PDF) Accident Report & Photos – Thai Aviation History. I waited for it to load.

The first words that stood out to me in the article were shocking. "*The crew bailed out.*" I sat back in the harsh glow of discovery. I had to read them a second time to absorb their full impact.

A photo inserted between paragraphs caught my attention, a towering, red fireball at its center.

Maj. Leaphart landed on a building and subsequently fell from it fracturing a bone in his right foot. Capt. Bernholtz also landed on a building suffering a cut over his right eye. The crippled Phantom crashed into the housing area on base, turning the entire area into a blazing inferno. Nine USAF men perished in the crash; most died as the pilotless Phantom plowed into the base radio and television studio. Flames destroyed nine buildings and one trailer. Property loss was estimated at $147,000.

Pilotless Phantom! I banged my laptop shut and laid back on the bedspread of the tiny guest room. On the wall to my right, framed photographs of the Milacek girls, yellowed with years, stared down at me. The cool touch of the pillow to my head was in stark contrast with the scorching thoughts inside it. *What the hell kind of decision was that? Who bails out at the last moment, and lets his plane kill his coworkers? Did they think it was going to land itself?*

How little I knew of war and its machinery. The painting of the plane popped into my mind, then my dream of the plane that could not be righted. And I thought of Al as a boy with the nightmare that corkscrewed across his sleeping hours.

Back in the living room, Al was napping in his chair. The breakfast dishes were gone already, cleared away to the kitchen. "Did you find what you were looking for?" asked Pat from over by the sink. She knew I hadn't really needed to go to the bathroom.

"Yes, ma'am," I said sheepishly. I busied myself with wiping a counter, so as not to appear completely useless.

"The crash of the F-4 Phantom had an effect on the men at Udorn," said Pat with her back turned. The knot on her apron string was coming untied. "It woke them up. Reminded them this war thing wasn't a game. It was the last tragedy Al ever informed me of. After that, he pretty much shut up when it came to reporting bad news from Vietnam. He didn't want me to be afraid." The dishes were slowly giving up their grease under hot water and suds. Pat shut off the water, and dried her hands on a dishtowel. She gazed out the window. A line of cows threaded through her neighbor's field, heading west for a drink at the trough. "He didn't even tell me about the Mackay mission until a long time afterward," she added.

"What became of the two pilots?" I asked. I heard the judgmental note in my voice as I said it. Pat did too.

She took a deep breath, and exhaled it like the whistle of a long, slow train as she turned to face me. "It wasn't their fault, Will," she said. "They had families back home, just like Al. Can you say what you'd have done?"

"No, ma'am," I said.

Pat stared at the suds. "I suppose they went back to work as soon as their bones healed. I almost hope they forgot about it. Sometimes that's what's best to do with pain and death."

The tone in Pat's words suggested she had tried unsuccessfully in the past to convince herself they were true – and before I could stop myself, I stumbled headlong into my next question.

"Are you afraid your husband's going to die?" I asked stupidly.

Pat glanced at me as if to fend off a blow, and immediately I wished I could melt into the kitchen floor. Then she turned back to the sink and grabbed a plate she had already washed. The water began to slosh again, the sponge squeaking as she retraced her steps. When the plate was clean, she washed it a third time. Finally, she turned to face me, leaning against the counter like it was the bar of an Old West saloon.

"Will," she began, "one thing you should know about me is that I'm a pretty tough old gal." She wiped her hands on her apron, then folded them across her chest.

"I've helped raise two girls and a couple hundred cattle. I've delivered the calves when they were born, and I've sliced off their testicles when it came time for that, too. I've baled hay and stacked it as straight as any man could. I've survived tornadoes, dust storms, droughts, locusts. I can bake a pie on short notice from things straight out of my garden, and I can haul it up to church in time for the elders' meeting. I moved more times in my first ten years of marriage than most women move in a lifetime. And through it all, I never asked much from life, just the occasional quiet meal with my husband, or a walk in the wheat with my Creator. But for the life of me—" Pat paused abruptly, as if to rein in her emotions. She turned back toward the window. "For the life of me, there are certain things I just don't want to talk about."

She went back to washing dishes.

Al slept throughout that afternoon, weak from the morning's activity. He was chipper at supper, though, even eating a second piece of pie when it came time for dessert. I noted that he never ate potatoes, though Pat kept serving them. I had never met a farm boy who didn't like potatoes.

In my years of growing up in Oklahoma, I had amassed an unofficial "Farm Boy Profile." It had the qualities that stereotypes demanded: the half-romantic hayseed chewing tobacco, tossing back cheap beer, and heartily stowing a diet of roast beef, potatoes, sweet tea, and pound cake. What the profile didn't involve was the skillful command of anything more technical than an Allis-Chalmers tractor, or a heart that cared much about the pain of a fellow human being. But here was Al, master of a legendary war machine and holder of one of the armed services' most prestigious awards, heartbroken over the fall of fellow pilots who probably had held him in contempt because they were crack fighter pilots and he was a lowly gunship airman. Al was nothing like the farm boys in my mind. He didn't dip or even drink.

When I laid down in bed that second night, again I couldn't fall asleep. I got back on the computer to finish my research of the F–4 crash. Apparently, a 48-Hour Mishap Report had been compiled in its wake, and transmitted to 13th Air Force at Clark AB in the Philippines. The report highlighted the fact that Major John Leaphart had flown for 13 years, and had 3465 flight hours in total, 1361 of which were in the RF–4C. Captain Joe Bernholtz had flown for nearly 10 years, with 2659 hours in total, and 372 in the RF–4C, as well.

In Colonel David S. Mellish's words, who filed the report: "The crew was medically qualified to fly the mission and had adequate food and rest forty-eight hours prior to the accident. Nothing was found which could impair their ability to perform the mission. A maintenance analysis of aircraft forms indicated there were no contributing factors due to maintenance performed or possible systems failure due to past history."

Commander Mellish concluded his report by saying that Falcon 34 was hit by an unknown number of rounds of hostile AAA fire which caused the loss.

So the report had all been neatly packaged and sent off to Clark AB, and the word had come back that no one was to blame. But in my mind, the story couldn't end that easily. Nine names leapt from my laptop screen, immortalized in pixels for my civilian voyeurism, begging for the story to go on. These were the men killed by the pilotless Phantom:

TSgt Jack A. Hawley, age 37, Wakeman, Ohio
SSgt James T. Howard, age 27, Denver, Colorado
A1C Andrew C. McCartney, age 20, Lakewood, Ohio
SSgt Alfred N. Potter, age 27, Forest Grove, Oregon
Sgt John Charles Rose, age 25, Bloomfield, New Jersey
Sgt Frank D. Ryan Jr., age 41, Mercer Island, Washington
SSgt Edward Wm. Strain, age 24, Myrtle Beach, South Carolina
Sgt Roy Walker, age 40, Albuquerque, New Mexico
A1C Thomas L. Waterman, age 25, Roanoke, Virginia

I was haunted by the ages of the men. Some had been younger than my own two sons when they died. I knew Al and I would soon begin our discussions about the "truck hunters" who flew with him, and I was hoping against hope they had all been grown men, with thick, greying beards and the bud of their lives far behind them. But Al had already told me that Firestone and Cofer were mere boys when they volunteered their flesh for service on the gunships.

Frequented by the many-faced specter of death middle-aged men can scarcely see, I lay on that bed and told myself the frightful truth. Sometimes a man does *not* have what it takes to make it home, or finish the race, or land the plane. Or complete a manuscript. Sometimes there are just flames and a list of names. Oh, what had possessed me to consider such a melancholy story? I closed my eyes then, and saw the painting above the fireplace. And I remembered why I was there.

And for the first time, with a rush of insight, I glimpsed the real reason I might tell Al's story.

It was only half for him.

I couldn't sleep.

About midnight, I wandered out to Al's backyard to see if the heavens had any advice for me. The night buzzed with the conversation of fireflies, electric with their starry change. As I gazed around me, Al's yard suddenly seemed claustrophobic. The sky was limitless, tempting me out past the cattle wire separating the Milacek lawn from the Milacek fields. It looked to be a whole world opened to me, a landscape wet with moonlight. I stepped over the wire, and out onto the great, red carpet of Oklahoma dirt.

It was a warm night for September. I walked along the newly plowed earth, listening to the 'slurp' of my tennis shoes between the tiller lines, knowing they would be ruddy and ruined by the time I got back to Al's house. But I didn't care. I felt a rush of exhilaration, a happy carelessness I hadn't often felt since my youth.

Above me hung the last of the "blood moons," supposed to be a harbinger of doom, a useless warning to a dying world. I cocked my head and stared at it, wanting to give it the benefit of the doubt. For a moment it *did* look redder than normal. *Maybe.* But then my eyes adjusted, and Mother Moon looked as cold and comforting as ever. In the distance, a coyote howled at her. And was answered by another. For the first time, I looked down from the sky. I was a long way from the house, its porchlight now a pinprick, my footprints leading back to it, punched in the soil. I traced their meandering path toward the light, mesmerized by the thought that each print was the record of a younger man, and increasingly so as their line traveled back to where they had begun at the cattle wire.

I don't want to write this old man's story, I thought. *I don't have to! I can get in my car tomorrow morning, and drive away, and forget I ever came to Waukomis.*

But then I looked down at my own two feet – glued to the ground by mud and indecision – and I had the sudden notion that if I *didn't* write Al's story, I might still be in his field twenty years from now, caked with regret for going my own way, calcified by the thought that I didn't give a damn about another man's steps when I had the chance to. Something moved in the dark behind me, and I turned around to face it. The coyotes had begun to sing again, and I could tell by the richness of their chorus that their numbers had grown. Where the distant fringe of Al's field blended with his neighbor's, I could see them congregating in the moonlight, a pack of them, eyeing me. I had never heard of one attacking a human. Or had I?

"I need to find a job!" I shouted at their gloomy silhouettes. "I need to make money! Pay bills! Work hard and die weary, like every other normal man! I don't have time to write a memoir! You wouldn't understand."

The coyotes didn't answer. But the space formerly occupied by them was now empty. I scrunched up my eyes to see if they were playing tricks on me. Sure enough, the coyotes were gone. My pulse quickened, irrationally. I began to move toward the house, my heart racing, my breaths coming in short, tight gasps. Along the edge of Al's field, I thought I saw six or seven grey ghosts floating swiftly, on a track to intercept me. *This can't be happening*, I thought. But I kept walking faster. The ghosts now looked like they had grown long, thin legs. And tails. Then it seemed that the pack of shadows really began to move, to lope straight toward me.

I turned to run, trying like mad to coax my middle-aged legs into a faster pace. But in the newly plowed field, each stride was slowed with the weight of red clay. Behind me, the ghosts were gaining ground. Ahead of me, Al's porchlight shone. I could hear my heart hammering in my chest as I ran, each footstep echoing in my jostling skull. When I got to the cattle wire – the one I had forgotten about, because I was too busy wondering what it would feel like to be eaten – the toe of my tennis shoe clipped one of the stakes, and I somersaulted into the safe patch of gold cast by Al's porchlight. Up I jumped, shouting something unintelligible, trying to get bigger than the beasts chasing me.

But as I stood there in Al's yard, my chest pumping like an oil derrick, all I could see in the field behind me were the dim lines of tractor tines, running westward under the blood moon.

I felt so stupid, a child afraid of the dark – and definitely a poor house guest. I opened Al's back door and slipped in quietly. It was pushing one in the morning. I took off my ruined shoes, so as not to track mud through the halls, and tiptoed to my room. Before I slept, I opened the curtains and looked out on the scene of my fearful flight. It was almost funny, but the taste of that primal fear was still in my mouth. Of being chased down. Caught. I could see nothing but darkness now.

And I was the only phantom that had been out there.

CHAPTER THREE

GOAT

Approximately 38% of Vietnam veteran marriages failed within six months of the veteran's return from Southeast Asia.

Sometime the next morning, with Al still sleeping and our third round of interviews put on hold, Pat found my shoes in her laundry room and asked me what to do with them.

"Proper burial," I said, as I took the rock-hard clodhoppers from her and pitched them into a trash can. It was a small price to pay for surviving an imaginary coyote attack. As I closed the lid on the can, I thanked them for their service. Pat never asked me how they got so muddy, but I assumed she had a theory. Perhaps she had heard me shouting at my fears.

After breakfast, Pat apologized to me for her emotions at the sink the day before, saying she had just been having a hard afternoon and that our conversation about things like Al's cancer didn't have to be curtailed on account of fear ... hers or mine. "If Al dies, we'll cross that bridge when we get to it," she said. And then she added, wistfully, "I just hope we go at the same time."

In the den, we found Al already in his chair, and the three of us got down to business.

"The nickname, 'Magnet Ass', was growing in Alan's soul long before anyone called him by it," said Pat. Because she was far less likely to philosophize about life than her husband, I made sure to underscore her words in my notebook whenever she added color to a particular memory. Around some of her comments, I drew stars.

"As long as I've known Alan, his backside has been on fire," she continued. "I wouldn't be surprised if God gave him extra padding from the start. Has he told you about the time he put a goat in the school library?"

"No, ma'am, he hasn't," I replied.

"Well, tell him, Alan," Pat suggested.

"Now, shug ... Will doesn't need to hear all that," said Al. But then he leaned toward me and, as if acknowledging one of his finer achievements in life, he asked, "Do you know how much mess a goat can make when left to himself in a room full of books?"

"Sizeable," I surmised.

"Legendary," corrected Pat. "There was paper blanketing the entire library, chewed up and wet with goat spit. The tables were all catawampus because of the long rope Al had fastened around the goat's neck. And there wasn't a single copy of 'Gatsby' left on the shelf by the librarian's desk," she added. "Which was fine with me, because I never did like Fitzgerald. But when the English teacher saw that the goat had defiled every last page of F. Scott's masterpiece ... well ... she broke down and cried, because she had come brand new to us from Oklahoma State University, and wanted to make a good first impression." As an afterthought, Pat included, "I think she intended to teach Gatsby that semester, and didn't have a backup plan."

"I got nine swats with a wooden paddle," said Al. "One for each copy of Gatsby the goat ate."

"His rear didn't cool off for a week," said Pat, stifling a grin.

"And our principal wouldn't let me participate in any school activities until everything was back in order," said Al. "I spent days giving the place a good scrubbing. It takes a long time to clean up after a goat. I learned that first hand."

Al paused for a few seconds, pondering the sins of his youth. "It was not one of my better ideas," he concluded.

Pat smiled, happy that one of her favorite stories had been unpacked for my surveillance. "And now you know the real story behind the name, 'Magnet Ass'," she said. "Alan's rear end has been drawing flak since he was a youngster. His crew just picked up on what was already there. They even made him a patch with the nickname on it, and they gave it to him when he flew his 100th mission."

"I assume the principal contacted your father," I said, looking at Al.

Al stared at the end table next to the couch, as if it had suddenly become the most interesting thing in the universe.

"Yeah, he heard about it," he finally replied.

I waited for a moment, because it seemed Al should have had more to say on this point. But without warning, he excused himself from the conversation, struggled up to his walker, and headed for a drink of water in the kitchen – though he had a full glass on the table next to his chair.

"Alan had a complicated relationship with his father," said Pat, once we were alone. "His parents divorced when he was fourteen. He chose to stay with his father, and his mother didn't pursue it in court. His sister and two brothers went west to Longmont with their mom. Barb was twelve, Carl was seven. I think L.A was four at the time of the divorce. 'L.A' stands for 'Leon Allen'."

"So the family split up," I said quietly.

"Yes," said Pat. "Probably for the better – but there's always pain when that happens. You know these things, being a counselor and all. Do you have a good relationship with your father?"

Pat's sudden question surprised me, and I realized it was the first personal thing either of them had asked me.

"I ... uh ... sure, we were close," I said, hoping my answer would satisfy her curiosity.

"That's good," said Pat. "There's nothing better than fathers and sons getting along."

"Nothing better," I agreed. Underneath my half-truth, a thin crack had opened up in my soul, running unabated across the bridge of trust between Pat and me. Eager to change the subject, I asked, "Was Al glad he chose to live with his dad?"

"Oh, yes," said Pat. "Al and Leon Sr. were buddies. They hunted and fished together as often as they could. The friend part came easy for the two of them. It was the father and son things that tripped them up from time to time."

"My father was an alcoholic," said Al, re-emerging from the kitchen.

"I'm sorry to hear that," I said. The look on Al's face said he much preferred talking about the goat. Nevertheless, he settled in his chair again and tackled the topic head on.

"Dad was a good man," he began. "Quick to laugh. A hard, hard worker. He built the house I was born in, you know ... a little, white one ... it used to sit out there by the big elm in the front yard. All that's left of it now is a mound, where the grass doesn't grow too well. You can see it, if you look hard. A local gentleman bought it years ago, and had it hauled away on a truck. Anyway, after dad and mom split up, he never said a negative word about her to me; I think he wanted to protect my childhood." Al paused and took a sip of water. "So, I ... I never want to say anything bad about him. And I don't want the book to say bad things about him either, if that's okay with you."

Al's voice trailed off, and he looked at me with desperate appeal.

"I'll do my best to treat your dad with honor," I promised, "But we've got to tell the truth, you know."

"Truth is good," said Al, nodding. "As long as it doesn't wreck someone."

"Agreed," I said.

"Dad was forty-six when he died of lung cancer," continued Al, "... just eight years before I went to Vietnam. He had me when he was twenty-four. So, he was a pretty young father. Playful. But hard-nosed, too. I learned not to cross certain lines. Sometimes, when he was drinking..."

Al looked at Pat for help.

"When Al's father was drinking, he wasn't always there for Al," said Pat.

Not wanting to appear eager, I put my pen down.

"Meaning he went AWOL," said Pat, anticipating my question. "He would come and go as he pleased. Sometimes, when he had too much to drink, he didn't keep his promises."

Pat glanced at Al, and a code of understanding seemed to pass between them, like Morse between two ships.

"Once when we were in high school – several years after the goat incident – an FFA banquet was held, at which Alan was slated to be honored for his service as club president," said Pat. "It was a fancy banquet, with white tablecloths and candles and everything, and a place for the honored guests at the front of the gymnasium. Each honoree was allowed one guest to accompany him or her, and Alan had chosen his best friend – his father. All through the meal, the chair next to Alan remained empty, and he kept his head down because I think he was embarrassed. The other honored guests were laughing and having a good time with one another ... fathers and sons ... mothers and daughters ... everybody seemed to have someone, and I could hardly stand to see Alan all alone up there. It was then I recognized he wasn't embarrassed at all ... he was heartbroken. Right before the program was to begin, I slipped up to the front quietly, came around behind the platform, and gave a little 'pssst' to get Alan's attention."

"She was the most beautiful sight I'd ever seen," said Al, quietly. "There's nothing worse in this world than being left alone, having everyone bail out on you. It was the first time I knew that I loved her – and that she loved me back."

"So, I sat next to Alan during the remainder of the evening," said Pat, "And when he went up to receive his award he looked so handsome." Pat paused to collect her thoughts. "Like Alan said, we don't want to say negative things about Alan's father," she said. "He did the best he could with the cards that were dealt him. He always admitted that it takes two people to make a divorce."

"And two to make a marriage," added Al.

"Fair enough," I said. "That's probably all we need to say about the goat and the banquet. I think they'll both make fine material for the book."

Al smiled and seemed content with my words. Later, when the sadness had cleared from the air, I took a chance on a particular philosophical question I had wondered about since coming into Al's household.

"What's the secret to a happy life?" I asked, choosing an open-ended question to probe the inner policies of the man.

"Don't worry about the stuff that hasn't happened yet," declared Al, without hesitation.

Struck with the breadth of his answer, I must have looked dumbfounded to Al.

"Were you expecting something else?" he asked.

"No," I replied. But it was a lie. I had expected something wooly and homespun, like, "If you want to change the world, start by making your bed every morning." Instead, what I got was the back of King Solomon's hand.

"Don't worry about the stuff that hasn't happened yet," I murmured to myself, feeling the blunt impact of the phrase. But as I personalized it and wrote it down in my notebook, it was strangely soothing, too.

"Right," said Al. "The stuff that hasn't happened yet ... and, believe me, there's a lot of it. But right now, the one thing that needs to happen is me going to bed."

"Don't forget your stretching exercises," said Pat, cheerily.

The last thing I saw before retiring down the hall to my room was Magnet Ass sitting on the couch, looking up at the ceiling ... then down at the floor ... up at the ceiling ... and down at the floor. So many organs had been rearranged inside him during his last surgery. The exercises were what the doctor at Mayo had told him to do to keep his neck from tightening up. And though I would have never told Magnet Ass this to his face, they were pitiful to behold.

Up at the ceiling....
Down at the floor....
Up at the ceiling....
Down at the floor....

The damn, devil cow had taken more than flexibility from Al; It had taken his dignity, as well.

Since it was my last night in Waukomis, I spent a few minutes reorganizing my notes and tapes, and packing my suitcase for an early start home the next day. While I packed, I remembered something Pat had told me at the dinner table that evening. She had mentioned that Al's co-pilot had gone through a divorce after returning from the war, and it had seemed strange to me that one trauma, (such as a deployment), could lead to a second one, more loathsome and long-lasting. She proceeded to tell me that nearly four in every ten married Vietnam vets found their marriages dissolved within a year after coming home.

As I threw my clothes in the suitcase and straightened up the guest room, I also thought about Magnet Ass's 'secret to life'. *Don't worry about the stuff that hasn't happened yet*, I said out loud to myself. How often I had been guilty of embracing a perversion of his motto, "Happiness comes to those who are best prepared," like something straight out of the Cub Scout's handbook. I had spent my entire life preparing for the future, and almost always being unprepared when the future finally arrived.

When I was done packing, I ducked outside again to make a phone call home – this time in the safety of the Buick. As I punched the numbers into my phone, I eyed the fields for good measure. But I saw no ghosts. Or coyotes.

"So, how's your book coming?" said Cindy, straight out of the chute.

"I don't have a book," I corrected her.

"Okay, so hypothetically, if you *did* have a book—"

"Look," I interrupted, "Maybe we shouldn't jump too quickly into this book thing. Maybe we should just wait until I have a salary in place, something solid under our feet. I can always come back to Al's story down the road somewhere."

"I don't think you should abandon the book," said Cindy.

"I haven't said 'yes' to the book," I repeated.

"Well, you should probably let Al and Pat know what you're thinking. It wouldn't be fair to lead them on."

Suddenly, something inside of me snapped. "This isn't my book! And this isn't my fault!" I interrupted, blind with the fear of failing someone. "And I didn't ask to be unemployed!"

Outside my car's windows, the stars careened westward, on a collision course with the horizon. And because the temperature in Waukomis had dropped dramatically since the day before, my windshield grew frostier with every defensive word from my mouth.

"I didn't say it was your fault," said Cindy. "This is not a matter of fault or blame. We weren't even talking about unemployment. Look ... can we just not argue on the phone ... please? Besides, it's late, and I've got a lot of things Sean wants me to take care of before tomorrow."

A ping of jealousy went off in my chest. Immediately, I recalled a photograph Cindy had shown me earlier in the fall, in which her handsome, 6'7" colleague was bending down to accommodate her small stature, his cheek nearly next to hers as they gazed happily into the camera. He was a fourth-grade teacher. She was his assistant. To make matters worse, a little boy student stood between them in the picture, giving the appearance that they were a family. Try as I might to beat the image back down, it would not go away.

"Why are you being quiet all of sudden?" asked Cindy.

"I'm not being quiet," I replied.

"Yes, you are," said Cindy. "The moment I mentioned something about my work, you got quiet."

"You're reading things into this."

"C'mon, Will, you're not acting like yourself."

Glad to have escaped suspicion of jealousy, I opted for a more acceptable truth. "I'm just tired, C – tired of not producing anything."

"Then *produce* something!" said Cindy sharply. And her words brought the conversation to a sudden standstill. There was tremendous power behind them, like the pressure of a trillion gallons of water against a vast, unwavering dam. I could feel the dam trembling with the weight of the words. But it was holding.

Strong. Resolute.

I had to hear them again.

"What did you say?" I asked.

"I said, '*produce something*'," she repeated. "Produce an old man's story. Produce his life's dream. Produce Al's book. Make it the best book anyone has ever read. Make it so good, people will want to make a movie out of it. Stop thinking about it. Stop talking about it. Just do it, Will, and find value in doing it."

"You mean, like ... forget about a real job and just focus on writing?"

"Yes."

"But I've never written a memoir before."

"Do you know anybody who *has*?"

"No, but..."

"Look, Will," said Cindy, "Why not call the people in Houston and tell them we're not coming for the final interview."

I couldn't believe what I was hearing. Cindy knew we had potential jobs waiting for us in several cities. We had talked about each one of them, before I left for Oklahoma. Including the lucrative one in Houston.

"Let me get this straight," I said, "You want me to say 'no' to a good paycheck, and good benefits, and a good board, and all of that?"

"Say 'no' to it all," Cindy asserted.

"Are you sure it's not just a 'Houston thing'?" I asked. "I know you don't like the bugs and the humidity down there. But what if a job came along that was in Cancun? Or Hawaii? Or ... or in Kansas City, next door to your sister's?"

"It wouldn't matter," she replied.

I paused to absorb the full meaning behind C's words, to test them and see if they were solid. "You know, there's not a lot of security in writing," I reminded her.

"Security is nothing if we're not happy," said Cindy.

"Are you sure?" I asked, one last time.

"Will! Sometimes you make me crazy. For the last time ... I'm sure."

"But how?" I persisted. "*How* can you be sure?"

There was a long, dramatic delay on the other end of the phone, so long that I began to wonder if C and I had been disconnected from one another. Then there was another sigh ... this time a peaceful one.

"I'll tell you when I get to know you better," she said, copying something my father used to say when I was a boy. For a moment, I felt as if my dad was right there in the car with me, his gentle sense of humor suggesting everything was going to be alright.

"Thank you, C," I said. "I don't know what else to say."

"Don't say anything," said Cindy, and she started to hang up, but something caused her to change her mind. "There's one thing I need to know," she said.

"What's that?" I replied.

"I've been telling all my friends about this book of yours..."

"It's not a book of mine," I reminded her.

"Alright, okay ... I've been telling everybody about this thing ... this project you're considering ... and nobody in Denver has ever heard of the Mackay trophy. Doesn't that seem weird to you?"

"I don't think so."

"So, what has Al told you?" she asked.

"He hasn't said a word about it," I replied. "I don't think he cares about the trophy at all."

"Wow," said Cindy.

I thought about Cindy's response for a moment, and the unusual nature of a man who wins the equivalent of an Oscar in the aviation world and then promptly forgets about it, and I realized there was nothing else to say. So, I just agreed with her.

"Yeah ... wow," I replied.

Then we said goodbye, and I went to bed one more night in Waukomis. As I turned out the lights, I was thinking about Al and his dad fishing and hunting together. I imagined them walking in the woods in the fall, the snap of winter coming on, the soft sound of china berries landing in the leaves, the *clash* of whitetail bucks locking horns in the distance, the smell of woodsmoke and bourbon ... a father's hand on his son's shoulder.

And I wished my father had been an alcoholic.

CHAPTER FOUR

FLINT HILLS

About a third of the Americans who died in combat were killed during the Nixon presidency.

Most people share my taste in heroes. We feel safer in a world watched over by beings who are nearly omnipotent. We understand that vigilance is the high price of freedom, but we would rather someone else pay the price. Thus, we need our heroes to be wealthier, stronger, smarter, and more charming than ourselves. We are reckless in our invention of these watchers. We create costumes for them, and weaponry, and fantastic powers that make them impervious to the things to which we commoners fall prey. Most importantly, we make our heroes capable of protecting the two treasures we hold most dear in our breasts – our safety and our significance. The best and brightest of these watchers we call, "superheroes", and we often assign them the gift of flight.

Sometimes our heroes are musicians or public servants, and we expect them to watch over us in specialized ways. At the time of Al's story, The Beatles had been standing guard over the planet for most of the sixties, keeping teenage boys and girls from slipping into the tractor-beam of their parents' Big Band music. On the political scene, the Kennedys put a youthful face on power, and promised to turn our nation into a Camelot of sorts. They certainly looked the part of superheroes, and many people were willing to follow them to the ends of the earth. Lyndon Johnson had his own appeal, though he was far less charming than his predecessor. His Great Society assured us we had seen the last of poverty and racial injustice. And, of course, Martin Luther King was a hero in his own league.

These were the demigods of the day, right up until the moment they disbanded, or declined to run for a second term, or took a bullet in the head. Then we moved on to other heroes. We are a fickle bunch, us commoners.

I always thought it odd that Richard Nixon rose to power without a single sign of being anybody's hero.

So many musicians sang about Nixon in the late 60s and early 70s, one might have confused him for a pop icon. But there was no such popularity. He was as duplicitous as a two-headed nickel, at one moment running for office on a platform of Communist bashing, painting political opponents as "pinko commies" to gain ground on them – and at the next moment, garnering votes by promising to bring the troops home swiftly. Thus Nixon, (as John Lennon, Frank Zappa, David Bowie, James Taylor, Neil Young, and others crooned,) waged war and retreated from it depending on the direction of the wind. Some say he prolonged the war by stalling the Paris Peace Talks, in order to secure his 1968 election victory. At any rate, Nixon seemed to need the war, like an alcoholic needs a drink.

In later musings, I even wondered if he might have been our story's villain.

Driving back to Colorado through the Flint Hills gave me time to think about what I knew and didn't know. For starters, I knew that Magnet Ass was not as frightening as I imagined he would be. He was kind, self-deprecating, almost pastoral in his treatment of his wife and house guests. At times, I found myself forgetting his immense service to our country, and relating to him as if he and I were on the same plain. Looking back, this may have been Al's plan all along. Nevertheless, I was uncomfortable with it, preferring my heroes bulletproof, indomitable, and far above me in stature.

On the passenger seat next to me, I had a notebook bursting with information about the Mackay mission, three 90-minute cassette tapes of Al and Pat pontificating on everything from marriage vows to blowing up trucks, and a half-dozen coconut-filled chocolates for Cindy – purchased at the Russell Stover's in Abilene, Kansas, and inspired by Al's tender cultivation of everyone in his circle of influence. He was already changing me as a man, and I never saw it coming.

I also had a handful of Oklahoma dirt, scraped from my tennis shoes before I threw them away, and stowed in a plastic baggie, which I borrowed from Pat's pantry in her laundry room. It was to keep me focused on the mission, until the last page was written.

These were the things I knew – the things that were solid in my life.

On the other hand, the Flint Hills are the perfect place for a man to think about the things he *doesn't know*. And as I drove through them, I could not escape my own obtuseness. Like a wall of water demolishing a levee, my most fearful thoughts burst through my defenses and flooded my sorry self.

Why had I quit my job in the first place? Did I really believe I could write a book about a war in which I never participated? Did I really think people would pay good money to read it? How could I have been so naive?

And then the nasty, lurking question I had been trying to ignore washed over me ... *What if Cindy gets tired of me being unemployed and leaves me for another man – one who has a job?*

I knew the thought was illogical, and I immediately stepped on the gas to put distance between it and me. But the thought persisted. Relentlessly, it poured through the fissures in my soul, and even though I knew there was no truth to it, I allowed its torture to continue. And the starkness of the hills held me captive.

They are hard and declarative, the Flint Hills – a vast land of light diffused by nothing, shining on everything. Through them runs a ribbon of asphalt, and on that ribbon run the souls of men on wheels, imperceptive of the glowing landscape on either side of I–35, where the blades of grass are bright with news, the undulating hillsides both concealing and revealing. There are reports to be had in these rugged haunts, rumors from the Overworld, revelation so startling that if a man would only stop his wheels long enough to receive it, he could share it with a sunless world – and the dawn would come for everyone.

But no one ever stops in the Flint Hills.

And their wheels just keep on turning.

Near Wichita, it dawned on me I had left Waukomis with only bare-bones information about the crew. They were names to me, and little else.

O'Brien....
Nash....
Clancy....
Russell....
Jones....
Wilson....
Firestone....
Cofer....
Lopez....

If I was to tell Al's story, I was going to have to know these men well. Otherwise, come chapter eleven or twelve, when the honeymoon of writing was over and the grunt work set in, I would have no comrades with whom to share the burden. It is true, after all, that books are written by their characters – not their authors. I suppose, too, that wars are won by privates, not by generals. But what do I know?

I know this....

Characters are everything. Without them, there is no plot, no story worth telling or listening to. Al had told me about one such character on our first evening together.

The F–4 pilot's name had long haunted Al's memory, because his actions were unforgettable. Like many pilots in the Southeast Asia theatre, this one was there to defend the helpless. Sometimes this took the form of relentless strafing of enemy troops surrounding unarmed, friendly villages. Other times it called for the pilot to be an escort for the gunships that flew "low and slow" and, thus, were an easy target for the artillery on the Ho Chi Minh Trail. At these times, Stinger's best friend was the F-4 Phantom.

Born in the McDonnell Douglas think tank, the F-4 Phantom II was a two-seat, twin-engine, all-weather, long-range, supersonic fighter-bomber, originally developed for the US Navy, but eventually adopted by the Marines and the Air Force. By the time Al served in Vietnam, the F-4C was as much a part of the Air Force fabric as any plane would ever be. With a top speed of 1473 mph, eighteen-thousand pounds of weapons on nine external hard points, and a 20mm M61 Vulcan rotary cannon, one could see why the F-4 was, in a word ... "invincible".

But a word can be misleading.

Al's recollection of the pilot was that he was a "GIB", a "guy in back", which meant he was a rated Air Force pilot, who could fly the plane and ostensibly land it from the rear seat, though he had a limited view and fewer flight instruments than the pilot in front of him.

On the night of this particular story, his plane was part of an escort for Al, and his request for help in dropping a load of bombs before heading back to base was not an unusual one.

"Stinger Two One ... this is Triple Nickel Niner ... need you to drop a log, so we can pickle my load and head home to Mom," said the GIB.

"Roger that Triple Nickel," said Magnet Ass. "Putting a log down for you now. Say hello to Mom for us. And thanks for your service."

In the back of Al's plane, Ed Lopez was already ahead of the game. Far below the gunship, one could see the jungle lighting up from the flare he had just launched. At seven-thousand feet, the tandem of pilots in the F-4 were already thinking of their warm beds on the base at Udorn. They had gone past bingo tonight, and were in need of getting lighter if they wanted to have enough fuel to make it back to those beds. The glow of the lu-lu on the ground was a welcome sight. They dropped their plane down to six-thousand to dump the bombs. But for some reason they kept descending. A few seconds later, the F–4 erupted in a fireball, on the edge of the Plain of Jars, and the GIB and his front-seater were nothing but a hole in the jungle.

As Al told me this story, he bowed his head and cried, and I didn't know whether to comfort him or be silent. So, I sat there like a stone. And I've always regretted not at least putting my arm around his shoulder.

"He just kept going toward the ground," said Al of the GIB he would never meet. "It happened so fast, there was nothing I could do ... nothing I could say."

After he had composed himself and dried his eyes, Al told me that the GIB and his fellow pilot were victims of "target fix-ation", but by that time I had learned to keep my mouth shut whenever he introduced me to a new term – opting to defer my questions until later, or to simply look it up myself. And here is what I found.

Target fixation is "*an attentional phenomenon observed in humans in which an individual becomes so focused on an object that his awareness of hazards or obstacles diminishes.*"

If one wants to understand target fixation in layman's terms, he need only ride his bike down a narrow, mountain path, trying to avoid rocks or logs by keeping his eye looking straight at them. Inevitably, he collides with the very things he tries to miss, and over the handlebars he goes.

So, it is a deep truth in life that the things we fear or fixate on eventually become our reality.

The story of the GIB's death shook me to the core, as had the emergence of another idiom with which I was wholly unfamiliar, but wanted to understand. The idiom was, "bingo", and it bugged me so badly that I pulled over on the southern outskirts of Wichita and called Magnet Ass on the phone.

"Are you lost?" said Pat on the other end, when she recognized my name on the caller ID.

"No, ma'am, I'm in Kansas," I replied. "Say ... Al wouldn't happen to be taking a nap would he?"

"I'll wake him for you," said Pat. "He'll be happy to talk." Before I could stop Pat, she put the phone down and traipsed off to retrieve her husband. When a groggy Magnet Ass returned, I apologized profusely for getting him out of bed, but, as always, he was eager to talk about anything that had to do with flying.

"What does 'bingo' mean?" I asked Al, getting straight to the point.

"It means, 'I have just what it takes to make it back to base'," said Al, automatically. "It's a pre-briefed amount of fuel. If a fella's smart, that's when he turns his plane around and heads for home. And everybody likes to go home, don't they?"

I thought about Cindy and my crazy, jealous, fixated thoughts in the Flint Hills, and for the first time in my marriage, home suddenly seemed less desirable.

"Will?" said Al.

"What?" I replied.

"You do like going home, don't you?"

"Of course I do."

"Then why didn't you say so?" asked Al.

"You wouldn't understand," I said, and then I changed the subject quickly.

"Al?"

"Hm?"

"Would you mind telling me a little more about the truck hunters?"

"Right now? On the phone?"

"Yes," I said.

Al heaved a long, labored sigh, as if considering my proposition. "I'm tired, Will," he said at last. "Can it wait until later?"

"Sure thing," I said. "How about tomorrow?" I waited in silence for Al to answer me, but he had already handed the phone to Pat and shuffled off to bed.

There are no billboards in the Flint Hills. No signs. No advertisements. No messages from the Ad Council. Nothing to clutter
a man's view or his mind. Only as one approaches the city do
the signs begin to appear again, like zombies lined up along
the highway.

Pulling into Wichita, I was reintroduced to the signs of
civilization:

OBEY YOUR THIRST! DRINK SPRITE!
FIRST BAPTIST OF WICHITA – TURN HERE!
BEEN HURT IN AN ACCIDENT? CALL 1-800-MYMONEY

What makes a life significant? I thought, as I drove through the
heart of Wichita. What kind of sign does one have to make in
order for others to say, 'Now there goes a mighty fine life'? Is it the
big things we do and say that give us value – or the small things?
The extraordinary? Or the mundane? A three-hour flight on one
wing? Or the quiet struggle against a fatal disease?

What if the next three hours of my life were so exceptional that
someone wrote a book about them fifty years from now?

The point in saying all this is that a person's life is filled with
countless three-hour missions, any one of which might be called,
"heroic" – but none of which is possible without the characters,
or the signs they make with their lives. Sometimes the characters soar all the way to the story's climax, then land safely at its
conclusion to the delight of the reader. Other times, they disappear in chapter three like the GIB and his front-seater, and the
story goes on without them. Occasionally, the characters are the
heroes. But whatever the case, as I said before, characters are
everything to a story. And all of them matter immensely.

Which brings me back to my problem; I knew so little about
Al's crew, and that which I knew could be summed up as follows:

Two of the nine characters in Al's story were dead and gone.
A third man wanted nothing more than to forget the story and

finish his life in peace. A fourth left the Air Force shortly after the Mackay Mission, citing "fear of flying" as reason for discharge. And a fifth crew member was apparently AWOL. So, before I had even written a single page of the book, half the crew had vanished, and I had no guarantee the others would engage.

What was it about the Mackay mission that made the truck hunters disappear? I wondered.

Over a sub sandwich in Salina, KS, I found a sunny, side street and opened my notebook. Like an archaeologist rummaging through rubble, I reviewed scribbled notes from Al's meager testimony about his men, hoping to find encouragement. Page after page of an old gentleman's recollections stared back at me, valiant attempts to resurrect what had long been buried beneath the task of raising daughters, wheat, cows and such, but so little about the crew with whom he flew a hundred and fifty missions. It was enough to drive an archaeologist batty.

Where, oh, where were the men of Stinger 883?

Then I saw it.

There amidst the rubble.

The tiniest bit of bone from which I could reconstruct a man.

He was one of the dead ones, but he would have to do. Perhaps I could bring him to life. I glanced at the page where the fragment lay in scribbled cursive, turning it back and forth in my mind's eye, wondering what ligaments once supported it, what organs it must surely have protected. Whatever the fragment was, it was all I had. And the fragment was simply this....

Airman First Class Donnell Cofer loved to sing.

CHAPTER FIVE

BODY OF THE BIRD

The first American to die in the Vietnam War was James Davis, in 1958. The average age of men killed was 23.1 years. The oldest was 62. The youngest, 16. Total ... 58,202.

Funny how I began my research of this book's characters with the youngest, most inexperienced, most deceased of all the crew-members. But that is all I had to go on. The bone fragment was right there in Al's words, in my notebook marked, "Magnet Ass And The Stone Cold Truck Hunters". And it was underlined with an exclamation mark after it.

Cofer loved to sing!

I had no sooner parked the Buick in the garage, walked in the back door of my home, and placed a phone call to the Air Force Academy in Colorado Springs, than I was connected with someone in records and I was trembling with excitement. With the phone to my ear, and a pencil poised to scribble on a gro-cery sack, I felt a warm body press against mine from behind.

"Hey, soldier," the body whispered, "You want to say 'hello' before you jump back into your book?"

I turned to see Cindy looking up at me. Embarrassed that I had ruined the homecoming with an immediate phone call, I kissed her and felt forgiven.

"Mmm," she said, "I like hello."

"I like it, too," I replied. "But it's not my book," I added for good measure.

Ever so slyly, I reached for her left hand on my waist, to see if her wedding ring was there, (which it was),... and I was just telling her how great she looked, when the historian on the other end of the line mistook our amorous moment for a prank call.

"No, ma'am," I said, quickly. "That was in no way meant for you—"

When she was finally convinced, the historian graciously gave me a slew of information on young Cofer, and I was off to the races. Three days later, when I received a package in the mail, I had even more bone fragments to deal with, and soon I had enough of Cofer's remains to stand back and see the whole man.

Born in Denver, Colorado, on May 26th, 1949, Airman First Class Donnell Hughes Cofer couldn't help but sing; After all, there was mountain air in his lungs, the kind that lowland birds in Waukomis, Oklahoma rarely breathed.

When he was six months old, Cofer's family moved to a slightly lower altitude in Albuquerque, but by then the die was cast. Cofer was a singer and a flyer ... and to those things he would remain true all of his days.

Strangely, Cofer's interests in music ran counter to the music of his peers. At Highland High School in Albuquerque, where the Beatles and Stones were all the rage, Cofer was the lead tenor soloist in a special mixed ensemble. The first three years of high school, he was accepted into the New Mexico All-State Choir. When puberty hit during his junior year, Cofer simply adapted to the change; Soon the former tenor held the bass position in the All-State Mixed Quartet.

But no Beatles for Cofer – that was noise, not singing. When he graduated from high school in June of '67, he immediately enlisted in the Air Force and was put on a waiting list where he remained until the following March. At the time he entered basic training at Lackland AFB, Texas, he had barely grown his tail feathers. From Lackland, Cofer went to Lowry, where he was back in the mountain air of Colorado. There he was trained as a weapons and munitions specialist. His first operational assignment was to the F–4D aircraft at MacDill AFB, Florida. It was during this tour of duty that Cofer decided to volunteer for a Southeast Asia assignment through the Palace Gun Program.

I remember reading the words, "Palace Gun Program", and thinking they sounded like a cotillion event gone awry. I wanted to shout some sort of warning to young Donnell Cofer, to alert him to the fact Vietnam probably wasn't the place for a mixed ensemble specialist. But every bird must choose his own flight path.

In March of '69, Cofer received his orders and reported to Lockbourne AFB, Ohio, for training in the AC–119K Gunship as an aerial gunner. He remained at Lockbourne with the 18th Special Operations Squadron until November, 1969, when at last he was deployed to Vietnam. At Phan Rang AB, Cofer completed his initial in-country training, at which time he was assigned to a Forward Operating Location at Phu Cat AB.

Finally, he was assigned to Udorn Royal Thai AB, Thailand.

"And that's how Cofer came to be part of Al's crew," I said to Cindy one night, as we sat by the fire. She was noodling around on her smartphone, and I was preoccupied with the only thing that had filled my life for the last seven weeks. Thankfully, I had settled into the insanity of a "full-time writer". But I still feared it could all come unhinged at any moment, spraying bits and pieces of author and manuscript all over the neighborhood ... like the Phantom at Udorn. I kept these thoughts from Cindy, particularly the weaker ones of insecurity and jealousy.

Being my polar opposite on the topic of literature and its supreme position in the pantheon of interests, Cindy had never really appreciated my previous five books – two of which were self-help books, the other three novels. She had read them as a matter of marital duty. But there was something different about this book, and both of us knew what it was.

"You love your boys, don't you," she declared.

"Of course, I do," I replied, looking up from my laptop. "And don't pretend that you don't love them, too."

Cindy smiled, and her smile told me I had pegged her.

Our own sons, Wes and Peter, were grown and gone, scattered

eastward toward the arch in St. Louis. Pursuing medicine and ministry. Helping others with their bodies and souls. Calling occasionally to check on ours. We missed them terribly.

By this time in the project, several of the truck hunters had begun to contact me, each with their own account of a roundabout path to Vietnam, not unlike Cofer's. I always thought it strange we referred to Al's crew as, "boys". Of those still living, the youngest amongst them was Firestone, and he was 68 when I began research for this book. Neither Cindy nor I could keep from freezing the crew in time, imagining them as young airmen, perpetually poised to defend the huddled masses until the end of time.

"So, what's the crew up to tonight?" asked Cindy, her eyes dancing in the light of the fire. She had grown accustomed to my nightly debriefs about the mission, and I delighted in sharing what I had written while she was away at school.

"Oh, you know ... they're over the fence again, as usual," I replied. "Shooting stuff, tearing around the neighborhood like they own the place, that kind of thing."

"It's crazy they volunteered to go to Nam," said Cindy, trying to sound tough with her use of war vernacular. "If it was our sons, I don't think I'd have allowed that."

"Well, there was this thing called, 'the draft'," I said.

"I know that," said Cindy. "But I'd have moved our family to Canada."

I smiled and looked into the coals, enjoying the warmth on my face. "Wait'll you hear some of the things they did over there. You probably would've moved us to Mars."

It had been two months since I first met Magnet Ass at his home in Waukomis, and I had received emails from five of the crew members. With each new introduction, I felt as if I was part of an expanding family. To my surprise and delight, they all welcomed the Cub Scout with open arms. But with the influx of information, there also came an overwhelming sense of responsibility – not so much to the writing of a book, but to the accurate portrayal of other men's lives.

I also realized I was going to need some sort of filing system for each crew member's data, or I would soon be in danger of the data taking over my life.

Fortunately, I began to see a natural order to the kind of information I received from each man, and this order transferred into a broader understanding of the way Al's ship was run. Eventually, I was able to categorize each man and his correspondence as if he were part of a living, breathing body – a bird's body.

Captain James A. Russell was first to contact me, and his emails were always bulging with fact. Without ever meeting the man, I knew he was probably not the kind who dealt in metaphors. Captain James Alexander Russell was a commissioned officer, one of the five CO's on Al's crew. Jim's job was to run the FLIR, which meant he detected enemy movement through "forward-looking infrared" and coordinated targets with Al, so that Al could pull the trigger.

Two things should be mentioned about Jim Russell for the sake of color – first, his hobby in high school was rebuilding cars and motorcycles, and second, he was engaged to his sweetheart just before deploying to Vietnam, and they married upon his return. In short, he was a man who liked things to run according to schedule, who didn't mind getting his hands dirty.

Captain Ronald Curtis Jones was the second man to contact me, which was more appropriate than the reader could possibly know, since it was Russell and Jones who always worked together in tandem. Jones ran the NOS equipment, or, "night observation scope". Coupled with the information that came from Russell's infrared, Jones' findings made it impossible for anything that moved along the Ho Chi Minh Trail to escape detection.

They were like birds of prey, Jones and Russell – and they never went hungry. Early on, I begin to describe them as "the eyes" of Al's crew; In one of Jim Russell's emails, he said my description couldn't have been more accurate.

A patch, drawn and designed by Jim Russell, prominently displays Jones's trademark red mustache and sheds light on why the crew often referred to Jones as, "The Red Baron".

If Cofer was the song, and Jones and Russell were the eyes, then Technical Sergeant Albert A. Nash was "the wings" of this swiftly evolving bird I had affectionately dubbed, "the stone cold truck hunters."

Born on April 8, 1941, in Easton, Maryland, Nash was the plane's flight engineer. My phone conversation with his widowed Wilhemenia was one of the highlights of my fall. Even though my interaction with Wilhemenia was short, I felt as if I had met the man. A photograph of the handsome, African-American engineer, with the compact frame and perpetually groomed mustache came to me in a packet from Jones, and I pinned it on the wall next to my desk.

If he was anything like sweet Wilhemenia, Albert Nash was okay in my books.

For weeks, I had tried to reach Captain Brent O'Brien, Al's co-pilot, but with no success, and I had resigned to the fact he no longer felt part of the crew. Then one day out of the blue, O'Brien called from Seattle, where he was on a business trip with his wife and had time to kill. He had hardly finished introducing himself, when he set the record straight regarding his departure from the Air Force.

"It wasn't really 'fear of flying' that caused me to leave," said O'Brien. "After all, I did fly nine more missions with Al's crew after the Mackay Mission. But eventually, I just felt like I had done my share – and I was tired of getting shot at."

"Fair enough," I said, glancing at a photo of the crew in my pile. It was taken on the day the boys received the Mackay in DC, and only O'Brien (far left) was wearing civvies.

"I noticed you weren't in uniform at the trophy ceremony," I added.

There was a good-natured chuckle on the other end of the line. "Yeah," said O'Brien. "That all happened so fast. I didn't even own a suit. My wife had to help me pick one out the morning we flew to Washington, DC."

Brent and I talked for nearly two hours in that first conversation, and I liked him immediately. When he told me Vietnam had blown a huge crater in his first marriage, leaving both spouses on opposite sides of the hole, I felt an enormous sorrow for Brent. However, when he divulged that his second wife, Joan, was seventeen years younger than he, I couldn't help but say, "Good for you, buddy." I imagined him trying to explain Vietnam to her, while she tried explaining 80's hair bands to him.

If there was a part of the "bird" that fit O'Brien's personality, it had to be the "feathers". He was the only crew member who spoke about getting away on days off in Vietnam, just to enjoy the beauty of the countryside.

"There was a hill near the base in Phu Cat," he told me. "I used to climb it and sit for hours. From that vantage point, the paddies and the hamlets looked like a chess board that belonged to some giant who lived in the sky. You never would've known there were dead bodies lying in the mud down there. It was nice to be far away from the war for a while."

Staff Sergeant Ronald R. Wilson was the "body" of the bird, the biggest part that carried all the innards and the vitals. Tall and lumbering, he appears strikingly handsome in some of the photos sent to me by Jones. My one phone conversation with him revealed a down home, rural boy, so laid back and countrified that he made Magnet Ass look like a city slicker.

Of all the truck hunters, Wilson was the only one who didn't use a computer – and the only one whose hometown was smaller than Magnet Ass's. He was a gunner, plain and simple. And when he got through hunting trucks in Nam, he planned on going back to Rosetta, and to hunting deer in Nowheresville, Missouri.

Then there was Sergeant Kenneth Eugene Firestone. Even in the first few sentences of his initial correspondence, I knew I was talking to the stereotypical Vietnam airman. If ever there was a part of the bird that could simply be classified as the "flit", Firestone was it. He was the "impulse" of Al's crew, the nervy, twitching, hopping part that couldn't wait to get to war, to see some action, to give the enemy what they had coming.

"Ken was a specimen," Al told me once, "Built with those long, lean kind of muscles that sneak up on you, and accomplish things you never thought they could. He could lift a full ammo can with one arm. Made it look easy even. It was the darndest thing."

As it turns out, the "flit" was also the one who, along with full ammo cans, pitched the tool box out the rear aft door on the night of the Mackay Mission. "That might have come in handy if we had to start unbolting the mini-guns," said Al. "But you couldn't be mad at Firestone for very long. He was too good-natured to hold a grudge against." Ken Firestone was second from the right in the group picture he sent me. Only his fellow-gunner, Ron Wilson, was taller.

So, these were the men who reported to me, and the order in which they reported: Russell, Jones, O'Brien, Wilson, Wilhelmenia Nash, (on behalf of her husband, Albert), and Firestone. Of course, Donnell Cofer was a reconstruction made possible with the help of the Air Force historian and the crew.

Captain Roger Clancy was still hesitant to engage.

Staff Sergeant Adolfo "Ed" Lopez, Jr. was nowhere to be found.

And finally, there was Magnet Ass.

At first, I had a hard time distinguishing which part of the bird he was. If I said he was "the heart", that would be cliché. If I said, "the head", that would not be accurate either. Too often, Al led his men in such a way, they hardly knew they were being led. O'Brien told me once that of all the bosses he had ever had, Al was by far "the finest". No, Al wasn't the head and he wasn't the heart. But no matter how I ransacked my brain for the perfect way to describe Al's place in the bird-body, I came up empty-handed. I even wondered if he was not a part of the body at all, but was, instead, the bird's "flight". This, however, left me with a picture of Al hovering above his crew, transcendent and superior, and I knew that wouldn't do.

At last it struck me. And when I saw it, I was stunned with the discovery, because it had been there all along. Silent, yet indispensable. Provisional, yet unseen. As vital to success as the very frame of any plane on any tarmac.

Al Milacek was the bones.

Once when Cindy and I lived in the Ozarks, I counted over two dozen species of birds in a single morning's breakfast on our back deck. Because our house butted up to four-hundred acres of deep woods, the birds felt safe to use our yard as a feeding grounds. So I put out seed and suet for them, and I sat back and watched the fun. Rose-breasted Grosbeaks ... Rufus-Sided Towhees ... Slate-Colored Juncos ... Indigo Buntings ... the list went on and on. As each came in for landing, I felt as if I was Ground Control, and the birds my beloved squadron.

The smaller of them approached with ease, touching down nimbly on the lip of my feeder with rarely a mishap. The larger birds, however, arrived with unpoetic grace, their final approach marked by theatrical flares and attitude corrections, and the occasional roll-out that took them right off the other side of the feeder. It was these birds – the raucous, obnoxious grackles and cowbirds – that I grew to love in a way only a father could, or perhaps a Captain.

Each bird had its own distinguishing chest candy, so to speak, and I prided myself on knowing them well. I would see a medium-sized, greyish bird with a fashionable mohawk on its head, and I would immediately say out loud, "Tufted Titmouse". The tiny, caramel and white bird with the disproportionately long beak and the pronounced eyeliner around its coal-black eyes was the, "Carolina Wren". Chickadees always took one seed from the feeder, then darted away to a nearby branch – "One and done", I would tell myself. But the finches – oh, my stars! – the finches would socialize at the feeder all day long, squabbling and tittering, culling out the sunflower meat from millet, until they had gobbled up ten dollars worth of seed, and scattered another ten on the ground for the squirrels to eat.

If a man watches birds long enough, two things will happen: first, people will think him to be two or three decades older than his actual age. And second, he will eventually see things that will make him melancholy as a Mourning Dove. I say this for

71

the obvious reason that all flight, even that of birds, is subject to the Law of Gravity. And birds, like men, can only tie the record for flying low.

It was a Saturday morning in October when the tanager decided the back of my house was as good a place as any to end his career in flight. With a loud 'thud', he crashed into the window of the French doors my wife had been polishing, then slumped back onto our deck, still as a stone. Cindy looked at the bird, then up at me with fat, urgent tears in her eyes.

"He's dead," she pronounced.

"Yes, I see," I replied.

Cindy went inside to comfort herself with cocoa, leaving me to preside over the bird's funeral. In the garage, I found a shovel and a piece of burlap in which to wrap the poor, unfortunate, former pilot of our neighborhood.

The deceased was a Summer Tanager, often mistaken from a distance for a common cardinal. A closer look revealed he lacked the cardinal's dramatic, black eye-mask, and I immediately added him to my "birds-I-have-seen" list. His mate, a pleasant, olive-colored bird, sat in a native cedar, watching me as I dug her husband's grave. He was the first tanager I ever spotted in the wild, and, come to think of it, my last, as well.

Ker-chippp! went the shovel, as it broke through the meager topsoil of my Missouri lawn and struck the limestone shelf that undergirds almost the entire Show-Me state. Three spadefuls later, I had my hole dug – he was, after all, a small individual – and I laid the burlap in the bottom of the hole like a shroud, waiting to receive the dead. His little body was still warm to the touch, his neck limp and broken. I wrapped him gently in the burlap, placed him in the hole, and covered him over with dust. In the native cedar, his mate watched the service, her round, black eyes shining with secretions from her lachrymal gland.

I chose to see them as tears.

So, one by one, the truck hunters reported to me for duty. Like birds coming to our feeder, they flew in at their own leisure, and I marveled at how unique each one was from the other. Captains. Sergeants. Staff Sergeants. A Technical Sergeant. And one Airman First Class, his pin-feathers still drying. They were all so beautiful and brave. Because one doesn't normally mention birds and war in the same sentence, it seemed unnatural to mix the metaphors of sweetness and savagery. Then again, a man whose nickname is "Magnet Ass" doesn't usually tell strangers he loves them either.

So, in the fall of 2015, when I was 56 and unemployed, I finally said 'yes' to the writing of Al's story, and I no longer told Cindy it wasn't my book. And forsaking all prospects of gainful hire, I went "over the fence" armed only with a laptop, and a wife who seemed willing.

Yes ... it was all so terribly unnatural.

PART TWO

"BETWEEN THE BLACK SKY AND THE BLUE."

00:02 / 8 MAY / 1970

The blast threw the plane into a sixty-degree, right dive, pinning Jones to the back of his NOS position like a bug on a windshield. He felt the throbbing crown of his head, and when he drew his trembling fingers back into the moonlight they were slick and red.

Surprised they had been hit, Jones grabbed the webbing that tethered him to Stinger's insides and pulled himself to his feet. To his right, the cabin was awash with firelight and engine fumes. To his left, fifteen-hundred feet of space, rancid with cordite, fell away into the moonlit jungle of Laos.

Further back in the plane, the gunners scrambled for their parachutes, while the insane slant of the cargo bay sucked them toward the open door. Here was the action Firestone and Cofer had longed for when they came to Vietnam. Now, all their piss and vinegar poured out into the darkness with everything that wasn't tied down.

"Where's my chute?!" shouted Firestone. He groped through a tangled sea of munition, where only moments before he and Cofer had been stomping links and cranking ammo into Al's M61 Vulcans. "It was right there on the rack, where I put it! Where's my damn silk, Cofer?!"

By the starboard cargo door, a lonely chest-pack teetered near the threshold, where the jarring blow had flung it. Cofer grabbed it just before it disappeared over the edge, and shoved it across the floor to Firestone. Then he scrambled away from the door and staggered to his feet with the help of the mini-guns.

"We're going to be okay, pal," said Cofer. He was twenty, and the crack in his voice was still perceptible.

"Of course, we are!" Firestone shouted above the recip's deafening roar. He swung the parachute over his head and tightened it to his body. As if to reassert himself as the calm and level-headed one, he added, "We should wear these things when we're working."

"But we're going to be okay," repeated Cofer, this time with questioning eyes.

Of the gunners, only Wilson was truly calm, his mind far away, over the ocean in Missouri. The sound of the engines winding up to light speed made him think of WWII movies he had seen, and he wondered if he would make it back to his sweet Rosetta. At the base of the Gatling guns, 20mm casings – spent and sizzling – spilled over the top of the hopper and onto the gun-deck, where they clinked together musically. Wilson kicked them with his boot, sending hundreds into the night.

From his position by the flare launcher, Ed Lopez saw a long, red torch blowing out the back of the engine, lighting the clouds like Cinco de Mayo. He still felt the effect of yesterday's whiskey, but as the crew's jumpmaster, he forced himself to act like a sober man. Soon, the atmosphere crackled with artillery, and Lopez shouted something in Spanish.

To the five men crammed onto the AC–119K's flight deck, the impact of the 37mm shell had sounded like a sledgehammer on top of the canopy.

"Mayday! Mayday! Mayday!" Captain Al Milacek called into his headset. His broadcast over emergency frequencies alerted Air Command that Stinger was hit and going in.

Navigator Roger Clancy looked at Jim Russell and noticed the FLIR's eyes were closed, his lips mouthing the Lord's Prayer as usual.

In front of the blackout curtain, Engineer Nash's mind was a snarled equation of damage assessment, fuel conservation, and the aggregate summation of a sixty-eight-thousand-pound airplane falling fifty-five-hundred-feet and breaking into a million pieces. He needed someone to give him a direct order, just to get his ass moving.

Milacek knew they were losing altitude fast. If he didn't get the plane to dish out in a hurry, they would auger in so deep the NVA would have to dig for days to find them. But a peace had settled over Al. He gave a nod to Pat and the girls on the dashboard, and glanced at his co-pilot, O'Brien.

"Full left rudder! Full left aileron!" he said, as if he had dreamed this scene all his life. "And give me full blowers in the right recip!" he ordered Nash.

Nash was happy to comply.

Welded together by a furious will to live, Milacek and O'Brien flew into action. They felt the belly of the plane being peppered by smaller caliber shells, and they knew they couldn't sustain another blow like the one that had hurled them at the ground.

The sky rained fire.

CHAPTER SIX

THAT THING IN THE BEETLE CELLAR

Construction of the Ho Chi Minh Trail began on May 19th, 1959, Ho's 69th birthday. At the height of Commando Hunt, the Trail contained an estimated 1500 artillery nests. All aimed at the sky.

We tease my mother about her survival techniques, back in the day when she was raising four kids – all of us under the age of six – while her ophthalmologist husband was out saving the world, one eyeball at a time. Family fable has it, she used to fasten our pajamas to our bed sheets with safety pins, so we couldn't escape during naptime and disturb her scant moments of sanity. Practically speaking, Jean Cunningham was going crazy. Once when I was four or so, and my sisters and I were battened down for the afternoon, my father came home midday from the office, hours ahead of his normal time. It was a summer day, and through my open window the sound of cicadas washed up from the driveway below, mingled with sumptuous honeysuckle. Because I was counting the tiny naval anchors on my wallpaper when he entered the room, I was not aware of Dad's presence until he was kneeling next to my bed.

"Get your clothes on, little man," he whispered, as he unpinned the safety pins and set me free.

Soon, we were in the station wagon speeding west toward the farm – the dark republic of my childhood receding rapidly behind me, the warm sunshine calling out to me through the windshield. Even at four, I was aware of a diabolical satisfaction welling up in me at the thought of my sisters back home, still in their beds, splayed like science experiments to their sheets. While I had our father all to myself.

When he wasn't practicing medicine, Bill Cunningham was a carnival barker. To this day, I know of no one else who can wash his hands with regular bar soap, then blow a bubble the size of a watermelon. Or wiggle his ears without raising his eyebrows. Or turn a traffic signal from red to green with the wave of his hand. (It was years before I realized he was watching the adjacent traffic signal out of the corner of his eye, so he could impress his children with his limitless wizardry the moment it turned yellow.) How sad it is when the magic of youth gets scrubbed away with logic.

"Have I ever told you how to make a cloud disappear?" he said, as we zoomed along.

"No," I said, standing up and eyeing the fishing gear in the backseat. We did not wear seatbelts in those days, and the idea of a car-seat had not yet spawned from a culture of litigation.

"Well, that needs to change right now," he said. "Go ahead, son. Pick yourself out one, and stare at it good and hard, until it goes away. You should probably start with a small one."

All the way to Piedmont I vanquished clouds that day, obliterating stratus and nimbus ... and occasionally attacking a towering heap of cumulus ... until I grew tired of my super power, and we arrived at the farm.

My father parked the car under a chinaberry tree, on the east end of the long, dirt road that ran from the little, green house to the sharecropper's place, and we gathered our things and walked silently toward the cattle ponds. I carried the snacks in a brown, paper sack: two Twinkies, a bag of potato chips, some beef jerky, and a bottle of Mason's Root Beer for us to share. Dad carried the fishing gear. As we walked, I became aware of something I had never known about my father – and though I am describing it now through a decades-thick lens of analysis, I saw it then with perfect eyes. *The less my father knew about a subject, the quieter he became.* By the time we reached the ponds, I knew in my heart he had never fished before ... and the gear he was carrying was borrowed from my uncle.

Tying a hook on the line was no problem for my father; After all, he made his living with suture as gossamer as a fairy's wing. But knowing what to put on the end of the hook was another thing. He searched my uncle's tackle box until he was convinced it held nothing of value for our purposes.

"We need worms," he announced. At that, we dug around in the sunbaked banks, until our fingers were raw with digging, and we came to the conclusion that every worm in Oklahoma had gone deeper into the ground, to escape the relentless sun. In the end, we used the jerky for bait.

With a flick of his wrist, my father sent the rig out into the middle of the pond. And we sat ... and we sat ... and we sat ... and we sat ... for a miserable, wordless eternity. Dad holding the one rod he had brought. Me sitting by his side, watching the muddy water. Behind us, on the ridge that overlooked the pond, three cows eyed the scene with parched contempt.

At last, Dad felt a tug.

"Got one!" he declared, triumphantly, and he handed the rod to me. "Go ahead, son – reel her in!"

Throwing my slight frame into the task, I cranked as hard as a four-year-old can, but to no avail.

"It's not moving," I said.

"Let me try," said Dad, taking the rod back from me. "It feels like a big one, son! I think we've really caught a BIG one!" Soon, the rod was nearing its breaking point, when – all of a sudden – the fish on the other end of the line shot out of the water, and landed with a "SPLASH" just a few feet in front of us, where it bobbed and floated and resembled no fish either of us had ever seen before. For a moment, we were both in denial. Then admission set in, followed by disappointment, and finally disgust.

"It's a tire," said my father, sitting back on the dusty, red bank. "FIRESTONE", it read, on the side of the faded whitewall. We stared at it for several painful seconds, and then it sank with a sucking noise, creating a little tornado of bubbles in its wake. "We should eat our Twinkies before they melt," said my father, reaching for the brown, paper sack. He was doing his best to salvage the afternoon, but I suspect his heart was somewhere on the bottom of the pond, with the tire and the soggy beef jerky.

Looking back now, I can see that my father wanted nothing more than to connect with his son. But something always got in the way – something that had to do with success, or *getting it right*, or ... or accomplishing something so perfect, so absolutely faultless, that it made up for failures from another lifetime I knew nothing about. To be honest, making clouds disappear would have been good enough for me. They were all gone from the sky by the time we pulled back into our driveway, and the stars were just beginning to shine through the branches of the elms in our front yard. We went inside, and my father hugged me, and we went to bed. It would be a long time before we fished together again. Even longer before I understood the things that haunted him.

In time, I lost my father to "*baseball blastoma*" in the shadows of a "dingy, beetle cellar", and I struggled to recover from the loss. These are the metaphors the psychologist told me as I sat on her couch years later, my fingers picking at a piece of fuzz on one of its cushions. Even as I wrote her a check for $130, I knew I wouldn't be coming back for a second session. The expensive decor of her office said we'd never get past diagnosis. Not that her diagnosis was wrong either; It was dead on, in fact. But I had known these things since I was a child, and I needed a remedy for my cares – not a better vocabulary to describe them.

Talking to Al about Vietnam was as good a remedy as any, I supposed – a strange, medicinal brew of sorts. With each new conversation we undertook, I was increasingly aware of an invisible line between the two of us – like an IV, running from his heart to mine.

Supplying something I lacked.

High in the sky over Laos, things are peaceful for the pilot. There are no signs to clutter his way. No ridiculous speed limits.

No Sunday drivers. Directions are found in color. Up is blue ... further up is deep blue ... the way to heaven is purple and violet ... black is for whatever else the Almighty has created out there. That is it. There is nothing more. The beauty is stark and simple.

Down is all the other colors....

...greens and browns and yellows and reds ... the hard and earthen colors of the tangible and the familiar ... calamitous if collided with ... these are the ones the pilot wants to avoid. He enjoys them for the view they offer, but he dares not fixate on them, lest he and the earthen colors should merge and become one. Above all, the pilot's immensely glad he's not walking amongst these colors, like the proud and valiant infantrymen he knew in college, back when they were all stateside and safe, with their books, and their homecoming games, and their ROTC functions to insulate them from the madness across the ocean. The pilot is glad to be an airman, and not a ground-pounder.

The air above the Plain of Jars – where Magnet Ass and the truck hunters spent most of the war in 1970 – was once fresh and clean, and only began to reek of cordite and sulphur when the First Indochina War began in 1946. At times, when the bombing was temporarily sparse, as it was for the two weeks between Lyndon Johnson's abandonment of Rolling Thunder in Hanoi and the commencement of Commando Hunt along the Ho Chi Minh Trail in November of '68, Al imagined a man might be able to smell the coconuts and the mangos if he opened up his plane's window and poked his head out. It was a beautiful land, and a beautiful planet....

... from the air.

On afternoon recce runs, before the sun sank and the Trail slithered and undulated with dark war-traffic, Laos was a sea of emeralds to anyone flying in a plane. It was an artist's paradise. An outdoorsman's dream. An entrepreneur's opportunity. Sometimes, when Firestone, Wilson, and Cofer had time on their hands, they would sit on ammo cans by the open cargo door and fire their .38's into all that greenery, picking out a solitary emerald they desired, taking aim at it, and possessing it with the squeeze of a forefinger. As always, they would dream about their homes far away.

Jones ignored this habit of the gunners, opting instead to fiddle with the NOS and to prepare himself for the mission ahead. Through the interphones, Al could hear the ping! ping! of his boy's pistols. But rather than chastising them for their waste of good ammo, he interpreted it as their way of coping, and he kept it to himself for forty-five years, until making it known to me in our interviews. Al was a good pilot, and a patient man to everyone who knew him. Some of the hunters even thought of him as a father.

As for Lopez ... he engaged in neither the view nor the levity. The heavens to him were as dark as a drunken binge.

The AC–119K had a ceiling of ten-thousand feet, a cruising altitude of four to six-thousand feet, and a combat altitude of fifteen-hundred to three-thousand feet. But though the scenery in the sky above the PDJ was breathtaking, the gunships could not stay up there forever. Eventually, Stinger had to leave that beauty behind, come down into the world, and do what she was sent to do, namely, to save some people – and to annihilate others.

The color of air, like the color of water, has eluded painters for centuries. There is no color known as "clear" on the painter's palette. Thus, he or she is left to capture the sky by imagining what is behind it, or above it ... or in it.

In the spring of 1970, the air above the Plain of Jars was the color of war, often grey and fouled from the continuous burning of grade-A, US shit in 55-gallon drums. Because Vietnam was a land with virtually no plumbing, the introduction of 2,709,918 Americans over the course of ten years, all with the need to eliminate, only made the problem worse. Being civilized, the US military set about to fix the problem by putting "piss pipes" everywhere. These were empty ammo canisters, sunk in the ground with their open end up and a piece of metal screen fastened over them for keeping flies out. A man couldn't walk ten yards without tripping over a piss pipe. But it beat the alternative, which was to have little mini-swamps of urine at every turn, and the chance of disease skyrocketing due to men whizzing wherever the hell they wanted to. One of the easiest distinctions between an NVA and an American fire base came to be the presence or absence of piss pipes. And one knew that if he stumbled upon a temporary artillery encampment that was dead silent, smelled strongly of urine, and was completely piss-pipe-free, he was about to have his head blown off.

Piss was easy.

Shit was something else.

Because the fire bases and LZ's were often established for no more than a few days or weeks, medics usually dug a slit trench latrine, placed a metal grate over it, then found some "throne-like" fixture, (i.e., an empty ammo can with a hole cut in the bottom of it), and placed it on the grate for grunts to use when nature called. There, the soldier could be alone with the flies and his thoughts, completely exposed to his fellow man … and often to the enemy, as well. No shortage of stories exists involving incoming mortars and surprised shit-takers, scrambling to shoulder their M16s, even before pulling up their pants. And it is no wonder that one of the most common terms used by Marines to describe combat was simply….

"The shit."

Larger, more permanent encampments were equipped with outhouses, usually "four-holers" for community-sake. Here, a steel drum was cut in half and fitted with a makeshift "seat", forming a shallow shit-pan. Every morning, the drums were hauled out by the lucky soldier whose turn it was for outhouse duty, then doused with diesel, set on fire, and stirred occasionally for several hours, until it's greasy contents were turned to ash and could be disposed of properly in a nearby hole. Some say the black enlisted man was assigned outhouse duty twice as frequently as his white counterparts. But one could never prove that with statistics. And if it's true, it exists now as a bitter stain on the hearts of certain, beautiful souls.

And so it was, that every morning, all over Vietnam, this scene was repeated, like the witches at their cauldron in the opening scene of Shakespeare's Macbeth.

And the thick, black cloud of war rose up to the blue sky and beyond.

It was this murky haze of Man-shit that planes and helicopters encountered first when they descended to the jungle canopy, and then further into combat. Men held their noses ... good men plunging down into the darkness ... coughing ... cursing ... wondering if there might be some other cup for them to drink.

Up close, the "emeralds" showed themselves for what they really were – giant pines, palms, gum, peach and orchid – vast tracts of deciduous woodland, denuded to expose the enemy's movements on the Ho Chi Minh Trail, withering beneath a shroud of dioxin. In its place, like an ungrateful son snatching his inheritance from the hands of a dying parent, fast-growing bamboo took root and sprang up. It was everywhere, thick-set and merciless.

Sometimes the UH–1B's, in order to create makeshift landing zones, were forced to use their rotors to cut through the bamboo, just to reach the ground. Like flies looking for the perfect pile of shit, they buzzed back and forth from one LZ to the next, dropping off grunts and picking up the wounded.

Their buzz was never ending.

"You never got used to the choppers," said Al one day, as I interviewed him in his hospital room in Enid, Oklahoma.

I had intended to visit his home again in Waukomis, but at the last minute, Pat had emailed me with news of Al's pneumonia. So, I met them at St. Mary's hospital instead, in Room 310. As always, I had the weapons of journalism with me ... the pen, the paper, the tape recorder for capturing quiet subtleties.

"Hold still, shug," said Pat, attempting to smooth his hair with a wet washcloth. "You don't want Will to think a couple of cats had a fight on top of your head last night, do you?"

"No, I don't want that," agreed Al.

As an afterthought, Pat knelt and wiped her husband's feet with the cool cloth, running it between his gnarled toes and across his dry, cracked shins and heels. Al closed his eyes and smiled at the soothing touch.

"Sorry the body's not ready for the viewing," he apologized, with a chuckle.

"You look fine to me," I assured him. "Can you answer a few more questions?"

"Cleared for takeoff," said Magnet Ass, just as Pat finished fussing over him.

"There's our pilot," I said, setting the recorder on his food tray and turning it on. Having heard nothing of the truck hunters' training, I was curious to understand how prepared they were for the unthinkable.

"Were you ready for war when you went to Vietnam?" I asked.

"I knew how to fly a plane, if that's what you're asking," said Al.

"But did you know what to do if you ended up in the jungle?"

"Oh, I see," said Al, "I'll have to think about that."

The soft 'beep' of Al's heart monitor kept time with the life in his chest, and he fiddled with the oxygen tube that led from his nose to the armrest of his chair, then disappeared into the shadowy recesses beneath his bed. He gave a weak cough, and Pat looked up at him with concern in her eyes.

"Every pilot and crew member did a little training," he said, after a moment or two.

Having read about the SERE program developed by the Air Force, I was familiar with the rigors associated with it. "And by a 'little', you mean a lot," I suggested.

"No," said Al, "That's not what I mean."

"But SERE..."

"No amount of training can prepare a man for war, son," Al insisted, his voice almost a whisper. "If you think we went over there with our t's crossed and our i's dotted, then you're wrong. We made a lot of things up when we got in country. There were just so many unknowns. The enemy preferred it that way. Have you ever heard of a fellow named, 'Dengler'?" asked Al.

"I don't believe I have," I replied, sensing a rabbit trail.

"You should know about him," said Al.

In 1966, a young man was rescued from the Laotian jungle. He was emaciated and babbling when the helicopter crew made contact with him. "I'm an American pilot ... I'm an American pilot ..." he kept repeating to the crew as they tried to calm him down. In his backpack were the remains of a half-eaten snake, and nothing else. In time, the young man was identified as Lieutenant Dieter Dengler, pilot of a downed Skyraider. The story of his unthinkable torture provides a small window into the lives of those who fell from the sky into the hands of the Pathet Lao.

When the crew found Dengler, he was covered with ant bites, and they lifted his skeletal frame into the helicopter as if they were lifting a child. Later, when Dengler was fed and rested, he told reporters the details of his torture. By day, his captors hung him upside down with his face in a pile of bullet ants, until the pain of their toxic bites rendered him unconscious. By night, they suspended him in a freezing well, so that if he slept, his nose would dip beneath the water and he would drown.

He never slept.

Other times, Dengler was dragged by a water buffalo through villages, while his guards laughed and goaded the animal with a whip. Broken and bloody, Dengler would then be handed a pen and paper, and urged by his captors to sign documents renouncing America. When he refused, tiny wedges of sharpened bamboo would be inserted under his fingernails, where they would fester and grow. Eventually, Dengler escaped – just before his captors grew tired of toying with him. To this day, he is thought to be the only American to have broken out of a prisoner of war camp in the Laotian jungle and lived to tell about it.

Naturally, I appreciated Al's story about Dengler, but he hadn't answered my question. And the more I pressed him for details about his training for Vietnam, the more he seemed to forget them, until at last, I gave up altogether.

The lighting in Al's hospital room had begun to fade by then. Outside the window, pale sun leaked through naked branches, and slowly marched west. Al's eyes looked sleepy. Pat's were moist with anxious tears.

"You take care, sir," I said.

"Don't call me 'sir'," said Al. It had become a game for us by then – Magnet Ass, the highly decorated war hero, giving orders, and me, the highly undisciplined Cub Scout, completely ignoring them.

"Roger wilco, sir," I replied.

I reached to shake Al's hand, but he wanted to stand for our goodbyes. Pat took him by his left arm, and I braced him from the right side, and soon the three of us were standing, shakily, next to his bed.

"I hope I'm alive to see the book," said Al, out of the blue.

I glanced at Pat, but she refused to look at me.

"Well, of course you'll be alive," I said, my words no more stable than Al's legs. We were praying when the nurse came in to inspect Al's IV. An awkward 'amen' cut the prayer short, followed by even more awkward farewells, and hugs, and playful salutes designed to ease us back from the edge of the unknown, over which the three of us had almost catapulted. When I finally left, Pat followed me into the hallway, and softly closed Al's door.

"We're scheduled to go to Mayo next week," she said. "I don't know what I'll do if they find more cancer."

A moment later, I found myself in my car, pressing the ignition button, pulling out of the parking lot ... thoroughly unaware I was doing seventy through the center of Enid.

I could not put the pain behind me fast enough.

From the beginning of the project, I suspected writing about the truck hunters' training would not be one of the easier parts. Because each crew member performed vastly different jobs aboard Stinger, the scope of the book would not allow me to explore each job with fair and equal analysis. I searched hard for a common thread in their preparation for the theatre of war, but the thread eluded me – that is, until Ron Jones wrote me about his experience in "jungle survival school".

"Out of our entire jungle survival class, only a couple of men successfully escaped. But our instructors made it perfectly clear there were no prisoners taken in Laos, and that those who bailed out and were captured by the NVA or Pathet Lao would not survive. So, most of us in Al's crew simply carried extra ammunition, and swore we would go down fighting – you had nothing to lose."

While reading Jones' account, an idea suddenly came to me....

An AC–119K'S crew may have been made up of two pilots, a navigator, an engineer, three gunners, an IO, a NOS, and a FLIR, but the moment ten men bailed out of a plane into the jungles of Laos, they all had one thing in common. They were no longer the predator....

They were the prey.

"Tell me more about this jungle school," I said to Jones.

Right away, my inbox swelled with information.

"In the unlucky event the truck hunters were shot out of the sky, they could take heart in the fact the Air Force wanted them to have a fighting chance once they reached the ground," said Jones next email.

Thus, in the fall of 1969, each of the truck hunters were required to complete water and jungle survival school, otherwise known as, SERE – which stood for, "Survival", "Evasion", "Resistance", and "Escape". Established by the United States Air Force at the end of the Korean War in 1953, SERE was extended during the Vietnam War to the Army, Navy and Marines.

"My water survival was located in Florida and lasted about a week," Jones told me in a follow-up phone call.

"A week!" I said, incredulously. It had taken me that long to program my DVR. Surely learning how not to die in the ocean or at the hands of the enemy should take longer than a week. I blurted out these things to Jones and, as usual, made a fool of myself with the stoic Night Observation Scope operator. It was so easy to forget I was talking to a seventy-year-old man, whose worldview involved being shot at with shells that were over a foot long.

"It's not like they had to teach us to swim," said Jones. "We were grown men, highly-motivated to stay alive in the jungles of Laos if we ended up there. We didn't need forever to accomplish it."

He paused to let his words sink into his interviewer's soft psyche. After a moment or two, he continued.

"The highlight of water survival was being placed into a parachute harness similar to the ones we would fly with in Nam," said Jones. "Then we would be lifted up around three-hundred feet or so with the help of a parasail, where you would release yourself from the line and float down to the water. Once in the water, you were required to get away from your parachute and into your life raft that was connected to you."

"Because my knife wasn't very sharp, it took me a long time to get the lines cut and to situate myself in my life raft. Then I spent several hours drifting around, gaining a perspective of what one could expect if he were to bail out over water. I passed the test with flying colors. And I think I got a pretty good tan that day."

I pictured a bronzed Ron Jones bobbing in the South China Sea.

"Jungle school was a lot more intense," said Jones. "It was located in the Philippines just north of Clark AFB. So, right away you felt far from home and closer to the theatre of war. It was twice the length of water school, and it culminated in a final exam that consisted of a simple exercise, where you were given some basic survival gear, then told to go anywhere you wanted. All you had to do was avoid being located by the Negritos that were sent out an hour after you left."

Jones paused again, as if recalling an important part of the story. "What I didn't know was that each Negrito was promised a pound of rice for every airman he located. And by the looks of the Negritos, some of them hadn't eaten in a long while."

Later, when I asked Jones to put it all down in an email for me, this is an excerpt of what he sent:

"After I took off from the others, I traveled up a trail close to an hour and felt that I was well away from anyone. I saw no person on my way. It was starting to get dark and I felt it was time to stop and hide.

I found a place that was heavily covered with vines and other vegetation overlooking a deep, steep gorge, and it seemed perfect. I stopped, took off my back pack and carefully separated the vines just off the trail. I placed my pack inside the opening, then crawled in myself. I turned around and again very carefully replaced each and every vine or grass stem I had moved. I then scrambled down the steep hill until I came to another area heavily saturated with vegetation. I stopped again and repeated my original efforts to hide my trail. I then moved along the side of the hill until I came to a tree I could use as an anchor to keep me from rolling down the hill if I fell asleep.

By this time, it was dark. There I was, by myself without any way to contact anyone in case of an emergency. I spent the night tightly wrapped around the tree listening to the sounds of the jungle ... including small, unknown animals. Around midnight, I heard a sound about fifty feet away from where I was straddling the tree. I held my breath as the sound drew closer and closer, and the breathing of whatever the thing was came in short, little puffs of air. Suddenly a light flashed in my eyes, and I could see that it was a Negrito, demanding one of the three tags I carried.

That tag earned him his pound of rice.

An hour later, another native located me. To this day, I have no idea how they did it. The best theory I have heard is that they could smell Americans due to the food we ate versus the food they ate. Navy Seals were convinced that this was true, and they would often eat Viet food before going on patrols. I've always wondered if those short, little puffs of air were the Negrito sniffing his way to my hiding spot. I never knew I smelled so badly."

I checked with some of the other truck hunters about their experiences with survival school, and their stories lined up with Jones' story. Firestone's jungle school was also conducted in the Philippines, but his recollection was that it only lasted a week, rather than two weeks, as Jones had said.

"There was never any sense of danger," wrote Firestone. "And probably most of the young, single crew members of the squadron were of the same mindset. Even the 'old guys' like Al, being twenty-eight or twenty-nine at the time and married, probably had some of this same care free, adventurous spirit. Remember, it was Al's choice to fly some one-hundred and fifty combat missions with anti-aircraft guns firing at him. The grit was already in him. Probably there since birth. So, jungle school was nothing to a pilot."

Though it was characteristic for the laid-back Firestone to have adopted this view of survival school, I couldn't help but think the crew's training had not been equal to the task awaiting them, should they have plunged into the Laotian jungle. I had read accounts of Parris Island boot camps, and was thoroughly impressed with the preparation marines underwent for hand-to-hand combat. So intensive was their training in marksmanship, that General John Pershing, founder of the "National Society of Pershing Rifles", was once quoted, saying, "*The deadliest weapon in the world is a marine and his rifle*".

Even so, with all their training, thirteen thousand marines were killed during the Vietnam War, and another eighty-eight thousand were wounded. In comparison to marine training, the truck hunters' survival school, though enlightening, seemed only slightly more rigorous than a church's summer camp, with parasailing and "counselor hunt" as thrilling diversions, but hardly the kind of preparation needed to keep a man alive in the jungle, with the enemy crawling everywhere ... like bullet ants.

Somewhere in the later stages of writing Al's story, I returned to the topic of SERE and learned that each trainee was required to sign a nondisclosure agreement upon completion of the program, thus preserving the element of surprise for future trainees. Tremendous degrees of exertion, stress, disorientation, and pain were, (and are), used regularly in SERE, along with severe food and sleep deprivation ... and even waterboarding. And although waterboarding was eventually done away with under pressure of great public outcry, the SERE program still stands today as the US military's best way to prepare its men to go through hell and return home alive, should they fall into the hands of the enemy.

All of this explained why Magnet Ass, Jones, and Firestone were determined to let me think their SERE training had been little more than a camp experience. If for no other reason than loyalty to the military way, they remained committed to their nondisclosure agreement, and for that I respected them.

So, I concluded that Magnet Ass and the truck hunters knew *exactly* what lurked beneath the canopy in Laos, and they were trained to wipe it out with ruthless efficiency. The problem was, I didn't have this same comprehension, and I suddenly felt like a storyteller without a villain.

I had always imagined that men like Al went to Vietnam on account of the Russian-backed North Vietnamese trying to impose their will on South Vietnam. This simplistic view had allowed me to think of the North as the bully on the playground, and the South as the bully's victim. It had also allowed me to think of the United States as the brave and popular classmate who, seeing the victim tormented, flies into action, vanquishes the bully, wins the day, and becomes the hero. But in light of the fact the US military began to withdraw from the war in 1969, leaving South Vietnam to progressively fend for itself against the bully, my reasoning broke apart like a plane in the canopy, and the lines between "hero" and "villain" grew fuzzier by the minute.

"Vietnamization" was what the Nixon administration called the withdrawal. But it looked to me more like the brave, popular classmate not finishing what he started. By 1975 Saigon was fallen ... beaten to a pulp by the bully, and leaving me to wonder... "Who really was the villain of Vietnam?"

So, I sat there with my notes and my tape recordings, blinking at the screen, while the cursor mocked my indecisiveness and foul thoughts rose up from the basement of my soul. *How can a man tell a story without a villain?*

Then slowly, it came to me....

No villain has ever entered our world except through the doorway marked, "Ideas". Once through that opening, the villain (disguised as an idea) behaves like a leak under the doormat. It spreads itself out and makes a moldy mess of the carpet, and the furniture legs, and the first few inches of the drywall. In the same way great bodies of water begin as trickles high in the mountains, so ideologies, both good and evil, begin as an inkling in the mind of a man. Over time, the inkling is fed by similar inklings, becomes a theory to be tested, grows into a thought, a preference, a habit, a movement. Eventually, the movement is bolstered by the approval of fellow inkling-holders, supplied by tributaries of debate, commerce, trial and error, even brute force, until at last, the inkling has become a swollen body of itself, spilling out in torrents of action, which are either a blessing or a curse, good or evil, depending on the original inkling.

The real villain of Vietnam was not a man at all, nor an army of men, I typed triumphantly. It was an idea, an embodiment, a ... a Thing more sinister than Nixon or Ho Chi Minh. I started to type the word, "Communism", but I stopped myself, because I knew the Thing was bigger than that, too.

It was darker.
Moister.
More slippery and cunning.

It was the sum total of every King Cobra, every Green Tree Viper, every unexploded ordnance, backwoods opium hootch, malaria-riddled puddle, leech-infested eddy, and barb-wired "tiger cage" built by the Pathet Lao to intimidate downed pilots into making anti-war confessions. It was the mud, and the muck, and the brown-eyed mamasans, who peddled ten-year-old girls to hopped-up soldiers for the price of a cold Beerlao. It was the fifteen-hundred artillery nests scattered throughout the jungle, some of them with cannons so big they could blow a hole the size of Saigon in the side of a plane. It was the Thing that makes people act like animals when cornered ... like an ordinary bitch with her tail between her legs, her teeth all wet and slavering.

Yes, the Thing beneath the canopy made all other villains look like a blustering, bluffing, playground bully, exposed by one stiff punch to his nose, reduced to a sniveling schoolgirl, but not the villain of Vietnam. No ... the villain of Vietnam was danker, and wetter, and greater than all the furred and feather-meated creatures that crept, prowled, loped, scuttled, slithered, hopped and scampered across the backbone of the Ho Chi Minh Trail. Even sixteen-thousand kilometers of hand-hacked footpaths, pocked with spider-holes, and built on the backs of conscripted Hmongs, could not contain the Thing beneath the canopy that the war had come to embody. The Thing was bigger than the Trail – older, too – as if it had been dreamed up in the mind of some grandfather's grandfather, then waterlogged in a Mekong eddy to make it good and shriveled, and finally trampled on by elephants and water buffalo, until it was hard as a week-old steam cake with all the sugar squeezed out of it. And when the rains came, all the Thing's hardness withered into a steaming goo ... like a sweaty, old woman, hunched over a story cloth, refusing to die.

At last I saw it ... and I saw it clearly.

The Thing was what Al trained for, even if he didn't want to talk about it. It was the reason for which men bled, and wept, and went halfway around the world to take their final shit. It was wretched and desiccated, ancient-old and crusty. As cunning as a snake with no escape. Darker than the darkest beetle cellar.

And so, I came to understand that Fear is the universal villain, haunting soldiers and sons, fathers and everything that flies.

Except for Al.

He seemed to fly far above it.

CHAPTER SEVEN

THE LIVES OF THE STINGERS

Twenty-six C–119s were transformed into gunships and sent to hunt trucks in Vietnam. None of them ever returned to US soil.

Two goals have motivated man since the beginning: the first is the assurance he can make it through the day without being cancelled out by, say, a Saber-Toothed Tiger, or the Praetorian Guard, or some fellow further up the corporate ladder. I shall call this goal, "safety", and though it is an important goal, it is not a very sexy one. The second goal, however, is tragically sexy, for its appeal has moved men throughout time – even decent men – to do terribly indecent things, merely for the sake of being known. I shall call this goal, "significance", and it is at the heart of every accomplishment attributed to Man, good or bad – from the Mona Lisa to the murder of men along the Ho Chi Minh Trail. In its Latin form, the word "significance" is "signum ficare", which means, "to make a sign." And if you asked a roomful of men which they would prefer – to be slowly eaten by a Saber-Toothed Tiger, or to reach a point in life where the signs they made no longer mattered to anybody – most would take the tiger.

Ho Chi Minh once said, "You will kill ten of us, we will kill one of you, and you will grow tired of it first."

And so, a day arrived during the Vietnam War when the US military realized the tiger it was stalking was an impossible one, and that they could not kill what they could not see. This began their search for a new weapon with new advantages. Ironically, it led them to something very old and seemingly insignificant – a plane that had long since ceased to impress anybody.

So, to the machines of Al's story we turn our attention.

Broken down into his base elements, Man is mostly dirt and water, evidence of the vast and humorous mind of his Creator. We are at once both sublime and shabby. But we are not alone in our universe when it comes to this dichotomy. The machines we make – the ones that float and fly and ferry around these bags of soot – are also impressive and infinitesimal. They are made not by God with limitless powers, but by sons of God who are fallible. And sometimes it is the machines with the flaws that are the most impressive.

In late November, I visited Magnet Ass at his home for the second time. His recovery from pneumonia had been tedious, and another trip to Mayo for a check-up had left both Pat and him on pins and needles as they waited for the results. We were sitting in his living room, when I asked him to tell me about the gunships.

"They were awesome," said Al.

"Yes, Al, I know they were awesome," I replied, "But what I need for you to do is describe them for me."

Al rubbed his head, a sign I had learned to interpret as polite disdain. "Okay, Will ... for starters, the AC–119K had two wings."

"No, shug," interrupted Pat, "What Will wants, is for you to talk about the planes as if they were alive. You know ... like *characters* in a story."

"Pat gets it," I declared.

"Characters in a story," said Al, still rubbing his head. "Well, that's the darndest thing I've ever heard of."

Bolstered by compliment, Pat charged ahead. "It's called an... thro...po...mor...phism," she stated, proudly. "Will tells me it will endear the reader to the planes, and will expand the list of personas available for plot development. You remember what he's always telling us, shug. Plot follows character! Plot follows character! Did I get that right?" asked Pat, looking at me again for approval.

"Like a champ," I replied.

"Well, it seems like a lot of falderal to me," said Al. "But if you say so, I'll give it a try."

Al looked up at the ceiling, as if the perfect anthropomorphized airplane hung there, waiting to be described. What he said next changed my view of his ability to remember.

"I first met Stinger at Clinton County Air Force Base in Wilmington, Ohio," he began, his voice low and serious. "She was a trash-hauler, just like everyone said she was. An aging cargo ship. Fat in the middle. Double-tailed and slow as Sunday. She was a waste of good gravity when she was on the ground, and an unwelcome consumer of air space when she was flying. Nobody liked the C–119, and it made perfect sense to retire her to the flight line. She was old and ugly as sin. Like a moth-eaten overcoat. Good for nothing but the closet."

Al took a breath and a sip of water, and the sunlight through his picture window illuminated every age spot and broken blood vessel on his sagging forearm. I glanced at Pat, and saw the sorrow in her eyes.

"Thank you, Al," I said. "I think I can find out the rest through research."

In the kitchen, Pat told me they had received the news from Mayo two days before my visit. The remaining portions of Al's esophagus and liver were clean and cancer-free. And for that they were thankful.

But there was a shadow on his pancreas.

Some say Stinger almost never came to be. Were it not for a handful of men who saw its potential, the AC–119K, and other gunships that preceded her would have never been adopted, and the story of the Mackay Mission would not have occurred. More importantly, had there been no gunships, the loss of innocent lives at the hands of Viet Cong and NVA would have been astronomical. As it stands, no outpost, hamlet, village or fort under a gunship's protection was ever lost to the enemy, so devastating was her power, so maternal her guardianship.

Hailed as a "trash hauler" before necessity called her from obscurity, the AC–119K was the original ugly duckling. Fat and drafty, and blessed with a double-tail, Stinger truly was like a girl at a dance with two left feet. Al had pegged her perfectly. From the get-go, she was nothing like her peers. And nobody liked her.

As my research on the gunships of Vietnam progressed, I noticed the planes' inseparable connection to the smattering of men who presided over their inception. In the same way the war was overseen by five presidents – Eisenhower, Kennedy, Johnson, Nixon, and Ford – there were primarily five men who were integral in the gunships' birth, adoption, and retirement from the Vietnam war as we know it. Their names were Flexman, Saint, McDonald, Simons, and Terry. And though this book is not the place to plumb the depths of these men's contributions to the reemergence of history's most devastating war machine, Jack Ballard's seminal work in, "Development and Employment of Fixed-Wing Gunships 1962-1972", is a fine place to start for anyone who is interested.

Suffice it to say that the US military recognized from the beginning that the Vietnam terrain provided an enormous advantage to the enemy. Shielded by a canopy of foliage, NVA truck drivers could carry troops, weapons, food, and other supplies to Viet Cong forces in the South, and hardly give a thought to being attacked from the air. Knowing US planes with front-mount weaponry would frequently lose track of them between first sighting and second pass, the truck drivers became brazen in their use of the Ho Chi Minh Trail, and the need for new counterinsurgency techniques was on every top innovator's mind.

One such man was Ralph E. Flexman.

In 1962, when Flexman was the Assistant Chief Engineer with Bell Aerosystems Company in Buffalo, New York, he became intrigued with the problems of counterinsurgency operations, and it seemed that US involvement in Vietnam and Bell's contracts to work on hardware associated with limited war were a perfect match. On December 27th, 1962, Flexman submitted to Dr. Gordon A. Eckstrand, Behavioral Science Laboratory, Wright-Patterson AFB, Ohio, several ideas he and his colleagues were working on:

"... with respect to aircraft, we believe that lateral firing, while making a pylon turn, will prove effective in controlling ground fire from many AA, (anti-aircraft) units. In theory at least, this should more than triple the efficiency of conventional aircraft on reconnaissance and destructive missions."

In short, the "pylon turn" was born – or born again, to be precise. It was not a new idea, just a forgotten one. The term itself was derived from the racing plane era and the pylon they sped around. As early as 1927, an Army pilot attempted to sell the side-firing concept to the Air Corps by fixing a side-firing .30 calibre machine gun to the wing of his DH–4 biplane. Tests were successful as he scored several hits on a ground target. The concept was brought up again in 1939, but as with earlier tests, the Army brass did not buy it.

Examples of the pylon turn and side-lateral firing went back to the swivel-mounted machine-guns on WWI aircraft. There were also the famed Flying Fortresses and the Liberators of WWII, which relied heavily on waist gunners to help ward off attacks of German and Japanese interceptors. And finally, the C–47 transports of the 443rd, which eventually became the infamous gunship prototype, "Spooky", carried .50-caliber machine-guns and fired from both sides of the aircraft.

But these successes had been largely packed away in mothballs, and it seemed American tactical air combat was boresighted on its front-mount ancestry. Meanwhile, all over South Vietnam, friendly outposts were being overrun by the enemy and Ho Chi Minh's trucks were streaming unabated to the front. Through a curious twist of history, it took a good-natured, Christian missionary to bring the pylon turn back into the public eye and the theatre of war.

Flexman had remembered reading about Nate Saint and his attempts to reach the Huaorani people, living in the jungles of Ecuador. Because the Huaoranis protected their privacy with violent resolve, Saint's first attempts at contacting them involved lowering a line from his plane to the tribesmen below, down which he passed tokens of peace and charity, while he circled lazily above them. Eventually, Saint landed his Piper PA–14 Family Cruiser on a lonely, jungle beach, and made several face-to-face connections with the people he so desperately wanted to influence for Jesus Christ. Plagued, however, by tradition, fear, and superstition, a Huaorani warrior killed Nate Saint with a spear through the heart, and Saint's ingenious use of the pylon turn was lost in the larger narrative of his compassion for the human soul. His story can be read in a book by his eldest son, Steve Saint, entitled, <u>End of the Spear</u>.

As Saint passed from this world to the next, he had no idea his mission to the Huaoranis would one day be resurrected in the jungles of Laos. But that is precisely what happened. Intrigued with the idea of gifts being slid down a rope to recipients far below, Flexman wondered if the same could be done with bullets. He recalled his experiences as a flight instructor, when he had pivoted his plane over a fence post and held the post in view at the tip of the wing. He therefore believed it reasonable that with a very small sight one could fire ammunition along the sight path to a target. All this pointed to possible counterinsurgency applications.

As is often the case when one has a bright idea, he realizes there is nothing new under the sun and he looks around to see if anyone before him has had the same idea. That's how Flexman found MacDonald. To be clear, Gilmour Craig MacDonald of Ames, Iowa, should be credited with the first formulation of the gunship. This highly inventive and imaginative individual initially suggested the pylon turn as a tactical method against submarines that had been forced to the surface. But with WWII waning, the proposal was scrapped.

Sixteen years later, under Kennedy's new emphasis for counterinsurgency, MacDonald tried one last time to resuscitate his old ideas. He suggested that by flying in a banked circle, the plane could keep its fire focus on a singular target, while avoiding the usual longitudinal strafing ... due to keeping one wing low and, essentially, pointed at the target. Again, MacDonald's proposal failed to arouse response.

Eventually, Macdonald ran out of steam.

But where Macdonald gave up, Flexman didn't. Having adopted MacDonald's work and continued it himself, he concluded on April 16th, 1963 that lateral firing from a pylon turn was definitely feasible. He reported to his Air Force professional colleagues the concept's advantages in limited war operations. As was the current case in Vietnam, aircraft often lost guerilla-war targets between first sighting and the time of the second pass. In contrast, an aircraft rolling immediately into a pylon turn could sweep a target with instant effective fire from a fixed aiming point. Flexman further foresaw that lateral fire from a low-flying, slow-speed aircraft could provide wider coverage, a higher angle of fire, and a capability for pinning down enemy troops. Nevertheless, the military believed Flexman's concept contained three major questionable areas: (1) ballistics and dispersion of the projectiles as they were fired ... (2) ability of the pilot to aim his lateral weapon and hold the target ... and (3) the reaction time necessary to change from straight-and-level flight to an on-pylon turn.

What Flexman needed was a pilot to test these questionable areas, and he found his man in Capt. John C. Simons. Flexman suggested to Simons that a test program examine these points and at the same time demonstrate the validity of the concept.

Receiving an "under the table" thumbs up from his superiors, Capt. Simon began testing Flexman's theories in T–28s at nighttime. With a grease-pencil marking on the glass as a rudimentary sight, Simon demonstrated he could track a target from a low-speed, banked pylon-turn ... even when that target was moving, i.e. a truck in the field below. He also observed that on-pylon tracking in low-speed aircraft was free of the "yaw rigidity" and changing control forces that often degrade the performance of high-speed planes. He marveled at the pylon turn's simplicity and the ease with which a target could be acquired and held in the sight. Finally, Captain Simons performed similar tests in C–131S, proving that lateral-sighting techniques could be accomplished in cargo aircraft.

From MacDonald to Saint to Flexman to Simon, the torch was being passed, and all along the clock was ticking in Vietnam. Now, they needed someone to drive the gunship project who possessed the subtle blend of tact and tenacity, self-confidence and openness, intelligence and common sense – someone with the guts of a fighter pilot and the shamelessness of a used-car salesman. Into the circle of resourcefulness stepped Captain Ronald W. Terry.

When I asked Magnet Ass about Captain Terry, he lit up as if the man's name was synonymous with the history of the gunships.

"Terry could sell ice to an Eskimo," said Al. And the way he said it made me realize that a sort of reverence existed between gunship pilots, enlightened by mutual brushes with danger and death. When I saw that there was a faraway look in Al's eyes, I suspected he was about to launch into a monologue, so I sat back in my chair and let the recorder do the work for me.

"The C–47's preceded Stinger in Vietnam," said Al. "They were a huge cargo plane – sometimes referred to as 'gooney birds'. But the more they proved themselves in combat, the more they gained respect. Eventually 'Gooney' was renamed, 'Spooky', because she struck terror in the hearts of our enemy. If it hadn't been for Captain Terry, there wouldn't have been a Spooky ... and there wouldn't have been a Stinger ... or a Shadow, or a Spectre either," added Al, speaking of the AC–19G/K and the AC–130 that would soon follow the first wave of gunships.

"Being familiar with combat in Southeast Asia, Terry knew exactly what we needed to get the job done over there," said Al. "He was like a fly on a horse's rump; The more the brass swatted at his ideas, the more he kept harassing them, until finally the brass gave in and the gunships were born. Sometimes that's what you have to do, Will," said Al, his voice weak and worn.

"When the chips are down, you just have to keep trying."

So, they took the old girl, and they propped her up, and they gave her a new call sign, and they sent her back into battle. Outfitted with two Fairchild-Hiller J85 turbojets, a night observation scope, infrared equipment, an illuminator, a flare-launcher, four 7.62 miniguns, two M61 Vulcan 20mm cannons, and a gazillion pounds of extra armor, the newly christened, "Stinger", was a nightmare to get off the ground. But once she was airborne, the old girl became a nightmare for the enemy.

Thus, the planes came to Vietnam in much the same way the men came – one by one. Some were proud, intimidating machines, like the F–4 Phantoms, and they left their mark on the land indiscriminately. Others came with meek heads bowed, like the gunships, and they did what was asked of them with merciful devastation. It has been said that an AC–119K could put an incendiary bullet into every square yard of a football field in three seconds, and leave little collateral damage behind. Comparatively, the F–4, with its napalm and its broad array of bombs, is widely known to have spread the burden of unexploded ordnance all over Southeast Asia, leaving behind shattered communities and numerous rebuilding campaigns – ones which the United States is still engaged in decades later.

Once, when we were saying 'goodbye' on Al's back porch, I heard the roar of a jet engine overhead. Being so close to Vance AFB, Al's farm was smack dab in the southern approach path and, thus, the perfect place for a pilot to retire. Without so much as a peek at the sky, Al looked at me and remarked....

"T–38 —kid's having the time of his life."

And he was right. The Northrop Talon swelled until it was nearly on top of us, then disappeared toward Oklahoma City, somewhere beneath its top speed of 858 mph – but still fast enough to impress.

"Does it make you sad that none of the Stingers ever came back home?" I asked him.

Al shook his head. "It was just a plane, son. It wasn't flight itself."

"But it was your plane," I countered.

"Hmmmph," said Al. "My plane's right here ... sitting on the flight line ... gathering dust."

It was the only self-defeating thing I ever heard Magnet Ass say. And in a way, it drew me closer to him. As he turned his walker toward the door, and started to inch forward, I reached for the door handle.

"Aren't we going to hug goodbye?" I asked.

"Of course, we are," said Al. "What kind of fool question is that?"

With that, Al wrapped his sagging arms around my waist, and clung to me in a longer than usual show of affection. Over his shoulder, I saw the Talon disappearing, and I thought to myself, *Surely there's a doctor in the world who can shove a couple of jet engines in the old man and keep him flying for a few more years.*

But I knew there was no such doctor. And I knew that all planes end up on the flight line eventually. I watched the Talon until it merged with the sky, leaving me with one last question regarding "significance", one that would be easy – even tempting – not to ask at all. To do so, however, would have made Al's entire story meaningless, by suggesting that men and machines are only significant whey they are young and useful. Such a thought haunted me, and I felt as if I could not go on with the book until I either killed the thought, or embraced it. If I embraced it, I would have to think of the twenty-six Stingers abandoned in Vietnam after the war as ugly, rusted out, hollow tubes, left to rot in faraway jungles, and forgotten. But I could no more embrace that thought than I could think of Al as a washed-up pilot, worthless because he could not even make his own breakfast, or walk without wobbling. So, I killed the thought. And I forced myself to answer the question I would rather have left unasked:

What becomes of a man's significance when he can no longer make a sign?

CHAPTER EIGHT

WHISKEY

"There is no hunting like the hunting of man, and those who have hunted armed men and liked it, never care for anything else thereafter."
   Ernest Hemingway

With a cargo hold full of dust and five of Al's crew on board, Stinger left Lockbourne, Ohio, in November of 1969, and headed west across the country's rooftop. In the cockpit, Clancy, Nash, and Dean joked nervously about what lay ahead of them, imagining the thrill of shooting trucks in the same way schoolboys anticipate lighting their first firecracker. Al rode quietly, listening to their chatter and enjoying the camaraderie that was building amongst his men. Because there was no need for FLIR, NOS, or gunners on this peaceful leg of the journey, the other five would hitch rides on C–141s, 130s, and commercial planes, then rendezvous in Phu Cat, via Saigon or Phan Rang. That left Ed Lopez, far back in the belly of the plane, alone with his ponderous thoughts. He wondered if his training had prepared him to kill... or be killed.

   The men's tactical training at Lockbourne had been an exercise in resourcefulness. There were no manuals on truck hunting in 1969, no protocol or best practices. Thus, much of what the Stinger crews had done to train for Vietnam resembled make-believe military play, disguised as sober-minded drills. They would take Stinger up at all hours of the day, (usually after dark), scour the landscape until they spotted a vehicle on the road below, then pretend it was the enemy. Rolling into a left-hand, pylon turn, Al and his crew would track the vehicle for miles ... hold it in their sights ... simulate attack sequences, without live ammo, of course ... score themselves in these imaginary scenarios, as if they were in a video game ... and so on. How unsettling it would have been to the passengers in the vehicle below had they known they were being targeted, stalked, used to improve the kill/death ratio of the US Air Force. Thus, soccer moms, and scout masters, and CEOs traveling home across the Ohio countryside after a long day at the office, played a larger part in the Southeast Asian theatre than they would ever know.

In short, there was nothing conventional, predictable, or quantifiable about the truck hunters' training; They went to Vietnam with only a vague idea of what they were doing. As the Dakotas passed under their wings, the men sipped coffee and thanked Uncle Sam for the warmth of arctic gear. They would be sweating like pigs by Adak Island, eager to exchange multiple layers for t-shirts and tiger stripes – the Rip-Stop fatigues that would be with them until the end.

Al's Stinger was not alone in her flight. Flanking her were several other AC–119s, fattened with armor and loaded to the gills with death and destruction. To the farm boy in Montana peering skyward through cupped hands, the convocation of planes flying over his father's barley field looked like their ordinary trash-hauler selves, rather than the birds of prey they had become. The boy could not have known they were heading to Vietnam, to kill people and break things. Al knew, though, and it bothered him incessantly. The only thing that kept his mind off the killing part of war was the sheer awesomeness of flight. If he could fly forever... and never have to pull a trigger ... he would do it.

Al had always loved speed. In quiet moments, when the pain and fatigue of his cancer drove him to the bedroom for a nap, Pat hauled out stories of her husband's "wild hair" days, revealing to me, perhaps, the genesis of her attraction to him. She remembered him rocketing along Wood Road in his father's '57 Chevy, racing his friends from Waukomis to Drummond – and never losing. She spoke about the early days of his piloting career, when, egged on by the untapped power of the T–38 at his fingertips, Al broke the sound barrier over Vance AFB and took what he had coming to him from superiors. This expedition to hell and back would be a "snap", Al told Pat. "Over before either of them knew it had begun." "Like a run through the gears down Highway 81 back home."

Men lie to their wives on the eve of battle. And their wives lie to themselves until they come home. Some continue lying even after their men return in boxes.

At the western extent of the Andreanof Islands, Al got his first glimpse of Adak, its landscape already flecked with snow. "Looks lonely down there," muttered Lopez over the interphone, as he stared blankly at the runway for which Al was aiming. He was aware of the small flask of booze he had hidden away in his left mukluk; It had been his only thought since leaving Lockbourne. But no matter how discreetly he tried to reposition it, the flask kept digging into his ankle.

"All right, boys," said Al, "We'll stay here just long enough to crew-rest, refuel, and mail these monkey-suits back to Lockbourne." He was tired of sweating.

Being the lowest ranking officer amongst the six gunship pilots trained at Lockbourne, Al had had no choice but to take off that morning in the six-slot, and try to make up airspace in whatever way he could. But he had steadily closed the gap for the last few hours, until at last he had caught up to the pack and was flying nearly wing to wing with the other planes. Along the way, he took note of his colleague's average speed, sizing them up, formulating a plan for a bit of fun he hoped would be talked about for years to come. After all, "A man should live his life in such a way that he has stories to tell eight-year-olds," his father used to tell him. So if he was going to have to fight, and die, and be carried home from a foreign land with a flag draped over him, Al figured he might as well make it interesting.

Al landed with a stiff wind rising from the tidal marsh at the end of Adak's runway. To his left, he glimpsed the dike and the system of drainage canals that had been constructed in 1942 to make the most of Adak's spongy terrain. Layers of sand, gravel, and pierced-steel planking – most of which were original materials – still felt firm beneath his wheels, as he touched down and taxied to a stop. Other than the standard crew rest required by the Air Force, they would waste no time on this island, and would be ready to go for the next FDP by mid-morning following.

"You keeping an eye on those Bensons, Ed?" Al said over the interphone.

From the back of the plane came Lopez's response. "Y-y-yessir, I know the d-d-drill."

"You're a good man, Ed," said Al, smiling inwardly at his scheme to insure victory. He had formulated the idea from a bit of childhood advice his father had once given him on a hunting trip. "Always pack enough water for you and your buddies," Milacek senior had said. "And when you think you've packed enough – pack some more." Imagining his colleague's cries of 'foul play', Al chuckled to himself, and glanced at the Benson tanks as he exited the plane, to make sure they were concealed. All that was left to do was spring the trap on his friends in the Philippines.

They spent the night on Adak in a shrieking wind, and were not remotely refreshed in the morning.

It was the fastest pit stop ever recorded on Adak, an island not unfamiliar with things coming and going at the blink of an eye. It is said that during the Aleutian Island Campaign of World War II, Brigadier General Simon Bolivar Buckner, Jr., once brought in hundreds of cedar trees and had them planted to boost the morale of his men on this bleak bit of soil in the middle of the sea. Sadly, all but a few of the trees died a quick death, killing the yuletide spirit Buckner had hoped to create, and leaving behind what came to be known as, "America's smallest national forest." With tanks refueled and unwanted layers of winter-wear left behind like grave clothes, Al and his men were happy to put Adak and it's sad collection of Christmas trees at their six.

Soon, Stinger was heading south across the wide expanse of the Pacific, lumbering along behind her comrades toward the most isolated place on the planet – Wake Island. Al turned down the volume on his headset and allowed himself to forget about the others in the cockpit. For a moment, he was alone with Stinger in the heavens ... no rank and order, or distant drums of war. Only solitude and sky. If Al leaned forward, he could see the end of Stinger's blunt nose brushing air aside like a dignitary at a crowded garden party, Queen of the Upperworld, Empress of Empyrean Blue. All around her indelicate figure, the gossamer filaments of cirrus clouds lent a silky sheen to the sky, transecting the sun's disk with scarcely a reduction to its brightness, affecting cloudish curtsies as the queen passed by. She was at once both terrifying and fair.

Somewhere between Adak and Wake, the engines gave a cough and a sputter, then grew silent altogether. Like a bird diving suddenly for it's breakfast on the ocean's surface, Stinger's descent was swift and shocking, catching everyone off guard... except for Al. His calm, three-word command over the interphone saved the day.

"Benson tanks, Ed," he said.

A moment passed, followed by another cough, then the recips sprang to life and Stinger dished out at the last safe instant, a mere football field above the ocean. For a minute or two, Al flew low and level, allowing the men a long look at the Pacific's hypnotic undulation. It was all so beautiful to Al – though to his crew, the surface of the sea looked like the grave that had nearly swallowed them. With a gentle teasing of the yoke, Al eased Stinger back into the blue, happy not to be scattered in pieces on the ocean swells.

"S-s-sorry boss," stuttered Lopez, when the plane was in the clouds again. He had guzzled the flask of booze a mile south of Adak, and its negligible effect on his sullen mood had rendered him even more disinterested in duty and deployment than usual, let alone his promise to switch from Benson tank A to Benson tank B before the first tank ran dry.

"Don't let that happen again, my friend," said Al.

"I w-won't, sir," said Ed.

Later in the day, through mountains of cumulus, Al spotted Wake Island floating on the limitless blue, a solitary fish, far from the safety of its school. From his vantage point, Al understood the island's vulnerability, imagining at any moment a great mouth opening up beneath the tiny crumb of land and swallowing it for supper. Indeed, larger forces had been affecting Wake Island for centuries, not unlike Typhoon Sarah that had pummeled her shores a year before Al's arrival, ravaging ninety-five percent of the buildings, and wreaking five-million dollars' worth of havoc. Al spied the new taxiway that had been built parallel to the runway since the storm, and he was thankful for the accommodations. He landed in a brisk crosswind, slightly behind the other five AC–119s, but still with enough afternoon light for the crew and him to deboard and scout around for a while.

To the north of where Stinger sat on the AWK tarmac, the runway stretched two miles into the distance. To the east the blue lagoon, ringed with sugar it appeared, stared unblinking at the sky. To the west, fifteen-hundred miles of water rolled lazily toward Guam. To the south, the Wake Island Launch Site, scarcely more than a groundbreaking, looked as out of place as a bombing campaign at a beach party. And all around, the island dozed in predictable November weather, the temperature somewhere between the average low of 76.1 and the average high of 85.5. Other than the rhythmic 'click' of Stinger's recip engines cooling down, the island was hauntingly silent, leaving Al to wonder if the sixteen-hundred-or-so government employees were all in siesta simultaneously.

"One more round of fuel should get us to Clark," said Nash. "Then it's a puddle-jumper to Phu Cat, and we're..." There was a hitch in Nash's voice, and both men knew he had nearly uttered the one word with the power to make a soldier a coward.

"Thanks for juicing her up," said Al, smiling at his new, engineer friend. He was pleased that at least one of his crew seemed to trust his leadership. "And check on Ed, would you?" he added, as he wandered away to stretch his legs.

Al had flown the line many times over long stretches of water, including refueling stops at Wake and other remote jurisdictions just like it. Nevertheless, the constant sameness of the sea and the sky, mile after mile, always settled over him like a stupefying vertigo. He could only guess what kind of impact such a flight might have on a man under the influence of alcohol. He had suspected Lopez's mukluk stash since they left Ohio, but had chosen to let it go at that, not wanting to drain the meager relational equity he had accrued in their few weeks of training together. As he strolled away from the runway, Al lifted his nose to the wind, hoping to revive his senses with the scent of the orange shrub-flower, for which Wake Island was famous. But all he detected was the sickening smell of diesel and aviation fuel, the result of the SS R.C. *Stoner* that had broken apart on the reef during Typhoon *Sarah*. Harassed by storms and black-tipped reef sharks, Standard Oil of California was still plodding through the cleanup process a year later, and paying out their ass in lawsuits. With a compassion welling up in him that transcends military branches, Al wondered if *Stoner's* captain had lost his command because of the incident – a reality in the military that made Al sad.

Knowing Wake would be his first stop in the South Pacific, Al had done some brush-up reading about the island during his training at Lockbourne, and was fascinated with the feather-poaching that had marked Wake's otherwise honorable history. As he stood on the shoreline, looking south toward Peacock Point, Al thought about the young, Japanese men who had risked their lives in sailing two-thousand miles from Tokyo to set up the illegal poaching camps, to harvest the sooty tern... the masked booby ... the black-footed albatross ... the lesser frigate ... and all because the richest women in Europe wanted to attend the theatre and not meet another woman with the same feather in her cap. As reported in the logs of the 1923 scientific expedition of the USS Tanager, upon discovering domestic artifacts and tools relating to the skinning of birds, as well as layer upon layer of bird bones in the guano-rich soil of

Wake Island – "*It seems that countless wings have been clipped in the name of greed and vanity.*"

After relaxing for an hour or so, the six crews convened over ice cream cones at the commissary, sapping the island's only soft-serve machine with their sudden run on it's simple pleasures. In pockets of four or five, the men stood licking and chatting, their conversations characterized by awkward gaps and interruptions associated with men thinly acquainted, yet bound together by heavier things they hurry not to discuss. A light meal of fish and fruit followed their dessert, and then the men were free to roam the island before turning in at the barracks. Some of them took a hike to the lagoon before bedtime, where they removed their boots and cautiously navigated the coral, until they were knee-deep in warm saltwater. One of them found a Type 96 machine gun, it's top-feed magazine rusted by decades below the surface, it's bipod-mount covered with calcified seaweed. A fired case was still stuck in the gun's chamber, leading everyone to wonder if the skeleton of a Japanese soldier might be, at that very moment, close by, staring up at them from the sandy bottom. They took the gun for a souvenir ... and waded out of the lagoon hastily, without looking back.

That night they slept fitfully, dreaming of birds, and broken ships, and Benson tanks ... and war.

In the morning, Al and the crew convened at "The 98 Rock", where they stood silently for several minutes, remembering the lives of the POWs who were taken to the northern end of the island, blindfolded, and machine-gunned by the Japanese garrison that occupied Wake Island in 1943. Then, without a word, the men boarded Stinger and fired up the engines. The last thing Al noted about Wake Island before they took off for Clark AFB in the Philippines was a small sign by the side of the runway. It was a reminder that Wake was situated west of the International Date line in it's own time zone and, thus, was a full day *ahead* of the fifty US states. The sign read: "Wake Island – where America's day begins."

After a short rumble down AWK's runway, Stinger lifted up and over the Island's highest elevation point – 23 FASL – and away toward the uncertainties of Vietnam. In spite of the soothing, tropical air, the men sat quietly with their thoughts, as if a sudden, cold gust of reckoning had blown through their souls. To comfort himself, Al rehearsed the details of his secret plan as he flew, and wondered when would be the perfect time to put it into play. He also decided it was time to let another man in on the secret.

Thirty-eight hundred miles later, the planes landed at Clark AFB, where the men stored their belongings in their barracks, had a tour of the base, took a nap, and ate what appeared to be the same fish and fruit they had eaten on Wake the night before. When the meal, (attended by the crews of all the various, Stinger gunships), was almost over, Nash stood up and gave his tea glass a little 'ring-ching-ching'. Having been invited into the circle of Al's secrecy just before supper, Nash had been rehearsing his speech as he ate. Now it was time to help Al spring his trap.

"Men," said Nash, "We are all aware that in a few short hours our lives will be changed forever. We will be asked to do things we would never ask of ourselves – and we will do them. We will be pushed beyond our limits, shoved into situations non-commensurate with the souls of civilized men ... shelled and shot at by the enemy ... until at last we emerge victorious, or blown away by NVA artillery. None of us knows the outcome. So, I turn now to Al Milacek, my new friend from Oklahoma ... a man less eloquent than I, but a darn good farm boy, with a darn good plan for having some old-fashioned fun on the eve of our journey. I give you, Captain Milacek."

To the sound of good-natured applause, Al stood up, tipped his cap to Nash, and said what he had been thinking about since leaving Lockbourne. As Nash had suggested, it was not eloquent. But it was clear and purposeful, the kind of language men appreciate, the only language Al knew.

"Tomorrow morning, I think we should race to Phu Cat," Al said, in his country drawl. "First plane to touch down gets a gallon of whiskey for every crew member, paid for by the money each of us puts in the pot, before hitting the sack tonight. 'Course,

I'll take off last as usual, being the lowest ranking pilot in the bunch. But I'll give it my best, and I plan on giving my share of the whiskey to one of you losers – me not being much of a drinker, that is."

At that, the room erupted in boisterous objections and vain declarations, and before Al even had a chance to announce the entry fee for his proposition, there was a hatful of money on the table ... and the men went streaming off to their quarters, spouting prophecies of blazing triumph for themselves and dismal defeat for everyone else.

Dawn found the planes already packed for departure, and everyone still so full of bravado, it appeared each man had spent the night thinking of clever things to say to his competitors.

As usual, the first five AC–119KS to depart from Phu Cat were specks in the atmosphere by the time Al's Stinger lifted off the runway. At first, he wondered if he might have bitten off more than he could chew, but then he remembered his arrangement with Nash, and a fresh wave of confidence washed over him.

"How much fuel you think the other guys are carrying?" Al asked.

"Just enough to get to Phu Cat," replied Nash. "I watched them do the fueling myself. They didn't want the extra weight, as I suspected."

"That's what I figured," said Al. "I scoped 'em out on Adak and Wake, and there's not a risk-taker in the bunch – maybe not even a real flyer. How much did we put in?"

"Enough to get to Phu Cat ... and burn the J85s the whole way. Plus, we have the Bensons."

"Hotdog!" said Al. "While everyone else is putzing along with their 3350S, we'll be screaming by with our hair on fire. You're a good man, Nash. Burn 'em, Dean!"

"Roger that," replied Ron Dean. And the roar of Stinger's General Electric J85 turbine jets coming to life was such sweet music, that even Clancy let out a little 'whoop'.

Halfway between Clark AFB and Phu Cat, Al overtook his pals, blowing past them with a defiant burst of backwash. By the time his wheels made contact with Vietnam soil, he was a full thirty minutes ahead of everyone. When the other crews arrived, and heard about Al's extra fuel, they were bitter beyond words. But in secret disclosures to one another, they admitted the idea was brilliant, and wished they had thought of it themselves. True to form, Al gave away his share of the booze.

The first few days in-country were marked by further training, basic acclimation to the Vietnamese way of life, and, in general, sheer boredom. It was good to see Russell, Jones, and the others had made it over from the States safe and sound, and though the men had only been together for a short while at Lockbourne, seeing one another again brought a lump to Al's throat. Even the gunners had become special to Al, and he could hardly wait to get started on the missions with his men. Soon, however, the days stretched into weeks without being assigned over the fence, and Al began to wonder if they would ever see action.

But on January 1st, 1970, all that changed when Al's crew was selected to fly the first AC–119K mission in the history of the Vietnam War – an honor Al would often attribute to the enthusiastic manner in which his crew came bounding off the plane in victory when they first landed in Phu Cat, eager to receive their whiskey. That evening, the CO's and the flight engineer met for the mission briefing, which was short and to the point, and contained nothing suggesting danger. They would cross over into Laos, due west of Phu Cat, and interdict enemy supplies moving from north to south – just like tracking soccer moms in their minivans back home. How hard could *that* be? Al's co-pilot for the mission, Colonel Rogers, predicted the night would be "uneventful", maybe even "boring. The briefing could not have been further from the truth.

When Stinger limped back into Phu Cat around 3 AM the next morning, her fuselage riddled with artillery, Al sat alone on the flight deck for at least an hour, thinking back on the mission, wondering what had gone wrong. After a while, Nash came looking for him, and the sudden materialization of his flight engineer startled Al. He had thought the man would be in bed already. But pilots and flight engineers often think alike, and failed missions are never shaken off easily by either of them.

"The men are in the rack, Al," said Nash. "You coming soon?"

"I guess sleep might be a good thing," replied Al, not budging from where he sat in the pilot's chair, staring at the bugs on Stinger's windshield.

"Can I ask you something in confidence, captain?" said Nash.

"Fire away," replied Al.

Nash looked around the cockpit, as if he believed some other crew member was lurking under the dashboard, listening to their conversation.

"Do you think tonight's mission is how it's going to be all year long?" Nash asked, hesitantly.

Al rubbed the stubble on his chin, recalling the fiery, orange tracers that had vomited up from the ground at them the moment they were over the target in Laos. He hoped he had appeared calm to the Colonel, but inside he had been a tangled mess. "I don't know what to think," said Al. "I've hunted all my life, but I've never had anything shoot *back* at me. Anyway, I've been sitting here thinking for a while, and it comes to me that getting shot at might be the one thing we *ought* to expect, maybe the only thing we should truly count on in this place."

Nash nodded, absorbing his captain's words as if they were medicine – needed, yet ghastly to the taste. "I don't suspect I'll see my wife again," he said, suddenly.

Al opened his mouth to placate his friend, but the soothing words got stuck in his gullet with a host of other truths that were hard to swallow. "We'll be alright," he said, but in his heart, he suspected none of them would make it home.

For a while the two men sat staring out Stinger's front window, mesmerized by the red and white lights of Phu Cat's only runway. Had they been able to put words to their thoughts, they might have both agreed that the longer they watched the blinking lights, the more they became aware of a third party's presence with them, one who was equally dilettante in the theatre of war – yet stoic, resolute, eager, and brave.

"Al?" said Nash, when the silence had grown thick and heavy.

"Hm?"

"Did you see that sign at Wake – the one by the runway?"

"Where America's day begins," murmured Al, unconsciously. He had seen it, and it had preyed upon his mind ever since. He was pretty sure his days were coming to an end, not beginning.

"Did you believe it?" asked Nash.

Al took his cap off, and ran his hand through his hair. "I believe the man who put it there believed it," he replied.

Eventually, the sun burned a bright, pink slash into the eastern blackness, and the two airmen, realizing the night was nearly over, gathered their things and trudged out of the plane, leaving Stinger alone on the tarmac....

Stoic, resolute, eager, and brave.

CHAPTER NINE

THE PINUP

"The miner came in '49, the whore in '51."
  Mark Twain

Vietnam in 1970 was dark, no doubt. But if one can believe it, there were darker things than war in Vietnam. Darker than the cloud of napalm. Darker than the smell of burning shit. Darker even than the blood-encrusted bayonet protruding from the socket of a soldier's half-decayed skull, as if the one who stuck it there, detached it from his gun and walked away, had finally no more need of it. Yes, if one can believe it, there were darker things than these.

They say a whole industry sprang up around American servicemen, one that was in its incubation stage when we arrived, but by the time we left was a full-on, crazy train. We call it "prostitution" in the West. The Vietnamese word for it is grotesquely beautiful. "*Maidam*".

Like birds, the young girls would congregate in bars where soldiers frequented, and they would sit along the walls together, tittering and applying make-up and crossing and uncrossing their legs, until at last a war-worn soul stood up from his table, walked over to the preening flock, and picked his favorite. Much ado attended these transactions between the working girl and the shell-shocked neophyte. Sometimes they would simply spend the day shopping together, or relaxing in the sun, or consuming fiery food and drink previously unknown to the boy from Wonder Bread, Wisconsin. Usually, however, untamed sex would break out between them – a daisy-cutter of carnal experiences that curried the boy's senses and forever made him partial to exotic flesh. Occasionally the girl would give the boy a disease. Occasionally, he would give her a baby. But as can be expected in times of war, there was always collateral damage at the edges of such scintillating bomb blasts. Marriages back home were blown away. Fiancés, far-flung in distant time zones, were amputated and soon forgotten. An estimated fifty-thousand Amerasian children were born and then abandoned by their soldier fathers, left to bear the derision of *bui doi*, or, "dirt of life", for the remainder of their own fictile lives. Some, if not most of these children were later forced into prostitution, as well.

In light of all this darkness, courage took many forms during the Vietnam War, some so disguised it would be easy to overlook them. One example is noticed in the testimonies of the pilots' wives, left behind to wait and wonder whether their men would return to them, and, if they did, in what condition they would be found. All this waiting and wondering took a toll on women, not unlike the war did on the men who fought and died. It was no secret that prostitution thrived in Southeast Asia during the war, and many were the wives who lived in fear of their men succumbing to it.

Unfortunately, life on base wasn't as insulating from the sex industry as they might have hoped. Hooch maids, like the ones at Udorn where Al's men were stationed in May, often cleaned up after soldiers in their barracks. Most were "good Catholic girls" who would flirt but never dreamed of dating an American. Others, however, were not averse to keeping the plumbing clean at every possible chance, if it meant a little extra money in their pocket. On some bases, attempts were even made to "humanize" the traffic in flesh. Cam Ranh Bay went so far as to create a system where a GI could actually "check out" a girl from the village, in the same way a schoolboy checks out a book from a library.

It worked in this way...

A young captain, stationed at the tactical fighter base in 1970, wakes up one morning and finds himself impassioned. Because he is in between missions, he has plenty of time on his hands. He sits up on the edge of his bunk, looks at the empty bunk next to his, stands, does three deep knee-bends and a set of push-ups to get his mind right, then walks stiffly down the hall to the head, where he splashes water in his face. In the mirror, the young airman sees the image of an F-4C Phantom II pilot staring back at him, and the image seems to be cocksure of itself. But as he walks away from the mirror, the airman feels terribly afraid inside. After all, he has never been with a woman ... other than his wife. He goes to the mess hall for breakfast, where he tries to forget the foolishness he is contemplating.

Later that morning, at the door to his commanding officer's office, the airman pauses to consider. Even as his knuckles are poised to rap three times sharply on the Major's door, as all O-3s have been instructed to do, he cannot get the image of his wife's face out of his head. *What am I doing?* he asks himself. *Do I really want to throw away everything for a roll in the grass with a stranger?* But then he thinks about the sacrifice he is making over here, the resolve and courage required of him on bombing runs, the many months that have passed since he has even heard his wife's voice, let alone touch her body, and the weight of it all brings his knuckles down sharply against the wood. Three times... as commanded. "Come in, O-3," booms the voice from behind the door. The rest happens in a haze.

After the O-4 signs the O-3's "letter of authorization", the young airman walks quickly to the "wall" that has been built around the village, next to the base. The "wall" is not really a wall; It is a corrugated barrier, twenty-feet high, with a chain-link fence parallel to it, creating a six-foot walkway between the fence and the wall, where young girls sit and ... wait. They are slender and sleepy-eyed, many of them having been up since yesterday at 9 AM, when the "meat market" opened. Noon is approaching, and the sweltering heat of the midday monsoon season has all the girls sweating, thinking past lunch, past shopping, past the line of MPS positioned strategically so that military personnel don't somehow slip unnoticed through the chinks in the wall, and into the village. The girls are thinking mostly of the beach and the bay, and the chance to cool off in the water. Everything else is secondary. The purses, the umbrellas, the shoes, clothes, radios, jewelry, and so on, will all be sold by tomorrow morning. On the other hand, the wide-eyed American boys, who buy all these items for them, are only thinking of one thing. And it is not the purses.

Sometimes money exchanges hands, but that is frowned on by Cam Rahn's commanding officers, who do not want to be known as a chicken ranch. "Without the wall, the men would run like dogs amongst the villagers, looking for any bitch in heat," the officers say. "We'd have no way to know where they were ... or what they were doing ... or with whom they were associating. Can you imagine? At least this system allows us to maintain some control. At least we can keep it all right here on the base. We like to think of it as our, 'guest system'."

The young airman has heard this line of thinking before. And it is one of the bits of logic that has lodged in his mind, and grown until it has become an accepted maxim, and, at last, has driven him here to this fence, to ogle the merchandise, and to select a companion for the afternoon. He scans the girls' faces... all so young, and fit, and tanned from the Asian sun. As he looks from girl to girl, he tries not to think about his wife's face.

"You," he says at last, beckoning with his index finger to a pretty one, wearing dark slacks and a floral shirt tied at her midriff. Because he knows no other language besides English, the airman is forced to communicate in signs, which only heightens the agony of the moment. The girl in the floral shirt, however, knows several languages, including, Stupid American. She stands up from where she has been sitting in the dust, smooths her slacks, says something in French to the girl next to her, and glides over to the fence, where she touches the airman's fingers through the chain link. Like centuries of Asian women before her, she has been taught that most of her life will be about pleasing a man. She has paid attention to that lesson and learned it well.

"Hello," she says, in soft, pleasant English.

"Hey," says the airman. His heart is racing.

An MP opens a gate for the American. Allows him to come inside. Asks for the letter of authorization he received from his commanding officer. Meanwhile, another MP frisks the girl in the floral shirt for drugs, weapons, and contraband. Once she passes muster, she joins the airman, and the two of them walk to a little hole in the wall, behind which sits yet another military policeman, and there they surrender their IDs through the hole, where they will be kept until they are picked up later in the day. In exchange, the MP slides a "day pass" through the hole, for the girl to wear as long as she is on base. On it, in cheery, gold letters, is embossed the word, "Guest", and it fits comfortably around the girl's neck. Something about the word makes the airman feel better about himself, even hospitable or gentlemanly. Deep inside, though, he knows he is really the girl's guest, rather than vice versa. And this realization casts a pall across the whole arrangement.

"Have her back by 2300 hours," the MP reminds the airman, as he walks away from the fence with his girl. He has heard those words before. Where was it? Where? Where? And then he remembers. It was back in Topeka, where he grew up. Back when he was a teenager. Back before the war. Before college. Before he had even kissed a girl. The words belonged to an honorable man – a man who would eventually become his father-in-law. "Have her home by 11!" he had said back then, because no one used to speak in military time.

Shit! the young airman thinks to himself, as the girl in the floral shirt tightens her grip on his arm. *What the hell am I doing?* But he has no time to answer himself, because the girl is looking up at him now with deep, almond-shaped eyes that are asking questions of their own.

Together, they walk off toward the beach.

In 1970, systems like the Cam Ranh Bay "meat market" existed all over Southeast Asia, and they were always operated under the names of "management" and "morale". Along with them, of course, came an ungodly amount of venereal disease on American bases, which became the subject matter of more than a few, short-length, black-humored, (depending on one's point of view), cinematic advertisements designed to encourage self-control amongst the soldiers. These "shorts", as they were called, were often shown in the on-base movie houses, between the featured films. They were never very effective. The VD epidemic just kept growing. The medical clinics just kept filling up.

And darkness grew fat on human flesh.

In the later stages of this project, when I had taken the best shots my editor had to fire at me and had reason to believe there would be no further surprises ... a surprise landed squarely in my lap.

"Here's a picture you haven't seen," Pat said to me one day, as we leafed through stacks of albums. She handed me the yellowed photograph, and when I turned it over to look at it, my heart skipped a beat. There in all her youthful beauty was Pat Milacek, wife of Captain Alan Milacek, mother of Christine and Diane, deaconess at the Salem United Methodist Church....

... clothed in just her bra and panties.

Not knowing what to say, I dropped the picture on the cushion between us as if it were a snake, and I locked my eyes on the "Footsteps In The Sand" poem that hung on the wall adjacent to the couch where we were sitting.

"Well, Will Cunningham!" declared Pat, "I'd have never picked you to be the shy one, not with the way you've slathered your manuscript with all sorts of colorful language. By the way you're acting now, you'd have thought I handed you a dirty magazine. It's just an ordinary picture, for crying out loud. If you weren't so scared to take a closer look at it, you'd have noticed everything is covered up nice and proper."

To be fair, when I finally *did* take a closer look at the picture, the parts of Pat one shouldn't be staring at were indeed, as she had pointed out, basically hidden by two suitcases and a sign that read: "See you in Hawaii". Comforted by the suitcases, I was eventually able to study the picture. Though to be completely honest, I never did pick it up again. This was "young", "spunky", "Daisy Duke" Pat ... not "matronly", "meatloaf-cooking", "grand-motherly" Pat. And I wanted to keep the two images separate in my mind. So I left the picture sitting on the cushion and I changed the subject.

Later in the evening, when my embarrassment had passed and I had time to talk more about it with Pat, I realized something very profound about the photograph. It had been part of a calendar she had started making way back at the beginning of Al's deployment. In it, each month of the calendar contained a picture of Pat in various states of repose – her moods, her eyes, her innuendos all intended to portray a message that mere words could not express. There was one of Pat and the girls in their Easter dresses, another of her lying on their bed with a caption that read, "Waiting for you to get home," and a very lonely one of her standing on the tarmac at Vance AFB, staring dolefully at the sky. When Al received the calendar, he put it on his wall in Udorn and used it to check off the days until his tour was over. Of course, the "suitcase picture" was his favorite. Strangely, it was the picture Pat had chosen for the month of April, the month before the Mackay Mission went down. Al must have looked at that picture a thousand times leading up to their R&R in Hawaii. And each time he looked at it, the darkness of Vietnam must have given way to Pat's coy smile.

The more I thought about it, however, the more the picture seemed to transcend coquetries; It was an act of courage by Pat, when everything around her must have screamed for her to shrivel up and die. She knew women whose husbands had cheated on them with strange girls in distant lands. She also knew wives who, in the absence of their men, frequented the O Club on base and went wild with indiscretion.

But instead of crumbling, Pat gathered her spirit and did what she could do.

She got down her single-reflex Kodak camera from the attic, where it had been gathering dust in the absence of Al, who was the family photographer. She looked at the roll count and realized she had twelve frames remaining on the roll. She scouted around for a tripod, until she realized it had been given away to the Salvation Army. And she enlisted the help of her six-year-old daughter, to make the most beautiful, most enticing, most prostitute-proof calendar (complete with pin-up photos), that her man had ever seen. It must have all seemed so strange to Christine, watching her mother fix her hair and apply her make-up and then strip down to her underwear to be photographed. This is what transpired between them forty years ago:

"Mommy," said Christine, as she got ready to snap the picture of her mother posing behind two suitcases. "You can't send this picture to Daddy. You don't have your clothes on."

"We want Daddy to come home, don't we?" said Pat, and she tousled her hair and threw back her shoulders and positioned the suitcases so they wouldn't reveal too much ... but just enough.

"Oh, yes!" said Christina, too young to understand the lengths love goes to to express itself. "I want him to come home *today*!"

"Then we'll give him the courage he lacks," said Pat.

So the picture was snapped.

And the envelope was sealed.

And the courage went flying over the mountains, and the oceans, and the endless miles of heartache between Waukomis and the war.

CHAPTER TEN

COUNTING HAWKS

7,484 women served in Vietnam. Of those, 83.5% were nurses. Eight of those nurses died. One was killed in action.

There's a little "Vietnam" in everybody's soul ... the conflict they don't understand, the one that brings them shame ... the one they push deep down, beneath the beetle cellar.

When I was a teenager, I overheard a conversation on a bus ride that provided context for the *baseball blastoma* from which my father, William "Alfred", had suffered. His father, William "Edward", the grandfather I never met, was apparently quite an athlete – not only in the annals of minor league baseball, but in the annals of his own mind, as well. Having just barely missed the American Association Championships in 1913 and 1914, "Bill" Cunningham pitched for the Milwaukee (Double A) Brewers during some of their lackluster years, prior to my father's entrance into this world. William "Edward" never made it to the big leagues, and was still suffering from "Almost Syndrome" when his son was born. Thus, he was destined to relive his shortcomings through William "Alfred", my father.

Keep in mind, these details came to me through the crack between the seats of a Greyhound bus, as my mother recounted them to a friend. We were on our way to Washington DC, on a church-sponsored Bicentennial trip. The year was 1976. I was a month shy of seventeen. I believe my father was sitting many seats behind me.

"At six-foot, four-inches tall, and two-hundred and thirty pounds, my husband had all the tools of an athlete," my mother told her friend. Since she spoke in increasingly hushed tones, I scooted as close as I could to the crack, to gather more snippets of the man I wished I knew. Here is the gist of what I heard.

Unfortunately for my father, God had made him an artist – a fact that didn't bode well for his relationship with William "Edward". Equally unfortunate for my father, his physique didn't develop until many years after his father died. Thus, he apparently wandered through his formative years as a sort of Norman Rockwell character, tall and gawking, and devoid of coordination.

"Well, it's obvious you can't throw a curveball, Billy-boy – so, you'll never amount to much," his almost-made-it-to-the-majors-father told him once, when they were tossing the ball around together in the front yard.

Not long after that comment, William "Edward" collapsed while finishing construction on the family home in the San Joaquin Valley of California, where he had worked to bring an electrical co-op to that community. Whether the cause of his death was heat exhaustion or a stroke, no one may ever know. But William "Edward" was in a box and in the ground before the week was over. My father was fourteen as he stood at his father's graveside, looking down at the man he could never please. And that was the last time William "Alfred" ever threw a baseball with his dad, or with anyone. Including me. William "Welborn".

Had I known this information during my own formative years, I might have understood why my father and I didn't play catch, or fish, or hunt, or hike, or do *anything* I imagined other boys did with their fathers. However, by the time I heard these facts at sixteen, *baseball blastoma* had already eaten away much of my insides, leaving a father-shaped cavity in my heart. And even though my father attended *every* baseball game I ever played in, cheering, "That's my boy!" unnecessarily loudly every time I batted, (even when I struck out), there always seemed to be a backstop between us, both literally and figuratively. It is a sad, sad fact that we can only bestow on our children what was bestowed on us, be it good or bad. What we give them remains "theirs" for life. What we don't give is often hard for them to acquire.

134

Meeting Al had brought all this back up from the beetle cellar and placed it in my lap, like an unexploded ordnance ... waiting to go off.

———————————

"Take me over the fence with you," I said to Al one day.

"Nonsense, Will," replied Al, while Pat re-tied one of his tennis shoes. "The war has been over for forty years. Even if I could, you'd get us killed, trying to anthropize the enemy."

"Anthropomorphize," I corrected him.

"That, too," said Al. He was smiling as he teased me, but I could tell he was also dead serious.

"I'm not talking about the fence in Vietnam," I pressed. "I want you to take me into the heart of your current battle."

"You mean 'cancer'," said Al. "Just say what you mean, boy."

Pat looked up from Magnet Ass's Reeboks, and the look on her face said, *I trust you, Will. But please – be careful.* I reassured her with a nod.

"Yes," I said to Al. "I mean 'cancer'. It's the connection between you and the common man, the point of contact with our readers."

"Point of contact," muttered Al. He closed his eyes and sat quietly for a moment, as if running through a mental, pre-flight checklist.

"It started when my doctor in Oklahoma City said he was sending us to Mayo..."

———————————

The first trip to Rochester, Minnesota was as cold as a cattle tank at Christmas.

It was February 19th, 2010, and Pat was driving Al to Mayo for his initial evaluation. The doctor's diagnosis, "Barrett's Esophagus", was the chief reason for their trip – and their hope was that his findings were nothing more than acid reflux.

"It's chillier here than Oklahoma," said Pat, as they sat in the McDonald's drive-through in Kansas City. She rolled the window halfway down, reached out, and tried to chip some of the ice away from her side-view mirror.

"Thank you for driving," said Magnet Ass. "I never imagined you'd have to do so much for me, Pat. But I..." Al looked out the passenger window, wincing at the pain in his chest, "I just feel so awful."

Pat rolled the window up, and inched forward in the line.

"I'm sorry you're feeling bad, shug. Dr. Neumann said you could expect your heartburn to get worse. Do you have that sour taste in the back of your mouth, like he said you'd have?"

Al nodded. Every word he spoke was irritating to his throat, so his conversations with Pat were more economical than usual. He tried unsuccessfully to stifle a cough, but it burst forth with smoke and flames. His throat was on fire.

"I'm so sorry," said Pat again.

In the backseat of their Chevy Tahoe, the things they would need for the three-day evaluation sat in a neat row of bags and satchels. Pat brought the kitchen sink when she traveled, always one for being prepared. Al had learned to travel lightly over the years, and his small duffel was evidence of a philosophy that had gotten him over many an obstacle. Barrett's would be no different, he hoped.

"Welcome to McDonald's," chirped the cheerful teenager at the window.

"Hello," said Pat. "I know we ordered two sausage biscuits back at the speaker-thingy ... but do you think you could change that order?"

"Of course," said the teen.

Pat looked woefully at Al, and his heart sank. He had hoped she would forget the doctor's moratorium on fatty, spicy foods, but she was always on top of things. He nodded his consent to another bland breakfast, glad at least for sustenance.

"We'll have two yogurt parfaits," said Pat. She paid with cash set aside for traveling expenditures, and they drove north toward

Iowa, consuming their sad, little meal. It would be Al's last solid food before the next day's procedure. That night, they stayed at a Motel 6 in Des Moines, and laid in bed holding hands, while David Letterman interviewed a guest whose bulldog rode a rocking horse. The world seemed so different to them now that they were old. Accustomed to a king-sized mattress at home, the tiny double-bed was barely comfortable, but also strangely comforting. They huddled close and drifted off.

In the morning they hit the road early, and Pat assumed the role of driver again, while Al tried to feel useful by giving her directions from a map. Neither of them cared for GPS systems. And since it's a straight shot up I–35 from the Milacek farm to Mayo, (seven-hundred and fifty-five miles to be exact), door to door, with scarcely a deviation, they both knew there was no need for a navigator. After twenty minutes of pretending he was leading, and another ten of map-folding, Al resigned himself to counting hawks on fence posts and the number of times he coughed between each mile-marker. Out of the corner of his eye, he eyed the driver's seat, and he tried to remember what it was like to be the master of his own machine.

Even as the wheels of Al and Pat's Tahoe rolled northward, the world was unraveling ... cracking, crumbling, being "un-made", as great writers have described it. In spite of wondrous technology, it seemed that each new time-saving device Man created freed him to get busy in twelve new ways. And each new victory won by Man was a victory over him.

As Magnet Ass counted hawks and coughs, he hoped the technology awaiting him in Rochester would free him from his pain.

Hawk.
Hawk.
Hawk.
Cough.
Hawk.
Cough.
Hawk.
Cough.

"How much further, Pat?" he said, a half-hour north of the McDonald's.

"Go to sleep, shug," said Pat. "It'll make the trip go faster."

In Barrett's esophagus, tissue in the tube connecting a person's mouth and stomach is replaced by tissue similar to the intestinal lining. It is most often diagnosed in people who have long-term gastroesophageal reflux disease (GERD) — a chronic regurgitation of acid from the stomach into the lower esophagus. Only a small percentage of people with GERD will develop Barrett's esophagus. Barrett's esophagus is also associated with an increased risk of developing esophageal cancer. Although the risk is small, it's important to have regular checkups for precancerous cells. If precancerous cells are discovered, they can be treated to prevent esophageal cancer.

The pamphlet Al read in the waiting room at Mayo was only slightly encouraging. On the wall, the clock ticked away, faithfully reminding every person in the room of their disappearing lives.

"It's just a biopsy," he whispered to Pat.

"Yes," said Pat, "Just a biopsy."

To occupy her time and to combat nervousness, Pat reviewed the list of questions she had jotted down on a piece of notebook paper for the doctors. Do Al's lab reports show abnormal tissue? How much of his esophagus is affected? Will I need to change the way I cook for him? She forced herself to read to the bottom of the list, where she knew she would find the most troubling question, the one that made her bite her lip and look away from Al.

What is his risk of esophageal cancer?

Pat folded the piece of notebook paper and put it in her purse. "Shug?" said Pat.

"Hm?" said Al.

"Are you afraid?" she asked.

Al rubbed the cover of the Gideon's Bible he had found in the drawer next to his chair. "Not with you here," he replied.

The upper endoscopy was more troublesome than traumatic for Al. He had wished for a less invasive procedure, something like a barium x-ray, where all he had to do was drink some liquid and have a picture taken of his chest. But Dr. Neumann in Oklahoma City had told him the EGD was necessary, which had led to this trip over the fence, and to this cold, sterile examination room.

Magnet Ass sat with the ridiculous gown on, fastened as judiciously as the meager ties would allow, his legs dangling in the air like worn out piñatas.

"It's important for you to know your procedure will be done under 'conscious sedation'," said the friendly doctor, as he administered the intravenous injection. "We need you to be vaguely awake and cooperative the entire time. Are you a cooperative guy, Mr. Milacek?"

"Like a lamb," said Al.

The doctor looked at Pat, and she gave a thumbs up.

"Of course, you're free to be in here if you'd like, ma'am," the doctor whispered to Pat, "...but your husband may be more at ease if you weren't..."

"I'd like her to stay," interrupted Al.

"As you wish," said the doctor. Behind his mask, his eyes suggested he was smiling, which made Al feel at home. Soon, the sedation began to work its magic, and the endoscopy nurse applied an additional topical anesthetic to Al's throat.

"I'll need you to lie on your left side," said the doctor. "And I'll need you to look straight ahead with your chin tucked in."

"You're doing great, shug," said Pat. "I'll be right here the whole time."

The endoscopy nurse repositioned the pillow under Al's head, but he barely felt the pressure of her hand against his forehead. He was slipping away already ... settling down into that warm halfway house between knowledge and oblivion. Soaring ... searching ... on the hunt again for bad guys in the jungles of his gut below. It felt good to be unaware for the first time in his life. And yet, he was still very aware of so many things.

A gloved finger probing his throat ... a gag response ... a mouthpiece being placed between his teeth ... a voice....

"I need you to swallow the tube, Al..."

"Say what?"

"We need you to swallow the tube..."

Down went the tube with the light on the end of it. Down and down and down and down. Through the esophagus ... and the stomach ... and the duodenum ... to the dark crevices of the trail below ... where the slippery, shadowy things marshal themselves undetected ... until someone goes searching for them ... dear Lord, Laos is lovely this time of year ... moonless ... moist and jungle-rotting ... is that enough fentanyl for you, sir?... perhaps more next time, should there be a next time ... man the guns! ... drop the flares! ... shed some light on your shiny insides! ... A prick and a sting! The armor is pierced ... the tissue taken ... yes, Laos is lovely this time of year...

"Breathe easy, Mr. Milacek ... you'll gag less if you just breathe easy ... that's good ... nice and easy ... nice and easy..."

Pale and glossy ... red and velvety ... the difference is everything when it comes to the nasty, little buggers that run on the trails below....

The entire procedure lasted just ten minutes.

In the recovery room, it took about an hour for the sedation to wear off, and for Magnet Ass to remember who he was.

"You did great, shug," said Pat, as she gave a little squeeze to Al's hand.

"I couldn't have made it home without you," said Al, groggily.

"What did you say?" said Pat.

For one moment, Al was standing on the tarmac with his wife, surrounded by well-wishers, and reporters, and fanatical airmen slapping one another on the back with vigorous blows. Then the next moment he was in this nondescript hospital room, with the flowers, and the subdued lights, and the cheeseburger smuggled in against Dr. Neumann's orders.

"I was mistaken," said Al, reaching for the cheeseburger with greedy fingers.

"They had your favorite in the cafeteria downstairs," said Pat, trying not to choke on her tears.

Three months later, Magnet Ass's biopsy came back positive, his Barrett's Esophagus was upgraded to cancer, and he and Pat began their long relationship with the good people at Mayo. From the start, he was a hit with the hospital staff, who, somehow, had already been briefed about the Mackay Trophy and were happy to have a war hero and his wife on their ward. Throughout their months at Mayo, nurses would find Al's Yoda-like wisdom charming, and doctors would marvel at his simple faith, refreshed by its contrast with the need for verifiable data that typified their lives.

"He asked if I would pray for him," said one physician, after a meeting with Al. "When I told him I haven't prayed since grade school, he asked if he could pray for *me*. I hope he gets well soon, and everything. But man, it'd be nice if Captain Al could hang around here for a while. Mayo's a happier place since he showed up."

In my months with Magnet Ass, the language of war had settled on my shoulders like a tongue of fire, smoldering with syllogisms, vulgarities, and curious acronyms. And sometimes, taking the yoke of my own native tongue, it made me blurt out things I would have never said prior to meeting Al Milacek.

"She's due an oil change," I told Cindy one day, speaking of our Buick, whose odometer had just passed a hundred and sixty-thousand miles.

"Since when has the car become a 'she'?" asked Cindy.

For ever so brief a moment, I looked at my wife and saw Flight

Engineer Nash, dressed in Nomex, kicking Stinger's tires. Then the vision dissipated like the smoke of a flare, and I was back from Udorn.

"Never mind," I said. "I was just thinking about the book. Do you know where the Jiffy Lube coupon is? I've misplaced it."

But even when I forced myself to think about other things, the language of war was always there, springing up in conversations, in commercials, in emails and phone calls. Like a child growing up in his parent's world, I was becoming fluent without even trying.

"'Bingo' again?" I would say to myself, when the Buick's gas gauge dipped below a quarter of a tank. "Seems like I just filled up two days ago."

"Roger wilco," I found myself thinking, whenever Cindy called me to the dinner table.

Recognizing it was inescapable, I finally yielded to the spirit and allowed myself to sink blissfully into its charm. But of all the terms and phrases associated with my new tongue, only one stood out as romantic.

"Over the fence." I loved it the first time I heard it, because it was pregnant with the possibility of greener grass, baseballs recovered, bullies eluded, a cigarette smoked clandestinely, whole neighborhoods hoodwinked with a bucket of whitewash. Of course, Magnet Ass and the truck hunters thought of "over the fence" in a singular, circumscribed, almost sacred sort of way. To them it meant, "It's time to go break things, and perhaps be broken."

I once read a lonely verse at the end of the fourteenth chapter of John's Gospel, that suggested Jesus was thinking these things, too, on his last night with his men.

"Get up! Let's get out of here," He said to his crew, as they lounged over supper together. They had a job to do, and they were burning daylight. So, at the word of their Captain, over the fence they went, the stone-cold truck hunters of a distant century, scared as hell, but pretty sure Captain Jesus knew what he was doing. Down the vine-choked hillside they went, picking their way along the shadowy, eastern slope of Jerusalem, across the Brook Kidron, and up to the Garden of Gethsemane, where the Romans were waiting for him. There, they arrested him, and beat the shit out of Him, and impaled Him on a tree.

Rochester, Minnesota was a long way over the fence for Magnet Ass. From the beginning of his cancer to its end, Pat and he went to Mayo twenty-five times. As was always the case when a gunship went over the fence....

...things were bound to be broken.

CHAPTER ELEVEN

BULLETS? BULLETS.

"Udorn brass made it very clear they didn't want officers helping enlisted men on their regular duties. I always appreciated chain of command and rules and everything ... but that was one rule that made no sense to me ... so, I broke it."
   Captain Al Milacek

Even from a distance, one could see the boy's face was covered with blood, as he stumbled down the block toward us. In his wake were a host of kids from the west end of 39th Street, the playmates of my childhood. Bringing up the rear of the entourage was a slouching, guilt-faced, older brother, with a fishing rod slung over his shoulder.

"Doctor Cunningham! Doctor Cunningham!" cried one of the kids. Why in the world they had not solicited the help of their own parents, at their own end of the block was a mystery to me. I could only guess that fear of punishment outweighed the need for immediate, adult intervention.

"He's in the house, reading," I said, as I inspected with awe the #8 fish hook protruding from the eyelid of the victim. "What happened to Kent?" I asked.

Everyone pointed at Kent's older brother, and I had my answer.

I don't recall the order of events that happened next, but somehow my father was there instantly, having transformed in some obscure phone booth from mild-mannered parent figure to "Asclepius the Healer", savior of the neighborhood. Setting his leather, medical bag on the retaining wall at the end of our driveway, my father helped the trembling patient have a seat, and then he leaned the boy's head ever so gently against the cool, red bricks. Above us in the trees, the cicadas buzzed with sibilant interest.

"Easy does it, Kent," he said. "We'll have you fixed in no time."

As my father assessed the situation, a loose testimony emerged from the circle of witnesses, and soon I formed the opinion that Kent's older brother, the one with the fishing rod now held discreetly behind his back, had been annoying his sibling by purposely casting in his direction, when he snagged him in the eyeball.

"There *are* less destructive ways to tease your little brother–don't you think, Matt?" asked my father, as he gingerly snipped the shank of the #8 hook with some magical snippers from his magical bag, dropped the eyelet into the palm of his hand, and slipped the barbed end harmlessly away from Kent's cornea.

"Yessir," said the elder brother, his head lowered in shame.

"No harm done," announced my father, taking his patient by the hand and lifting him to an upright position, like Jesus and the paralytic. Later, when the excitement of the crisis had faded, and the neighborhood whirred again with the drama of "Kick the Can", and we had all forgotten that young Kent had almost been rendered a blind man, reduced to begging at the gates of Oklahoma City for the remainder of his life ... I recall seeing my father and Matt, sitting on the wall, with the fishing rod propped against it. My father's hand was on the culprit's shoulder.

He was a busy man, my father the doctor – but never too busy to restore the wounded. He was, after all, "Asclepius the Healer".

Great men always invest in lesser men; Magnet Ass's men sensed this from the start. Nowhere was this more evident than in the fact Al *never* let his gunner's crank ammo alone.

"It was a grueling task," said Ken Firestone, "Made worse by the fact it was often done after a long and edgy mission. It entailed getting the spent casings from the storage area under the plane, and then loading them onto a trailer that brought ammo for the reloading. We would reload both 20's and the mini's if they had been used. We also had to restock the ammo rack with the extra ammo needed for inflight reloading. Now this could work up a good sweat. I'm not sure how long it took, but I know it would have taken a lot longer if our entire crew hadn't stayed and helped until the job was finished. Each member of our crew completed the entire mission, and that included preparing the aircraft for the next crew. That wasn't everyone's job; It was the responsibility of the gunners. But that's what made our crew one of the best. We were in it together. Had it not been for the CO's helping the NCO's with such menial tasks as this, I don't think we'd have ever won the Mackay Trophy. I don't even think we'd have made it back to Udorn with one wing shot off."

In this way, Al's crew grew in unity, fueled by the humility of the commissioned officers, and fused together as a formidable weapon to achieve the purposes of a nation that had long ago forgotten what it meant to dwell in harmony.

Now, there is tremendous empowerment that occurs when an "insider" – who has already basked in the warmth of his fellow man's applause – grabs hold of an "outsider", drags him into the "circle of belonging", and hands him the keys to the neighborhood. Conversely, irreversible damage is done to the "outsider" when the "insider", upon securing his spot within the coveted circle, makes entry to its club twice as hard as it ever was when he was on the outside. It is a hushed and wicked truth that all men fear the "outside". So, we clamor to avoid it, doing anything in our power to at least appear as "insiders".

But there were no "outsiders" in Magnet Ass's crew. No tenderfoots. No neophytes or fledglings. Everyone was on the inside. And the cruel Outside was held at bay by the molten bullets of acceptance and love.

As the first draft of this book drew near its end, I finally accepted the fact I would have to include in the manuscript a letter that came to me in the closing months of my father's life.

It was at once both terrifying and reassuring, and I hoped it was the beginning of something good for the two of us. But it also reminded me of the beetle cellar, which was the deepest reason I had, throughout my life, felt the haunting possibility that I was....

... an outsider.

In the spring of 1990, when my sons were two and four, and I had settled into the routine of raising kids and paying bills, I received a letter with the handwriting I had often tried to copy as a teenager. Marked by the fluidity of an artist and the rigidity of a perfectionist, the name in the top, left-hand corner of the envelope peeked out from under the other letters I had retrieved from my mailbox, and I tore into it instantly.

"Beloved Son," it began, in its flowing script. Right away I heard my father's voice, as if we were sitting on his back porch together. He had a penchant for the dramatic, often referring to my sisters and me as, "beloved daughter", or, "son of my loins", or sometimes simply, "Beloved". Of course, I failed to appreciate this drama when I was living under his roof, thinking it weird and Shakespearean. In later years, however, long after I had moved away, such language made me feel like the subject of a master artist's painting, sitting patiently and still, while he slathered me with color.

After a paragraph or two of cordialities and news from Oklahoma, Dad settled into the reason he was writing, and the letter became a living thing, pregnant with possibility.

"*It has long occurred to me that I have failed you in the friendship department,*" he admitted. I recall my hands trembling as I read these words, trembling because the words were true, and I had lived them quietly and painfully, longing to hear them spoken from his lips. "*But with the years has come the realization that an old dog can learn new tricks, if, that is, a young dog is willing to be patient with him. And with that realization comes the thought that a fishing trip might be just the thing for two dogs– like you and me – to discover whether friendship is within their pedigree."*

As I mentioned, my father had a flare for the dramatic. If you were to duplicate that last paragraph in everyday, normal language, it would read something like: *"Hey, son, what a jerk I've been for not hanging out with you lately. What do you say we put a fishing trip on the calendar as soon as possible? It would do us both some good."* Then again, such a mistranslation would cause you to miss out entirely on the feeling of being splattered with aching love and vivid sorrow.

I have grown to appreciate the way my father painted with words.

And so it was, that in the fall of '90, four months after I received the letter above, my father showed up at my front door, to make amends of his own. Up to his chest in rubber waders, and carrying what looked like a gigantic, plastic filing cabinet, he looked like an Orvis manikin, freshly-escaped from the retail store. The whole get-up must have cost him a mint. So, right away I recognized he had skin in the game.

"Come in," I said to the manikin. With the squeak of thigh on thigh, my father crossed my threshold for the first time as a novice, rather than an expert. We spent the evening mapping out our plan to conquer the trout in Taneycomo, while his daughter-in-law and grandsons eyed with wonder the colorful baubles in his tackle box. At midnight, we went to bed dreaming of the day to come.

The following morning, after a hasty breakfast of juice and store-bought pastries, Dad and I threw our gear in the car and headed to Lilly's Landing, where I had rented a small fishing boat and paid for it with my own money. With the strange rush of prominence that comes from footing the bill while one's father looks on, I loosened the figure-eight knot that held the bow of our vessel to the dock, and we floated off into the green current of Taneycomo. Because I was at the rudder, I recall the way my father's grey hair looked, with the sunlight spilling through it like oil. Even though his back was to me, I could tell he was smiling.

Much of that morning was spent drifting and talking, and getting our lines untangled from hidden snags and root-wads. At the height of the sun, when the fishing was poorest, we anchored to a fallen tree and ate a lunch of cheese and summer sausage, washing it down with ginger ale, my father's favorite. Late in the afternoon, I caught an enormous, male Rainbow, barely lipping him with a brown Rooster Tail, and when my father reached for him with the net – he missed him badly. As the lure came loose from the huge, hooked jaw, the fish broke free in a burst of color and light. For a painfully long time, my father stared at the sad, concentric circles that fled away from our boat and hid themselves in the shadowy cuts of the distant shoreline.

At last, he looked up at me.

"I'm not much of a fisherman," he said, his eyes apologetic, his words rotten with a lifetime of repetition. By a stroke of luck, I saw the curve ball sailing over the bow of the boat, and I checked my disappointment.

"You're a damn, fine fisherman, Dad," I declared, and I handed him my rod with the lucky Rooster Tail. "Make a few casts and see what happens."

My father took the rod and sat up a little straighter on the bow seat. And far back in the recesses of his eye, where the retina records life's brightest and blackest moments, I thought I saw the red coals of friendship smoldering.

On my desk at home sits a photograph that chronicles that perfect day perfectly. In it, my father is holding up two fish on a stringer. They are in no way impressive. In fact, they are so meager, one might wonder why they weren't released immediately, rather than photographed in their wretched, gasping state. However, when one looks from the fish to my father's smile, then back again to the fish, the correlation is evident. As far as Dad was concerned, he had landed "Moby Dick" and "Orca" in the presence of his admiring son. And that was good enough for him. It was perhaps the most golden day of my life, but it was destined to dangle on the boughs of my existence as a singular, sparkling knickknack. For it was never repeated.

On Christmas morning, my father announced his lung cancer to the family. In May, my mother called me with the news of his death. Four days after that, we buried him at our farm in Piedmont. His stone says, "He was kind", and it stands in the wheat like a defiant middle-finger to the city of Milwaukee. At least, that's how I see it.

My father would have never meant it that way.

Perhaps the last thing people want to leave behind when they exit this world is "unfinished business". This is probably why Richard Nixon spent so much time in his later years writing about the mess he made of things in Southeast Asia. At times, a sort of apology hemorrhages through the words in his memoirs, running between the lines, settling in clotted pools at the bottoms of the pages. To be fair to our former leader, he was making amends, and there is always value in that.

And so, the writing of Al's story was fast becoming two things for me: the hope of a vital friendship filled with brimming possibilities, and the aching reminder I had spent much of my life cranking bullets alone.

I also began to wonder if anyone had ever died from writing a story.

CHAPTER TWELVE

KNIFE

15 out of every 100 people with esophageal cancer will survive for 5 years or more after diagnosis.

They say the knife was the first tool to be developed. But it was thousands of years before Hippocrates spoke of the knife as an instrument of surgery, using the word, "machaira" to describe it. How interesting that the famous historian chose an old, Spartan sword – not unlike the one Peter used to cut off the servant's ear in the Garden of Gethsemane – to denote one of modern medicine's most well-known pieces of equipment. And so we see that knives, like many of the things people invent, can waste a man or heal his wounds with similar efficiency.

In late January, when the feeders were empty and the water in my birdbath was hard as stone, and the finches sat in the pines, staring at my backdoor as if to say, "Well?"... I climbed into my wife's Honda and headed east again to Oklahoma. This time I was going for a short visit to Waukomis, and then on to see my mother in Oklahoma City, who was slowly turning to dust in body and mind. She was eighty-seven.

The kiss goodbye to Cindy had been cursory at best, the weight of the book having settled on our marriage like heavy snow on brittle branches.

"Well? said Cindy, as if she was a bird in the backyard, too. "Is that how we're going to leave it?"

"It?" I repeated, playing ignorant. My wife has always hated it when I do that – and I'm not sure why I continue. I suppose it's the pain-thing I mentioned earlier, and my need to keep myself separate from it. Even my own pain has never been a place where I felt welcome.

Choosing not to press the issue, Cindy let me go then. I saw her in my rearview mirror, standing on our porch, biting her lip and waving until I got to the stop sign on the corner, turned, and vanished out of view. I did not wave back.

By the time I reached Limon, I was far enough from the pain that I could stand outside of it and study it, like a researcher observing a live specimen, pinned to a wax board. The night before had been a miserable one.

"Are you okay?" Cindy had asked, as she slid under the covers next to me. She was lying in the gentle glow of the reading lamp attached to our bed, the one we had picked out together at a consignment shop and nicknamed, "Narnia", because it was like a sleigh, painted silver all over. The prospect of intimacy hung heavy in the space between us.

"I think I'm going to go write for a while," I said. What I meant to say – what I had intended to say, if it were not for the pain-thing – was that I couldn't fathom a woman wanting to be with a man whose financial bottom line had a big, fat "zero" scribbled across it, and whose only current contribution to society was ideas on pages, and even those pages weren't real, they were ghosts floating in cyberspace, unable to scare up a single cent of income. But I didn't say any of that. I just left the beautiful woman in the Narnia Bed alone with her own pain, and I went to sleep on the couch in the den, which was a stupid, low thing to do ... darker than the darkness of a beetle cellar.

And then I left her again the next morning. Without so much as a wave.

At the border, where colorful Colorado grows monochromatic and fades into dismal Kansas, one can always expect to see cars pulled over and excited drivers photographing the sign that welcomes them to the "Mountain State". This phenomenon may seem strange to the uninitiated, since Eastern Colorado looks exactly like Western Kansas, and, except for this one sign, contains nothing that merits even slowing down, let alone stopping for a picture. But over the years of traveling between these two states, I've concluded there is something about the promise of mountains that makes westbound travelers pull over, grab their cameras, capture the iconic photo, pause to chat with strangers about the wonders that must surely lay west of the sign, and imagine, as they stand there on the breast of discovery, that they can already see the Rockies' purple outline, even though two-hundred miles still lie between them and their dreams.

I took that very same photo thirty years ago with Cindy. It lives now in a shoebox ... in our basement.

At Colby, KS, I stopped for gas and bought a microwave burrito inside the desolate convenience store that squatted on the edge of an even more desolate wheat field. As I returned to the Honda, I paused to admire its sleek lines and shiny exterior. It was a Christmas gift from me to Cindy, no more than two weeks old, a brand-new car, the only new car we had ever purchased in our marriage. I had done it quietly without my wife's knowledge, ransacking the savings I had laid up over years of employment, and plopping it all down at the dealership before I could change my mind. I had even put one of those giant, red bows on it when I gave it to her, just like the commercials on TV. Cindy had loved it immediately, and insisted I take it on this road trip, so I would be comfortable. The gift had been "all about love", I told myself as I stared at the car. But then my mind leaped to an image of Al and the truck hunters flying in their converted trash-hauler every night, making do with what was handed to them, and my gift of the Honda to Cindy suddenly began to feel as if it had been motivated by something other than love.

Frustrated, I pitched the burrito, still in its wrapper, into the trash can, and drove away ... anything but comfortable.

Pat had told me once that she had been keeping a diary since her childhood, and had never missed a single day's entry. Eager for what it might mean to the book, I had asked her to make a copy of it for my use, and she had burst out in spontaneous laughter.

"The diary's not just one book, Will," said Pat. "It's dozens and dozens of them – over sixty years' worth at least."

"Well, then maybe you should just give me the parts that seem relevant to our story," I said, "And I'll take it from there."

Happy to help as usual, Pat had granted my request, laboring long hours over the many, separate diaries to cull out the pertinent stuff. Thus, as I flew past Wakeeney, and Hays, and Salina, and Wichita, I had balanced on my right knee all the important parts of an old woman's life, and the weight of it felt no heavier than a bird's wing. With one eye on the road, I scanned Pat's journal entries, making note of the interesting things and speaking them into my tape recorder.

"*Hi, Will*," the entries began. As I read the words out loud, I could hear Pat's country twang going up and down like a steel guitar, warm enough to make me forget the mess I'd made of things back home. "*We left home on November 30th, 2014, for Alan's one year checkup on his esophagus surgery, only planning on being gone about 4 days. It was a cold, 4 deg. On Dec. 2, they did a CT scan on Alan's esophagus, requested by his surgeon, Dr. K. All appeared ok as he scanned the pictures. Then he told us that there was a spot on Al's bile duct, near the liver...*"

Those last three words, "near the liver", got my attention.

My hands gripped the steering wheel a little tighter, and my heart pounded like a faraway drum. Sometimes when a plane is shot, the blast takes out a wing and, though the damage is significant, the pilot believes he can bring his craft under enough control to fly it home. But other times, unbeknownst to the pilot, collateral damage has been done, as well. The tail has suffered loss ... or the rudder ... or the landing gear. Control begins to slip through the pilot's fingers, and he blows through a barrack full of slumbering souls, like a rhino through a quiet glade.

As I careened across the lunar landscape of western Kansas, I thought about my life since September, when I began this project. I recalled the end to my comfortable salary ... a flatly rejected first proposal ... a second proposal only slightly less rejected... expensive trips back and forth from Waukomis ... an even more expensive flight to see my editor in Portland. The money was just flying out the window – money I didn't have. And the end was nowhere in sight. But when I read Pat's words about her husband's liver, it was the first time I had considered that Al might die before this book came to life. That was the final turning point in the project for me – and there had been a lot of them – the day I stopped whining about my plane, and started thinking about someone else's.

So, "over the fence" I went again with Al, because I realized another part of his plane had been shot off, and I wanted to learn about it. This time I went with the help of Pat's journal, and with Dr. Kubrick – the best liver surgeon available at Mayo.

December 2, 2014–

"Hepatectomy," said Dr. K, when Pat asked what the procedure was called. "Other than taking Al's whole liver, it's the only way for us to get the cancer out," he added. "You can be thankful your husband's healthy enough for us to leave him with a portion of a functioning liver. Otherwise, he'd need a transplant."

Right," said Pat, "I can be thankful." She squeezed Al's hand, and he looked at her with faraway eyes.

Dr. K scheduled Al for an MRI at 7:15 that evening, to see how extensive the damage was to his liver. After the MRI, Al and Pat went back to their motel, tired and hungry, and shocked at how fast this was all unfolding. Just a few hours before, they had been setting their sights on Waukomis, eager to get back to the farm. Now, they were facing another surgery, and the unknown. They went to bed without watching the news, and slept fitfully.

The following morning found Al and Pat like a couple of gunship pilots between missions – plenty to think about and nothing to do. To occupy their time, they ate breakfast together and went to the mall for some window shopping. Then they went back to the motel, called their girls, and waited for the MRI results. Later, they paid a visit to Dr. Kubrick's office.

"Al needs surgery ASAP," Dr. K said, when they were finally able to discuss the MRI.

"How soon is ASAP?" asked Al, his voice ragged and worn.

"First thing in January," Dr. K said, bleakly.

Pat cringed at the thought of making the long drive to Minnesota again. But then she smiled, and took control of her emotions. "Okay," she said, "If that's the soonest you can fit us in, we'll be here with bells on."

The two co-pilots went back to their room, packed their belongings in silence, checked out at the front desk, and were on their way out of Rochester, when Dr. K called again and asked them to return to the Gonda Building at the Mayo complex. They had scarcely exchanged 'hellos' and sat down in his office, when Dr. K gave them the news.

"I've had a cancellation in my schedule," he said. "I can do Alan's surgery in the morning if you're willing to stay until then. The sooner we do it, the better the odds."

Al looked at Pat, and they both nodded their consent.

They went immediately for blood work, then to the anesthesiologist for a lengthy conversation that was one part comforting and two parts clinical, and finally back to the same motel, where they were lucky to find their room still available. After laundry, there were more phone calls home, and a light supper for Pat only, since Al's surgery required a twelve hour fast. At last, they prayed and fell into bed exhausted. All the while, in the back of their minds, Dr. K's use of the word, "odds", rotated round and round like a roulette wheel, keeping them both awake until the early morning hours.

Check-in on December 5th was at 7:45 AM, and Al and Pat were there five minutes early. After more paperwork, and the obligatory donning of the gown that never fits, Al was wheeled away to pre-op. Pat was not permitted to accompany him. She stood waving until he reached the intersection of two hallways, where Al asked the nurse to stop and turn the bed around so he could see Pat one more time. With tubes wagging back and forth, Al raised his arm in a feeble salute, and Pat burst into tears.

1300 hours / 5 December / 2014

On the afternoon of Al's hepatectomy, Dr. K went over the fence with all the bad intent of a Stinger crew, hunting down the disease smuggling sons-of-bitches that had attached themselves to Al's insides, and were moving with lethal efficiency from organ to organ.

"Harmonic or Ligasure?" asked the nurse to Dr. K's right. At her disposal, she had every energy sealing device in the world available to surgeons. The one that would be used for Al's surgery depended on the doctor's preference. Unfortunately, the nurse knew the machinery at Mayo better than she knew the medical staff. So she waited for Kubrick's answer.

"Decisions, decisions," replied Dr. K. He had been on his feet since early morning, and the prospect of many more hours in surgery didn't excite him. "Let's see," he mumbled, "I'm more concerned with burst pressure than getting this patient sealed quickly."

"So ... harmonic? Or Ligasure?" repeated the nurse.

Dr. K's patience grew thin. "If you have to ask ...," he began, but then he caught himself. "Let's start over. How about the Ligasure at first, and then I can shift to the Harmonic if I want lower thermal speed."

The nurse handed Dr. K the device he requested, and waited for his next instruction.

The body on the table had been prepped-in for Pfannenstiel, with the wound protector and specimen bag already in place. Standing between his patient's legs, Dr. K looked down and pondered what he knew about the man. Of all the patients he had ever had, this one was the most unusual.

"They don't make 'em like they used to," he said.

"Pardon me?" said the anesthesiologist, at the head of the table.

Unaware he had spoken his thoughts out loud, Dr. K rephrased the question. "Stephen, have you ever had a patient pray for you before you cut him open?"

"You mean ... like ... verbally?"

"Never mind," said Dr. K. He was tired, and it was getting harder and harder to set aside his humanity and shift into deity-mode. Nevertheless, he took a long, cleansing breath of sterile air, cracked his knuckles for good luck, and glanced at the crash cart, the room's one reminder that he was not, in fact, God.

"Okay, people ... what do we have here?" said Dr. K.

"Left lateral hepatic resection," replied the nurse, unaccustomed to Dr. K's love of the rhetorical.

Dr. K fought the urge to respond, continuing instead with his inspection of the body on which he would soon be cutting. "Both arms tucked in ... good ... foley catheter in place ... good ... patient prepped and ready to go ... very good ... no central line..."

"We're running this one 'dry', doctor," said the young anesthesiologist.

At the interruption, Dr. K. kept his eyes down, for fear he might eviscerate his colleague if he looked directly at him. He felt 'the snap' coming on, but he couldn't stop it from coming. Like a flood through a pixie straw, Kubrick's ire burst upon the anesthesiologist with devastating force.

"Of course, we're running this one dry, Stephen," said Dr. K. "That's what we discussed two hours ago, when I told you we wouldn't be using a central line. That's why no more than seventeen seconds ago, in plain and understandable English, I said, 'no central line' into the microphone, so that everyone in this room, and all future generations of human beings could harken back to this moment in time and say, 'Yep ... that's what the doctor said ... no central line ... he said it just like that.' If you'd like, Stephen, we can wait while you check the tapes for yourself. Maybe that way you can be assured that we are, in fact, running this patient 'dry', as we both have now made abundantly clear, and we can move on with this surgery. Or were you just making small talk?"

Except for the sound of the anesthesiologist swallowing the last bit of moisture in his mouth, the operating room was as quiet as a cemetery. Dr. K closed his eyes, wondering what life might have been like as a realtor or an insurance salesman. His mind raced back to his internship long years ago. He saw the old hospital building in the inner-city of Atlanta, where he had spent his early residency and sacrificed the prime of his life serving the indigent. Seventeen stories of hellish sleeplessness and the walking dead in scrubs. He saw himself, eye-bags and all, the newly minted doctor with the newly minted initials behind his name, falling asleep with a retractor in his hand, waking up only as he fell toward an open abdominal wound. He saw the eighteen-room ER, with its two rooms set aside just for the gun and knife and highway carnage. He saw the crazed assailants, following their victims into the hospital, and finishing them off enroute to surgery with the deafening roar of a firearm. He saw the mistakes that were made ... the artificial valves sutured upside down, then corrected amidst blinding execrations ... the kidneys, intended for transplant, but ineptly dropped ... bouncing, skidding, coming to rest on the linoleum surgical floor, then washed down and utilized nonetheless ... and all of this related on one level or another to fatigue. Dr. K had never been a military man, but when he remembered his residency, he felt sure he had served his country in some capacity. It was like being in Khe Sahn – with the smell of chicken and waffles instead of napalm.

Dr. K felt his face flush and a slight dizziness coming over him, and it was times like this he wished he didn't know so much about the symptoms of high blood pressure. For God's sake, what was wrong with him? These were *good* people to his right and his left, without whom the patient would soon be dead. Sure, they were green. But they didn't deserve to be yelled at. He opened his eyes and looked around at the souls who shared his sterile existence. As always, the body on the table seemed better off than each of them. He took a deep breath through his nose, and the suction of the mask against his nostrils reminded him his world was closing in.

He needed coffee.

"I'm ... sorry, people," said Dr. K, wearily. "But this is modern surgery. We do it every day here at Mayo. And as Stephen has so thoughtfully reminded us all, we are running our patient dry today ... no central line, no blood drip ... no Pringle maneuver if we can avoid it ... and all because we want to minimize the recurrence of tumors, and the possibility of reperfusion injury when we restore blood to the organ ... as I'm sure we all remember from the textbooks. So, from now on... or at least until the end of this procedure ... please, people ... only tell me the things I *don't* know."

Unsure if what they had just heard was an apology, the anesthesiologist and the nurse glanced at one another, and then back down at Al, who was fortunate enough to be far away in Vietnam. Dr. K proceeded to make five small incisions, including the Pfannenstiel for specimen extraction, and four trocars for the passage of cameras, surgical instruments, and body fluids. Then, he got down to business.

"Taking down falciform," said Kubrick, in a haggard monotone. Above the operating table, the sensitive microphones picked up his every word and recorded them digitally. For future generations, of course.

"Staying high to prevent dangling fat", said Dr. K. "Moving lower now"... "scoring out the plane"... "confirming extent and margins with ious"... "dividing up to pedicle"...

Dr. K's feet were systematically killing him, their diabolical plan to do away with everything below his waist first, then proceed upward in a massive Blitzkrieg, until there was nothing left of Kubrick but his milkmaid scrub cap. Slowly, the hours passed, long and languishing – the *beep*, *beep*, *beep* of the heart monitor keeping time like a metronome. With an hour left, Dr. K asked the nurse to dab his forehead with a wet cloth, and he waded back into the fray.

"So far so good," said K, "Now it's staple, staple, staple ... everybody loves stapling ... am I right? ... am I talking?" Dr. K looked at Stephen, hoping to make up for his rant with friendly banter. But the anesthesiologist just nodded and went back to monitoring Al's heart rate and breathing. He was new at Mayo, and he wondered if all the hard work to get his foot in the door had been worth it. One thing was clear to him, though. There would never be a friendship between the omnipotent and the flawed. Of that he was sure.

Kubrick rambled on.

"As suspected ... I'm having to mobilize more falciform and triangular ligament ... par for the course, though ... everything looks fine and dandy"...

Through the scope, Al's insides looked like a grocer's meat display after a power failure. The Ligasure and the stapling device flashed in and out of the picture, cutting, cauterizing, closing things up with an impressive economy of movement.

"Thinning out remaining parenchyma," said K. "...more stapling now"... "Alright ... here we go ... moving into final hemostasis".... "As usual, I like to over-sew the pedicle staple line" ..."that way, there are no leaks" ... "no blood, no bile" ... "no unsightly mess, kids, as we like to say in the business"...

The nurse made a face, and was immediately glad she had her mask on.

"Torch me, sweetheart," said Dr. K, holding out his hand triumphantly. The nurse retrieved the Argon Beam Coagulator from the metal tray to her right, and placed it in Kubrick's open palm.

"I do good work, don't I?" he said. Everyone around the table nodded obligatorily, but Kubrick didn't notice. He was only being rhetorical. He focused on the end of the coagulator, and the lulu's in the jungle far below.

Down through the port went the coagulator, like an A–10 Sandy in close support of troops.

"Easy does it," said K. "That's good ... that's nice ... ohhh, that's exxxcellent." It was all very casual to Dr. K, as if he had been over this fence a thousand times before. He was going beneath the canopy now ... setting fire to the "unfriendlies"... supporting the TIC ... giving hell to the enemy who thought they could just stroll in and take over the village like they owned the place. He could see the palms' fat leaves flapping from the rush of chopper wind ... the bastard neoplasms defoliating everything they touched ... the landing zone just ahead by that hepato-caval ligament ... he would have to bring the Huey in just right... dissect it with the rotors ... divide it between a clamp ... tunnel it ... connect it ... loop it ... Damn! He'd have made a fine pilot, if he hadn't gone to med school....

"Extracting via Pfannenstiel and closing the ports," said Kubrick, a little over eight hours after beginning Al's hepatic resection. He placed the last bit of diseased tissue in the specimen bag, uttered a meaningless "thank you" to the other humans who had gone to war with him that evening, assured Pat in the waiting room that the surgery had gone swimmingly, and was in his BMW and gone from the hospital fifteen minutes after the final suture, trying all the while to forget that the man on the table had prayed for *him*! This god of the operating room!

And another piece of Magnet Ass's plane was sent away to the lab for study.

Surgeons are soldiers of fortune. When they are young, and just beginning their careers in mercenary work, they often serve ungodly hours. Thirty-six on, twelve off, thirty-six on, twelve off. Day after day, week after week. Like a marathon, with only zombies for athletes. Like the fourth quarter of a football game played in sub-zero ice and snow. Doctors often wonder what they were thinking when they declared biology as their major back in college. They live numbing lives. Dehumanizing. And grotesque. They learn firsthand about the primary drives, and recognize soon enough that they have nothing to do with hunger, or thirst, or sex, or procreation ... and that sleep is the only thing that really matters.

How one chooses this lifestyle of self-flagellation, sacrificing everything for the grind, is utterly beyond comprehension.

My own father was a surgeon, but he was able to sit down while removing cataracts ... a procedure that often took less than twenty minutes, where there was no dissecting through four inches of blubber, and a "major" bleed could be absorbed on the end of a Q-Tip. If my dad had performed an elective, ophthalmic case that ended at 2100 hours, he'd have been called up for review by the hospital surgical board.

As I drove east, past frozen stubble and abandoned homesteads, I realized that the real heroes of peacetime America are a lot like the ones during wartime. They are the orthopods, and the heart surgeons, and the gut doctors. They are men like Dr. K., and they almost always have blood on their hands. The fact that Magnet Ass offered to pray for Kubrick before the liver surgery must have, at first, seemed an affront. What need does a god have that a mortal can meet? In the end, Al's prayer for K let him feel like a human again, a little boy even – lost and alone, and terribly afraid of what comes next.

More than one million units of stored, whole blood were transfused into the critically wounded during the Vietnam War. No wonder they called the HCM, "The Blood Trail". It was covered in Asian blood from Ban Ban to the DMZ, then recovered with the ripe, red juice of American sons. Blood was everywhere, in the shattered remains of beast and bird, in the torn orifices of male and female rape victims, spurting up from the rice paddies and the poppy fields, as if the land itself had suffered a deep and severing blow.

Some say that bleeding is the most feared complication of the hepatectomy, like the one Al had in December of 2014. But the real complications have nothing to do with the surgery at all – and everything to do with the surgeon. Leading others into hell will always require a special person.

Leading them out requires a saint.

For one who's view of the world had included so much tragedy, this window by Al's favorite chair must have provided peace and comfort.

Don't be fooled by the perfect part in his hair. Magnet Ass's backside had been drawing fire from a very early age.

I always thought it interesting that both President Nixon and Al Milacek grew up in little, white houses built by their fathers.

Cofer loved to sing! And, apparently, he played a little cards, too!

When the war was over, Ron Wilson went home to Rosetta, and vanished into the Missouri countryside.

Al once told me that if it weren't for Nash, all the fancy flying in the world couldn't have gotten them back to Udorn. Somehow, he just kept coming up with the gasoline. The whole crew owed an enormous debt to Albert Nash.

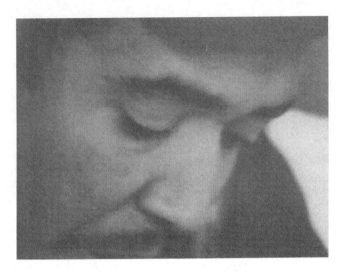

Albert Nash was a humble man and a phenomenal flight engineer—happy to serve his fellow airmen by taking good care of the plane.

Here the boys are in DC, receiving the Mackay Trophy for their famous mission. As always, the CO's are mingled with the NCO's—a theme consistent in their relationships over the course of many years.

A young Al Milacek, fresh out of flight school.

The only photograph I had of Brent O'Brien by himself was this more contemporary one, taken by a stranger on a trip to one of the 80+ countries he and Joan have visited.

Al was so impressed that Ken Firestone could lift a full ammo can with one arm – he mentioned that fact at least a dozen times during our interviews. Bragging on another man was the closest Al ever came to bragging on himself.

Even in a black and white photo, one can tell Ron Jones' mustache was fiery red.

Ed Lopez was the oldest man on Al's crew – and perhaps the most mysterious.

Here, Jim Russell and Ron Wilson enjoy a cigar and a good laugh in the O-Club.

Donnell Hughes Cofer was the youngest man on Al's crew – and the embodiment of optimistic, American spirit.

Roger Clancy was the quietest man on Al's crew, and the only one – other than the deceased – who wanted nothing to do with being interviewed. But he knew the lay of the land better than anyone, and it was his understanding of topography that helped get them over the top of Phou Bia.

Seeking to make war more tolerable, Ron Jones came up with his own fashion-forward flight suit. However, because it didn't meet regulations, he was not allowed to wear it into battle. Years later, it still fits him.

In honor of their, "Dirty, ole Magnet Ass" and his 100th mission, the men had this patch made for Al.

This patch, designed by Ron "The Red Baron" Jones himself, depicts Ron at his nightly chore – spotting the enemy with his night observation scope, (NOS).

When they landed on one wing, the crew were given a royal welcome home – Crown Royal, that is. Ironically, Al was a teetotaler. But the look in Lopez's eye says, "It's going to be a long night."

There is no way of knowing how many drinks Jim, Ron, and Nash had consumed when this photo was snapped. But a close look at their eyes suggests they are trying to forget what they've seen over the fence.

Though these rickshaws weren't quite as speedy as the motorized tuk-tuk Ed Lopez rented for his drunken spree, they do provide a picture of the romantic pace at which Udorn traffic ran.

A young Pat beams over a gift from Magnet Ass. Though it wasn't one of the pinups, it should have been.

Mustache intact and wife, Pat, by his side, an older Ron Jones still fits well into his mess dress.

They say Al shrunk five inches with the esophagectomy. But he was a giant in his heart.

Here is Pat by the sink, where I broke her heart with eight thoughtless words.

Had it not been for Ron Jones submitting the crew's one-winged flight for consideration, the Mackay Trophy might never have been awarded to them.

The first time I heard Wilhemenia's voice on the phone, I knew she was a beautiful woman.

One of the sadder aspects of the writing experience was that Al Nash was long gone before I got involved with the project.

Simple and unadorned, this photograph reminds me of the importance of teamwork – like a crew that stays together, no matter what.

As the Milacek family poses with the Mackay Trophy, their smiles seem to be saying the same thing: "We're glad to be together again."

Back when wedding cakes were serious works of art – and marriages were forged in courage and commitment. Due to her husband's service, Pat moved fourteen times during their marriage. "It was Velcro drapes and curtains," Pat told me, "I just kept putting them up, and taking them down."

A child is often inspired by his or her parents – just as a nation can be inspired by the brave citizens who serve it.

Though others were afraid to test Stinger's rebuilt wing, Al and his crew never worried about the stuff that hadn't happened yet. They were the first to take Stinger back into the theatre of war.

She may have been a nightmare to look at, but when Stinger went to work, she became everyone else's nightmare.

Seventeen-and-a-half feet off the leading edge.

If one looks closely at this map, he or she can see the handwritten words, "Plain of Jars", "Ban Ban", "Parrot's Beak", and "Mekong River". In the same way characters mean everything to a story, so the settings in which we find ourselves often demand a fitting response. For these settings, only courage would do.

The Mackay Trophy ... the US Air Force's award for the most meritorious flight of the year.

"Colonel Al Milacek with the first draft of his story."

Decades after they streaked across the Laotian sky on one wing, Jim Russell paid a visit during Al's darkest hour.

PART THREE

"WAY PAST BINGO."

01:06 / 8 MAY / 1970

Like a great, obsidian whale with one fin missing, Stinger turned until its underside no longer peered at the surface of the heavens. At last she was level. O'Brien caught his breath and hailed the escort, hoping they had someone tonight who could hit the broadside of the universe.

"Triple nickel two one ... cleared to fire on 37's and any known AAA. Get some iron on those targets. Fangs out!"

"We got a second rhino up top," said Al, of the additional F–4 that had just joined the party. As much as he wished for a Sandy, Al was thankful for the extra escort. "Much obliged, AC," he added.

Behind the blackout curtain, Clancy had discovered less-than-cheery news. He buffered it with a compliment. "Good stick, Magnet Ass. Your new heading is Hanoi. In case you're interested."

"Copy that Naviguesser," replied Al. "You're always telling me where to go."

Clancy's heart pounded in his chest, but he had flown seventy-five missions with Al Milacek, so he trusted the man. "You got this, golden hands," he said.

Rumors of American pilots being tortured in Hanoi crept into Al's mind. He did his best to fight them off, but he couldn't help envisioning the "tiger cages", where prisoners were kept for months on end in tiny, barbed-wire enclosures, and taken out only occasionally for beatings. Though he and his comrades were supposed to be protected under the Geneva Convention, North Vietnam's stated position from the beginning was that American prisoners were "war criminals" who had committed crimes against the North Vietnamese people in the course of an illegal war of aggression. As such, they were not entitled to the privileges and rights granted to prisoners of war. If there was one thing Al hoped to avoid, it was a crash landing in enemy territory.

Keeping one hand on the yoke, Al shook out his other fore-arm and glanced at O'Brien. "You okay, pal?" he asked. O'Brien was silent for a few moments, lost in that place men visit when pondering life's brevity. He had never envied the life of a ground-pounder. Tonight was an exception. An especially loud flak-thump brought him back to reality.

"Piece o' cake," he replied. "I always wanted to see the world." "That's the spirit," said Al. "We're in the weeds now. But we'll be okay in a minute."

Al knew what he and O'Brien were in for if they had to fight the nose of the plane for an extended period of time. But he kept his thoughts to himself.

"We can maintain this heading all the way to Hanoi, in which case I'm pretty sure they won't be happy to see us," said Al. "Or we can rudder on and off a few seconds at a time, to see if we can turn this bird around. What do you think?"

O'Brien thought that idea sounded good, and the two men set out to accomplish the impossible. Over and over, they repeated this maneuver, sometimes standing on the rudder together, sometimes taking turns. *Rudder off … rudder on … rudder off… rudder on.* Sweat soaked their Nomex suits. Artillery from the trail below pounded away at them relentlessly. Still, the nose of the plane resisted like a stubborn child.

Above the wounded Stinger, the two F–4ES flying CAP were hot on the six artillery nests that had engaged 883 – their nine tons of ordnance poised and pickled with the flick of a finger. In the blue-black broccoli tops of the jungle below, plumes of orange and yellow suggested O'Brien's wish for a sharpshooter had been answered. But their daisy cutters were a pin prick in the arsenal being flung at them. All around the plane, the air sizzled with shells. If it were not for the Kevlar shield by the plane's left door, Jones would have been splattered all over his NOS position.

When the plane was finally facing Udorn, and the barrage of artillery had, if anything, intensified, Al swallowed dryly and made his first difficult decision... "Silks on, men. We may be punching out."

At their captain's command, several of the men donned their parachutes and hurried toward Stinger's rear, preparing to jump. But the rapid movement of their weight frustrated Al and O'Brien's attempt to maintain stable flight, and the plane began to yaw.

"Get back up here!" barked Al.

After the men repositioned themselves, and the plane limped along level again, Al admitted, "That was my fault, men. Let's all just keep our wits about us."

Behind the blackout curtain that separated the pilots from the NAV and FLIR, Roger Clancy checked the altimeter and thought about the mountain that loomed between their sputtering plane and the Royal Thai Air Force Base in Udorn. With a 9165 ft. summit, they'd be lucky not to run into the side of the mountain. Clancy broke the news to Al.

"This mountain's nine angels high. We're seven-thousand AGL now. Quite a climb, boss."

On the other side of the curtain, Nash was calculating fuel consumption on the right two engines. He knew his machine well, right down to the rivet and screw. But the detail that suddenly concerned him most was the plane's maximum rate of climb–950-ft-per-minute. He wondered how long they had before they slammed into the massive, dark wall rising up before them.

"How far out are we?" said Nash. "Minutes," said Clancy. "Three ... maybe four. Depending on speed."

Nash knew if they pulled back power on the damaged engines, they would drop into the jungle. But he also knew the damage they had suffered might never permit them to make it over the mountains. His analytical mind was on overload There had to be a way.

Suddenly, it came to him. "We gotta get lighter," he said.

Even with Stinger's guns inactive, the noise in the plane lingered around 112 dB, making it difficult to hear at times.

"Say again?" said Al.

Nash shouted into his headset. "We're way past bingo, Al. We gotta get lighter *now!*"

"Alright, pal," replied Al. "Don't boresight. One problem at a time. Keep us juiced, and we'll be fine."

Al allowed himself the brief thought of a high-speed collision with cold granite. Then he gave the command to the rest of the crew.

"Pickle everything we don't need, men! ASAP!"

The crew flew into action.

The first thing out the door was the toolbox, something that might've been helpful in unfastening the mini-guns, which would have made the plane a lot lighter. Like mourners at the funeral of a friend, the crew stood in silence, staring out into the darkness, as if it could bring their toolbox back to them. Once they got over their stupidity, the men started tossing everything they could get their hands on. Firestone hoisted ammo cans, one in each hand, and pitched them over the edge – each can weighing a hundred and fifty pounds. Thousands and thousands of rounds of ammunition, personal possessions, even the M16s went out the door. Lopez took off his wristwatch and threw that out, too. One of the men even pitched a paperback book he had been reading. The only things they kept were their parachutes.

Slowly the plane gained altitude. But she still hadn't reached the summit.

O'Brien glanced out the window of the cockpit, and saw that the right reciprocating engine was a glowing chunk of metal, full blowers and pushed to the limit. He wondered if at any minute, the engine's pistons would stop converting pressure into rotating motion, and the plane would smash into the mountain. But if the crew had any chance of making it home, they had no choice than to push the recip. In the dim light of the cockpit, O'Brien looked at Al and thought he detected a smile on the captain's face.

"You ever been in a glider, Obie?" asked Al.

"Always wanted to," replied O'Brien. "But never got the chance."

"Well, you're about to be in one now," said Al. "Feel free to chime in if you think this idea is hair-brained."

Suddenly, O'Brien was certain of the smile, and he felt a little hunk of Al's peace separate from the older man's soul and drift over to his side of the plane. One never knew what might happen when the 'farm boy' in Al took over.

"When we make it over this mountain here, we're going to be considerably higher than before," Al continued. "At that altitude, we should be able to pull back the engines and reduce our speed. We'll glide on in to Udorn, soft as a goose."

O'Brien looked at Nash, who was already way ahead of the conversation, wondering how in the world he was going to manage fuel consumption, particularly with the right recip burning gas like it was ten cents a barrel.

"Nash?" said O'Brien. He reached back and touched the engineer, deep in thought behind the console.

"Right – yes," agreed Nash, appreciating collegial warmth at such a cold crossroads. "Glide on in. Soft as a goose. It'll work if we can get over this mountain."

"*When* we get over this mountain," corrected Al. He relaxed the other forearm, and introduced the next looming challenge.

"Once we get to Udorn, we'll have to bend the throttle to land this bird. Faster than we're used to landing. Probably faster than the plane is built for."

"How fast are you thinking?" asked O'Brien.

"One-sixty-five … one-seventy … something like that," replied Al. "No flaps for sure, since we don't know what condition they're in."

O'Brien swallowed cotton, while Nash ran the numbers in his head. Considering the plane's maximum speed was a hundred and eighty-one knots, he wondered how fast they could touchdown without killing themselves, or someone on the ground. A drop of perspiration lingered on Nash's eyebrow, and he brushed it away.

"Udorn's concerned about control," he said.

"Can you blame 'em?" said Al.

It was dead silent on the headsets, each man recalling the recent crash of the battle-damaged phantom on its final approach to Udorn. The memory of broken plane and burning bodies washed over them. Al broke the silence.

"We'll do a controllability test up here in the sky. Figure out how the nose will respond in a flare or a stall, and go from there. Speed is our friend. When it's time to touch down, we'll hope somebody's at the end of the runway to catch us."

O'brien checked himself before chiming in. "We're cleared to land at Vientiane," he said, looking straight ahead into the dark. "It's a little closer. And ... you know ... with us past bingo ... we could ... but it's your call, Captain."

Al had always prided himself on leading democratically, but he also knew that sometimes leaders have to do the hard thing, the unpopular thing. He took a deep breath. "Vientiane doesn't have near the firefighting crew as Udorn. So, we might as well land at a place that can put out the flames if they have to." Al glanced at O'Brien. "If it comes to that, I mean."

"Right," said O'Brien. "If it comes to that." He gripped the bracket on his control yoke, and stared at the black mountain that seemed to be rushing towards them.

It was the tallest mountain in Laos.

CHAPTER THIRTEEN

BOTTLECAP

"All in all, I flew roughly 150 missions, most of them with the stone-cold truck hunters, a few of them with virtual strangers, all of them while being shot at. But, there was the occasional distraction..."

Springtime in Vietnam found Al and the boys bored stiff and, if anything, anesthetized by the routine of shooting and being shot at. So, it was that in a world of rank and precedence, drill and ceremony, even protocol for offering toasts at formal dinners, anything that offered a break from the routine was welcomed by Al's crew, regardless of personal safety. But one night in early-April, just a few weeks before the Mackay mission, while running through the motions in southern Cambodia, the crew received a call over the radio that would make them appreciate the ordinary.

The RTO's voice, thick with Australian accent, sounded so young and shaky on the airwaves, that Al figured he was eighteen, maybe nineteen – fresh from high school at best. His circumstances, however, had all the trappings of a grown man's world, blown apart by a Claymore mine. At first, his message was muffled, barely distinguishable, like a cry for help from the bottom of a well. But then the kid must have changed the battery in his PRC–25 and attached the whip, because his words grew blunt and clear.

"Flash. This is Bravo Two-Six ... requesting immediate dust off for three WIA and one KIA ... over."

Al's mind scrolled instantly to the letters he had received from pals in the infantry, back when he was still in training. Their recurring themes were always the same. The terror of leaving the wire at night ... going out for the millionth time on ambush patrol

... walking in darkness so thick, one has to tuck his hand in the ammo belt of the fellow in front of him ... watching the supply routes from the edges of moonless mango plantations ... firing at muzzle flashes in the inky blackness ... memorizing the sound of a bullet as it crashes through the front of a buddy's cranium and exits the backside, taking bits of brain and helmet with it.

Although it was still weeks before the monsoon season when the call came in, it was raining hard as hell, and the wind threw great sheets of water across Stinger's window, making it difficult to see anything. Al looked at O'Brien, and without saying a word he pulled back on the yoke and away from their target below. If the call was about troops in contact, the trucks could wait.

"Bravo Two-Six ... this is Stinger Two-One ... 7.62's and 20's available ... are you currently under fire? Over."

"Affirmative, Stinger Two-One," the kid replied. "Bravo Two-Six in heavy shit, sir. Bottlecap has a bullet in his head ... butterbar is a facking wreck ... doesn't know his arse from a hole in the ground. I'm the six now, as far as I can tell. Over."

By now the kid's voice had drawn down to a shrill whisper, as if Charlie was so close he could smell the fish sauce on his breath. Suddenly, Al heard the crackle of AK–47s, then the "w-h-o-o-s-h" of an RPG, and the kid, peppered with tiny bits of shrapnel, let out a string of profanities.

"Where's the action, Bravo Two-Six?" asked Al, requesting the beleaguered company's coordinates.

Somehow, in spite of the mayhem that had broken loose all around him, the kid shifted into the five-line, GTA close combat attack briefing, and gave Al and Clancy everything they needed for clearance.

"Stinger Two-One ... this is Bravo Two-Six ... fire mission ... over."

"Bravo Two-Six ... this is Stinger two-one ... go."

"My position is ... ECHO, CHARLIE, LIMA, ECHO, WHISKEY, SIERRA, CHARLIE, WHISKEY, WHISKEY ... marked by ... shit! ... I dropped my claymore bag in the trees back there ... with all my flares and smoke grenades. I'm a bloody bogan, sir! I got nothing to mark us with. Over."

"Easy, son," said Al, trying to calm the kid, before he got what was left of Bravo killed. "Say again those numbers," he added, wanting to make sure of the exact coordinates. Al could never forgive himself if he blew away his own men.

"Repeat," said the kid, his breaths coming in short snatches of air between every third word. "Our position is ECHO, CHARLIE, LIMA, ECHO, WHISKEY, SIERRA, CHARLIE, WHISKEY, WHISKEY. OVER."

Clancy immediately began working with the numbers, offsetting the computer to calibrate a CCA parameter acceptable for the 7.62 mini-guns.

The kid was frantic with fear now, and Al could picture him lying face down in the mud, wishing he had stayed in school ... wishing he had taken a job at the pub ... wishing he was watching cartoons with toast and vegemite, back home in Broome, or Broken Hill, or Coober Pedy, where the best salt and pepper squid on the continent is known to make grown men cry. Wishing he was anywhere but here.

"Charlie's almost on us," the kid whimpered. Little boy tears bubbled up beneath his grown man words. "Repeat. Target location a hundred meters east and closing. Description VC. Shit, sir ... we're broken arrow! The fackers are on top of us! You gotta hose us down! Cleared danger close! On my command!"

"Ready to fire, Bravo Two-Six," said Al. "Hang on, pal. We're close enough we can almost see you. We'll be coming in from north to south. Can anybody put a flare through the canopy? Over."

"Negative, sir," replied the kid, "The men are all dug in but me. Over."

"Can you put a flashlight in a helmet and hold it over your head? Charlie won't see it. FLIR will pick it up. Over."

"Roger that flashlight. And ... no disrespect, sir ... but you need to hotel alpha! Over," said the kid.

"Roger that, Bravo Two-Six ... we're coming in hot ... suggest you dig in now, son. Over."

"Stinger Two-One, give me a minute for dig in. Over."

"Wilco. Over."

At their NOS and FLIR positions, Jones and Russell scanned the ground for the flashlight in the helmet, and O'Brien tried without luck to hail the closest Medevac chopper.

"Dust off says they can't get up in this weather," said Obie, glancing at Al.

"Then, we need to get in there and do some damage control," said Al.

"Hell, yes, we do!" cried Cofer, from the gundeck. Being the youngest on Al's crew, he must have felt a certain, generational bond with the Aussie and his company being shot at down below.

"We got heat at Bravo's numbers," Russell confirmed, when he spotted the kid's flashlight with his FLIR.

Al glanced at his reticles, to get a feel for where to lay the fire down.

"Parameters are set—" said Clancy, "It's going to be tight."

"Minis on line, sir ... ready to rock!" shouted Cofer.

"Easy, Cofe," said Al. "We gotta let the kid dig in. If we keep our wits about us, we might just save his life."

Suddenly, there was another burst of gunfire on the radio, and the kid shouted, "Bravo Two-Six is red! Repeat – Bravo Two-Six is red! Cleared for fire, sir! Cleared for fire!"

For a solid thirty seconds, Al rained hot hellfire from the sky, each three-second burst sending a molten incendiary into every square yard surrounding the coordinates provided by the Aussie, allowing just enough buffer for the fire to be effective, but not friendly. Though he couldn't see the damage he was inflicting, Al envisioned thick stands of vegetation exploding ... branches splitting ... wood, and vine, and pulpy fruit pieces cascading down upon the jungle floor, where ... hopefully ... they would cover the remains of the enemy like a burial shroud, and where... hopefully ... the young Aussie and his company would be left alive, untouched, aghast and agape ... staring up at their savior, through a hole in the trees.

Hopefully.

When Al released the trigger, it was dead silent – all the sound in the universe sucked down into the jungle through the giant crack in the canopy, then exhaled with a rattling gasp.

"Bravo Two-Six ... come in," said Al. A great silence lifted from the earth, accompanied by the beat of rain on Stinger's windshield, and the *boom* of distant thunder. Al touched the earpiece on the side of his head, as if by doing so he could reach through the radio and resurrect the fallen Aussie and his bottlecap.

"Kid?" said Al, dropping all radio protocol. "You out there, kid? How copy?"

Nothing.

Al glanced at O'Brien and Nash, but neither man could look at him. They stared at the rivulets of water that ran from the top of Stinger's windshield to its bottom, where they congregated in lonely reservoirs reflecting the terrible, Cambodian sky. Suddenly the kid's PRC–25 sprang to life.

"Crikey!" he exclaimed. "We didn't stand Buckley's without you bastards! Half of Bravo is cactus, but the ones that aren't swear they'll buy you a butcher first chance they get! Tango Mike Stinger Two-One! Tango Mike! Over."

The sound of Cofer and the gunners cheering in the back of the plane was so loud that Al had to lift the headset away from his ear. But his smile said he was glad they had decided to come to Bravo's aid. And though he had no idea what a "butcher" was, he would be happy to share one with the ground-pounders if he ever got the chance.

"Bravo Two-Six ... this is Stinger Two-One ... reading you five. Be safe, boys." And then out of curiosity, Al asked one more question. "You are the RTO, aren't you? Over."

"Hell no, sir" said the kid. "I'm just a digger. Our dittybopper took a blooper in the chest. He's all over the bush in facking bits. So, I grabbed the thing and gave it a go. Sorry I was such a bellowing big calf of a boy back there."

Al looked at Obie, and both men just shook their heads. "Bravo Zulu, son," said Al, "You did a fine job. Bolo back to the wire, Bravo Two-Six. Over."

"Roger that bolo, mate," said the Aussie, obviously choked up. Then as if he had been an RTO for years, the last thing he said was....

"Bravo Two-Six ... Out."

They were brave in many ways, Al and his men – and to this fact, the young Aussie would attest. Before returning to the wire the following day, he and the remaining men of Bravo company probably did their own "mini-BDA" for personal reasons, knowing a recon team would soon arrive on a slick, make the insertion, snap some pictures, and send the official report up the chain. What they found in the jungle, beyond the little area where they had dug in, no doubt made the kid cry again. *No less than fifteen holes per NVA soldier*, the LRRP reported. *Some within a few feet of the shallow bunkers dug in haste.*

It was one of Al's most memorable missions of the war, certainly the most satisfying, considering, for once, he and his men were actually defending US soldiers caught in the throes of battle. But as always, they were back to shooting trucks the following night. And the routine continued that way until the end.

Throughout my writing of this book, we had an arrangement for the times I was unable to visit Waukomis for face-to-face interviews, wherein Al would dictate the details, Pat would type diligently, and then the entire mess would be sent to my email, for me to sift and shine and sprinkle with fairy dust. Sometimes in the middle of her typing, Pat would pause to question Al's reasons for sharing this detail or that. Occasionally under such inquiry, Al would grow short with her, saying, "Pat ... just type it, please." But I never took this to mean he didn't appreciate his wife's help or optimism. And because her husband was in such discomfort, I don't think Pat took it that way either. Instead, I understood Al's lapse into acrimony in the same way I understood the Aussie's tears during the firefight. Al's health was failing fast, plain and simple, like a ship disappearing over the horizon.

Right about that time, I wrote a little poem to express the thick melancholy that had descended on me regarding Al's health, and I promptly tucked it away in one of my notebooks, where I didn't find it until many months later. But I always hoped it would make it past the phalanx of critics who protect the narrow beaches of literary acclaim.

It's easy to be brave when the sky is blue.
Harder when it turns grey.
Harder still as evening yawns....
And swallows day.

CHAPTER FOURTEEN

IN THE BLIND

"Nobody used stamps in Vietnam. As long as he wrote, 'FREE',
where the stamp usually went, Uncle Sam saw to it that the letter
made it home."
  a truck hunter's recollection

We have all at one time in our lives received a word for which
we had been waiting on tiptoe. And when at last, it came, we
wished it hadn't.

After several months of Al's deployment, Pat received a phone
call from an airman's wife she had met while Al was training at
Lockbourne, and she had walked back through its dialogue multiple times, turning it over in her mind like a stone in a riverbed.
The woman's opening line was meant to reduce anxiety, but it
had the opposite effect on Pat.

"*By now, you've heard of the AC–119K going down in the South*
China Sea," the woman began, erroneously assuming Pat had
already caught wind of the recently published piece in the Stars
and Stripes. In her defense, the woman was trying to comfort
Pat, but with each word she spoke, Pat's anxiety doubled. "*The*
fact it was a Stinger doesn't mean it was your Al's Stinger," the
woman blundered on. "*Even if it was, they say everyone made it*
out alive – except for one, that is. And I'm sure it wasn't your Al.
It can't have been – I don't think."

After the woman hung up, Pat immediately went to the base
and secured a copy of the 'S and S'. And though, as the woman
surmised, it wasn't Al's Stinger that had crashed into the sea,
the assault on her peace of mind was complete and total. From
that point on, everyone who loved Pat and were near enough to

take action, forced her to combat her fear by getting busy. She sewed fourteen blankets during the remainder of Al's tour, and when that diversion left her alone too often with her thoughts, her father and her uncles invited Pat to fish and hunt with them.

"I was a hunter's worst nightmare in the duck blind," Pat told me, "Always talking when I was supposed to be quiet. I scared away more birds than I shot at, and I probably ruined a lot of good hunting for everyone. But my daddy was determined to keep my mind off of Vietnam."

"How long had you been married at that time?" I asked.

"Almost ten years," said Pat, staring pensively out the window. "But I was still my daddy's little girl. Fear makes everyone a kid again."

In spite of all Pat's busyness, the thought of the downed AC–119K was not easily dismissed by pastimes. Its details were so haunting, that Pat would often lay awake at night, imagining her own Al parachuting into the cold sea waters. More often than she cared to admit, she dug out the Stars and Stripes article and re-read it to remind herself that Al was still alive and well.

One particular detail of the story chilled her to the bone.

Beset by a sudden failure of the landing gear and unable to land at her home base in Da Nang, Stinger 839 had headed out over the South China Sea, where its entire crew parachuted into the waters and waited for a rescue boat. Eventually, every crew member was snatched alive from the frigid swells by a Navy vessel – all except for one. Forgetting to sever his parachute lines when he landed in the water, the airman was caught by surprise when his chute became tangled in the rescue boat's propellers, and he was dragged beneath the surface. By the time they could get to him, his lungs were filled with saltwater. Sometimes Pat would dream about the airman's face disappearing beneath boundless waves. And always at the last second, the face would become Al's.

Throughout the spring and for the remainder of Al's tour in Vietnam, Pat doubled her sewing and hunting, and tried not to worry about the stuff that hadn't happened yet.

Sublimation is a wonderful mechanism in both war and peace-time. A man with a fear of falling decides to become a pilot. A woman who dreads the feeling of the cold spot in the bed where her husband used to lay next to her sews a lifetime's worth of blankets and passes out warmth to friends and family members. Sometimes a boy with a terrifying story at the bottom of his soul studies English Literature, learns to tell new stories, turns them into print, and parlays them into publication.

In the end, though, sublimation has its limits.

At last, we have arrived at the page where I must tell you about the beetle cellar. Other than the fact it lives in my mind as surely and solidly as my father's gravestone, there really is *no such place*. It is the stuff of a nightmare I had when I was five, and I have shared it with so many therapists I've lost count of their interpretations. Diagnosis is helpful, but only to people who want to remain sick – or to those who make a living off of them.

In the nightmare, I am with my father on a lonely, country road. To our right, a moon-soaked field opens out to the east. On our left, a dense wood, restrained only by a tottering fence, reaches for us with hungry limbs. My father is holding my hand.

Suddenly, my father's long strides grow longer, and he increases his pace. Try as I may, my little legs are incapable of matching his. My fingers slip from his grasp. He pulls away. Loping at first. Then jogging. Then galloping like an animal on all fours. "Come back!" I cry. And even as I call to him, he is transforming into something no child would desire ... a beast ... with a tail ... and sharp claws flinging chunks of earth behind it, as it gathers speed and melts into the shadows.

"Come back! Come back, Daddy!" I scream. But the beast does not turn around.

Far ahead on the road, I watch the beast turn left into the woods, and when I arrive at that point, I do the same.

Suddenly, the woods are not the woods at all. I am standing in the den of my childhood home on 39th Street. To the right is the old, blue couch. To the left is the television set. And in front of me I see my father, now changed back into a man, smiling at me, lifting the round, crocheted rug in the center of the room, ducking underneath it, and letting it flop over him, as if in a game of hide-n-seek with his son.

"There you are!" I say, as I run to the rug. With great relief, I hoist it above my head, thinking my father will be there to hug me to his chest ... to fling me playfully in the air ... to shout, "Hooray! Hooray! My little man has found me!"

But there is no such reunion.

Beneath the rug, lying on the floor of our family's den, is the decomposing carcass of a wolf, matted with the crusty casings of a thousand assorted bugs.

It is the beetle cellar.

CHAPTER FIFTEEN

EVERYTHING HAS A DRIVER

In 2006, the Department of Defense made it a crime for a service member to hire a prostitute anywhere in the world; the penalties can include up to a year in prison, forfeiture of pay, and a dishonorable discharge.

"So, the biopsy came back positive?" I said, making sure I had understood Magnet Ass correctly.

Al nodded, and his blue eyes blinked at the sunlight that somersaulted through the picture window, casting a happy rectangle of light where his chair sat in the corner.

"It might be good to talk about something else now," suggested Pat. "How about if Al tells you more about his younger days?"

"I don't mind getting old, Pat," said Al. "And I don't mind talking about it either."

"But readers might want something a little livelier," said Pat. She thought for a moment, then brightened. "Tell Will the stories you used to tell the girls," she insisted.

A puzzled look settled over Al. "When they were little girls?" he asked.

"Not those," said Pat, "The ones when they were older, the ones about the truck hunters and their carrying-on in Thailand."

"Oh, those stories," said Al, smiling. Like a bridge that joins two opposite river banks, Magnet Ass's memory stretched back in time and connected him to younger days in Udorn. "We probably should begin with Lopez," he said, with a chuckle.

"All in all, Udorn was a hot, boring place," said Al. "Not like the beautiful spots down in the Gulf. So, when we weren't hunting trucks, there wasn't much to do." Al thought about what he had just said, then reversed course. "Then again ... Udorn was whatever you made it. And because Ed Lopez made it his personal playground, he never had a shortage of things to do."

This is going to be good, I thought.

"Now, I don't want to talk down any of my crew members," said Al, "But if there was anyone with a wild hair to him, it was Ed. It wasn't unusual for him to drink his lunch, if you know what I mean."

"I know what you mean," I said.

"One day, after a full night of truck-hunting, Ed got up early and hired himself one of those rickshaw things with an engine. I believe they called it a 'Tuk-Tuk'. Ed told the driver he wanted to spend the morning just sightseeing around the city, and that he would appreciate it if the fellow didn't try to converse too much."

"What he wanted to do was drink the bottle of whiskey he had purchased at the BX on base ... and he didn't want to be interrupted," said Pat.

I had checked out the RTAFB on Google Earth, and most of the old wooden buildings appeared to have been leveled, leaving room for a new terminal on the west end of the property. But the BX and the metal BOQ still appeared to be standing, decades later. I pictured a weary Ed Lopez, haggard from his night over the fence, setting off on new adventures that would surely set new records for haggardness.

"What did a morning's worth of Tuk-Tuk cost back then?" I asked.

Al deliberated for a moment about a monetary system long erased from his memory. "I think it cost one baht," said Al. "About three cents in US."

"Three cents!" I exclaimed. "Why didn't Ed just buy the whole Tuk-Tuk?"

Al shook his head, and I could tell he was laughing inside about how green and untraveled I was. "Life was cheaper back then," he said.

"Much," added Pat.

Al continued. "In any case, Ed's driver must have carted him clear to Bangkok, because by the time Ed got back to the base, there wasn't a single drop left in the Crown Royal bottle he began with, and he was barely sober enough to jump out of the Tuk-Tuk and escape into the barracks, before the driver could collect his baht."

"Oh, my," said Pat, with a giggle.

"When the driver realized he was about to miss out on a whole morning's wages, he also jumped out of the Tuk-Tuk, ordered someone to watch it for him, ran after Ed Lopez, and caught him just as he was entering the BEQ."

"I thought you guys lived off base?" I said.

"We did ... but that was only after the base ran out of room. Come to think of it, only us commissioned officers ever used the hotel arrangement. The NCOS were always on base, if I remember correctly. At the time of this story, we COS lived in the Bachelor Officer Quarters. Anyway ... where was I?"

"The driver catches Lopez at the BEQ," Pat supplied.

"Right ... so the driver catches Lopez at the BEQ, and there is such a ruckus, someone has to run back and fetch me, because I'm his Captain."

"Babysitter," corrected Pat. "And Ed was the oldest of the truck hunters," she added, to emphasize the ridiculousness of it all.

"Yes, he was," said Al. "Thirty-six at the time. He didn't always act his age, though."

"I guess not," I said.

"So, I finally get to the scene," said Al, "... and the driver is shouting at Ed in some kind of Lao dialect. Of course, Ed is hammered and he can barely keep from falling on the ground ... and I'm doing everything I can not to bust out laughing."

"Baht! Baht", the driver keeps saying. "So, I turn to Ed and I say, 'C'mon now, buddy' ... 'why don't you just pay the man his baht, and we'll go take a long nap. We have to fly tonight, and by the looks of you right now, you're in no condition to drop flares'."

"So, Ed pays the guy," continued Al. "And I literally drag him to the BEQ, and help him off with his clothes, and put him to bed."

"Was he ready to go over the fence that night?" I asked.

"He was launching lu-lus by zero-thirty," said Al, "Same as always."

"What did your girls think of Lopez?" I asked.

Al looked at Pat, and the two of them conferred in shrugs and grins. "They thought of him like you would think of a long-lost uncle," said Al. "I always painted him as a jolly kind of guy ... and that's what he was ... happy-go-lucky ... but he pretty much kept to himself. Jim Russell and I were talking not long ago, and we wondered if maybe alcohol had gotten Ed bumped in rank over time. He had been in the military since the 50's. Longer than any of us, that's for sure."

Al paused. "Most of the things I told the girls were tamer than the Tuk-Tuk story. I usually just shared about the crew's good-natured monkey business."

"How about the flight suits Jones made?" said Pat.

Ron Jones had sent me a photograph of a special suit he had made for missions, along with a note that said, "I wore this to a party a few years back, and surprisingly it still fit ... kind of. We only wore our suits on one mission, and then brass caught wind of it and told us they weren't regulation."

I had this image in my mind of Ron Jones hunched over a sewing machine in the BOQ, making fashion-forward apparel for anyone in the barracks who was bored ... or scared to death of what lay over the fence. There are an infinite number of ways a man copes with the unknown.

"Bottom line," said Al, "We just had fun together. Sometimes, when we had completed a mission and we weren't quite bingo yet, the truck hunters would ask if we could go on a 'safari', and I never refused. The Ho Chi Minh Trail was crawling with movement ... trucks, bicycles, people driving donkeys ... and water buffalo that were loaded to the gills with food and ammunition."

"Sometimes, Russell would see a roundish blip on his FLIR, and Jones would shout out, 'I got an elephant! Clear to fire, sir.' I was known as the 'great white elephant hunter' while I was in Vietnam, because I shot more elephants than any other pilot." Al looked down at his lap, a mixture of pride and shame coming over him. "I don't know what I think about that now."

My next question was asked with fear and trembling, because I had formed a certain view of Magnet Ass and the stone-cold truck hunters, and this view was vital to Al's story.

"Were all the crew members *like* Ed?" I asked.

"What do you mean, 'like Ed'?" Al replied, suspiciously.

"You know ... 'derelict'," I said, swallowing dryly.

Al shook his head sharply, and I could tell it hurt his neck. "I said Ed Lopez was 'crazy' ... I didn't say he was 'derelict'!"

I started to defend myself, but Magnet Ass cut me off.

"'Crazy' in Vietnam isn't the same as 'crazy' back home. The things we saw there were..." And then Al paused, as if he believed the very words he chose next would determine the thoroughness of his recovery from the war. "The things we *did* there were enough to make anyone crazy." He lapsed into silence.

"It took a long time for Al to forgive himself for his missions," said Pat. "He and the crew told themselves night after night that they were only shooting trucks and other kinds of vehicles ... when all along they were also shooting people. But they were doing their duty ... and they were keeping the enemy from reaching the front."

"Every truck had a driver," said Al, staring a hole into the carpet. "I still think about it today."

Play during wartime will always seem out of place. It's as if we believe when a soldier goes to war, he leaves all remnants of innocence at home and morphs into a killing tool, stone cold and divested of emotion. From our safe vantage point, we picture the theatre of war filled with smoke and flame and wall-to-wall razor wire. We hear the explosions. We smell the burning flesh. We flinch at the screams and the sirens and the curse words of the heartless. Far be it from our minds that a child has gone to war, or a cleric, or a saint. Only beasts kill for God and country, we tell ourselves.

The civilized stay home.

A story exists in apocryphal literature of the boy Jesus making twelve sparrows out of clay, blowing breath into them, and setting them free to the delight of observers. In it, we sense the role of joy in the midst of suffering. Though the validity of the story is debated, it is reminiscent of a more ancient tale, one of God using the lowest elements of the universe to fashion Man and clear him for takeoff. He could have used gold or diamonds, but He didn't. Like a child playing in the mud, He took the simplest things He could find and made people out of them.

Before we were anything, we were nothing.

In the truest sense of the word, we are all *dirt-bags*, each one of us ... doing our best to scramble through this world, coping and enduring, and hoping the pain doesn't get to us before the curtain falls. Who am I to fault a man for yukking it up in the middle of a war? Who am I to judge Ed Lopez, or the truck hunters ... or even Ho Chi Minh, for having a laugh or two?

They say that during Vietnam's dry season in 1970, poverty and homelessness were so widespread that an expensive toy from nearby China was never more than a dream for a Vietnamese child. Instead, they invented their own entertainment, fashioning fun out of simple songs and household items, such as melons and chopsticks.

Thus, if we envision the truck hunters shooting elephants in the clouds, and the offspring of their enemy kicking a pumpkin around a field, while white phosphorus napalm burns down their imaginary bleachers....

We are not far from the truth.

CHAPTER SIXTEEN

A TASTE OF CURRY

"Writing a book is an adventure. To begin with it is a toy and an amusement. Then it becomes a mistress, then it becomes a master, then it becomes a tyrant. The last phase is that just as you are about to be reconciled to your servitude, you kill the monster and fling him to the public."
  Winston Churchill

Since my first book in 1987, I had flung five monsters to the public – none of them, however, to the agnostic public. On the contrary, they had all been published in the Christian Booksellers Association, the final resting place for stories about characters with tamed adventures and sanitized vices.

But <u>Magnet Ass</u> was different.

Even its title suggested danger, and it never failed to make me chuckle – like a junior high boy who has just heard a dirty joke under a bridge. I particularly felt this way one Sabbath, when my mother's blue-haired friends surrounded me outside the door to their Sunday school class and insisted I tell them about my latest literary project. Cautiously, I proceeded, doing everything in my power to conceal the title of the book. But, inevitably, they wanted to know what to *call* it. So, I gave in and blurted out the two words I had tried to avoid. And because they had held me in their minds in a cryogenic stasis since I was three, the thought of me writing anything that had a coarse word in its title was a shock to them, equal to the denouncing of one's faith.

"Did you say, 'ass'?" one of the women asked me. And before I could answer, another of them jumped in on my behalf. "I believe he did," she asserted. "But he always seemed like such a *nice*, young man," said a breathless third.

Soon, all them were talking about me in third person, as if I had been dismissed from the conversation. "Looks can be deceiving, Helen, looks can be deceiving." "Yes, but I always thought a Cunningham would be on the up and up." "Well, a good name doesn't make a good man." "Yes, I suppose. But still, you would think. Oh, dear – look! They have bear claws!" At that, they all turned simultaneously and marched off toward the donut table, little wisps of dust billowing up from their feet with each solemn step.

For some sick reason, this kind of thing always made me smile.

Truth is, the writing of Al's story had challenged my faith more than any singular event in my life, because it touched on the most troubling questions of man's existence.

"If God is so good and so powerful, why do horrific things still happen in this world? And if God is so loving, why do so many of these horrific things happen to those He supposedly loves?"

More specifically ..."Why were the M-16, war wounds of Vietnam so graphic that the US government labeled them, "classified"?" "Why were handsome, young soldiers scarred for life with napalm ... and transported like meat on canvas stretchers ... and deposited on sawhorses ... and operated on by the thousands, while they cried out to heaven for a god they didn't believe in to save a body they no longer recognized?" There were not many answers to these questions in Vietnam, then or now. I kept looking for them, though, listening especially to the repercussions in Al's story – which I had come to describe in my notes as *echoes* – hoping to find meaning in things that are repeated. But I was losing my mind with all this listening, mostly because the main thing I listened for never came around. There was no echo in Vietnam of the Drummond Methodist Church back in Oklahoma. Nothing remotely close, in fact. So, I finally gave up my search, assuming God had played no part in that twenty-year war.

But I was wrong.

All along, right under my trembling fingers, every time I touched them to the keyboard, every time I typed the words, "Al", or "Captain Milacek", a little spark of electricity shot up through my arm, across the gaps between muscle and bone, through the roadblocks of doubt that exist somehow in every cell of a man's body, all the way to my brain, where it lodged, made its home, and hung its message on the wall of my mind.

"God *was* there," the message read, "Right there in the heart of that dirty, ol' Magnet Ass – and in the simple things that cannot be corrupted."

As in life, much of war is unremarkable. A gunship airman rises to the sound of a clock, not a bugle. He showers. Shaves. Puts a flight suit on like business slacks. If he can find an American newspaper and isn't in a hurry, he reads it. But he's usually in a hurry. He's in the destruction industry. There is work to be done. Things to be broken.

Early in the book project, this *business-as-usual* nature of war made me uncomfortable, and I recall pressing Al for facts that would make war seem more eccentric to the reader. But he always downplayed my concern by offering to have Pat refill my water glass. Likewise frustrating was the fact that Al's memories of Vietnam were almost exclusively focused on the Mackay mission, target-fixated on the story that brought us together, and very little else. It was as if the memories that might corroborate his contribution to a once Arcadian society, had all been embalmed and buried. These I began to label as Al's "curried recollection". I knew it was there, deep inside of him. And there was nothing I wanted more than a taste of it.

"I can't just say you guys jumped in a plane and took off and destroyed stuff," I'd remind him. "I need to know things, for credibility sake."

"What kind of things do you need to know, Will?" Al would ask. This would get me excited, and I would turn on the recorder, and grab my pen and paper. "Oh, I don't know. Things like pre-flight checklists, mission briefings, weapons inspection, that kind of thing." Then I would sneak in my real requests, the ones that involved local color, movement, sights, sounds ... curry. I was sure that if I prompted Al enough regarding Vietnam's wild side, Captain Lazarus would come forth from the grave dressed in tourist's shorts, with a camera around his neck. Al would bow his head in thought, and I would slide the recorder closer to him. Through the window, just beyond his shoulder, I could see the wind kicking up dust devils in his wheat field. I knew I was pressing him for things that had ceased to matter to him long ago. But I had a book to write. A story to construct.

"Well, Will, we all just kinda did what we were supposed to do. The young guns made sure the ammo cans were loaded. Obie and I would chat about where we were going that night. Jones and Russell checked the recce equipment. Clancy read maps. I think Lopez was messing with the illuminator. And Nash probably walked around the plane and kicked the tires – sorta like you do with your car, when you're about to go on vacation. Is that enough to make you credible?"

"Kicked the tires."

"Yes."

"Vacation."

"That's right."

The long periods of silence on the tapes during these early conversations are me picturing the packing process for a vacation in Vietnam. "*Don't forget the napalm, honey.*" "*Thank you for reminding me, dear. It's always the little things I leave behind.*"

When I began receiving emails from the other crewmen, I was happy about the ones that dealt with the Mackay mission in detail. But I salivated over the ones that helped me experience Vietnam as a *real and colorful place*, a place that used to be on every tourist agent's pamphlet rack. These were the things that would make the story sing, I thought. A package from New

Jersey, meant the Widow Nash was sending me vibrant tidbits from her husband's journal. One from gunner Ken Firestone in Normalville, PA, was sure to be white-hot with intel, and usually anything *but* normal. He could have sent a bottle of beer, and it wouldn't have surprised me. Jim Russell, (FLIR), and Ron Jones, (NOS), were particularly helpful in the "curried" department. Their recollection of facts and nuances ushered me into the world of Vietnam in a way Al was hesitant to. They spoke of weapons, planes, sweat and adrenaline, rice wine, the French influence, the paddies, pork and peacocks, and the pheasants strutting on the skirts of dusty villages. At times, as they unfolded their experience for me, I could almost smell the mountains of human feces, heaped up, set ablaze, and mingled with the aftermath of sizzling shells. Day after day, this factual tsunami came pouring in through the mail, and I was immeasurably thankful to the perfect strangers who were sending it. I learned more about Vietnam from them than I ever learned from Al. But I did not see their hearts.

Only Al showed me that.

One fact I collected from the deluge was that May 7th was Jim Russell's birthday. At 5 PM, on the evening of the Mackay mission, Russell took a taxi from the hotel to the base, where he had dinner at the Officer's Club, checked his mail at the squadron, and hung out until the mission briefing. "*I don't remember if I went alone to the O Club, or met someone there,*" Russell wrote me, a month into my research. The briefing, however, was crystal clear to him, forty-five years after the fact:

"As always, we were tasked with the armed reconnaissance of Route 7, from the Plain of Jars to the North Vietnam border, as well as Route 6 from Ban Ban to the border. Route 7 runs from the POJ to Ban Ban and then turns southeast toward Vinh. Route 6 starts at Ban Ban and runs north and then east into Hanoi. Both routes were just narrow dirt roads. The Mackay mission was focused on Ban Ban, where the two routes come together. Our Intel Officer, Bob Curry, outlined the threat analysis, which was the same as every other night ... 23mm and 37mm AAA sites. It was information we had provided to him from our previous mission, but we listened to it anyway. He then briefed us on the escorts' call sign, radio frequency, etc. There was nothing out of the ordinary about that evening. All five of us officers were there, as usual, plus the Chaplain. I'm sorry, but I don't remember the Chaplain's name. He was an integral part of each mission briefing, though, always praying for a safe and successful mission. This was common practice at most of the bases we operated from. Speaking of religious things, the only time I remember attending church on a semi-regular basis was with Al at Udorn, after we moved on base. Al was more faithful than I was. He even went to church after some of the late, Saturday night missions. I, on the other hand, did not!"

Birthday boy Russell then went from the briefing to Life Support, where he picked up his equipment and hitched a ride from Crew Transport to the plane. At the plane, he made sure the FLIR and other gear at his position were operating properly. As always, the crew was hunting trucks that night, and if they were going to fail it would *not* be on account of his infrared. This thought moved Russell to repeat his inspection of the FLIR, more thoroughly the second time around.

Equally curried were Ron Jones' correspondences about the Mackay mission. Though they confirmed Al's description of war as ordinary, they left no misunderstanding about what kind of "vacation spot" Vietnam had become. Some historians estimate the total war-related casualties to be 1,353,000, including allied forces, NVA, Viet Cong, Pathet Lao, Khmer Rouge, and North and South Vietnamese civilians. One undisputed fact is that civilian deaths accounted for the greatest percentage of the total.

One of Jones' first emails about the Mackay mission began with the sentence, "*This is one of those rare occasions when I am home with no grandkids climbing all over me. So, let me answer a few of your questions.*"

His was a casual arrival at Udorn on the night of the famous Mackay mission. Because of the approaching monsoon season, Jones and Al had taken a boat from the Siri Udorn hotel to the Royal Thai Air Force Base, partially because the streets had already begun to flood, but mostly because they wanted to enjoy the ambiance of the city as long as the weather would permit it. Soon all travel, whether by road or waterway, would be soggy and miserable. For Al and the others, this was the seventy- fifth time they had been over the fence together. Only Co-Pilot O'Brien had logged a different number, having just recently joined Al's crew on 27 Apr 70 when the regular co-pilot, Ron Dean, was upgraded to aircraft commander and given his own crew. Tonight, was Obie's seventh mission in the seat next to Al.

Like Russell, Jones gathered his gear and was driven to the aircraft, where his preflight consisted of a close inspection of his night observation scope, (NOS), insuring he had backup batteries, and checking the condition and placement of his parachute. Jones had described to me on one occasion his irrational fear of snakes, in particular the ones that would be waiting in the jungle for him if he were ever forced to bail out. "*With my luck*", said Jones, "*I'd land right on the biggest, most pissed off King Cobra in Southeast Asia.*"

Thoughts of snakes aside, Jones would frequently practice putting on his parachute in the dark, often repeating the procedure multiple times between takeoff from Udorn and the evening's designated target area. In some of the pictures Jones sent me, I noticed the parachute on the floor, to the left of his NOS position. Seemingly insignificant – until needed. In fact, many of the combat accoutrements described for me by Al's crew belied the life or death necessity one associates with the machinery of war, replacing it with a sort of paltriness. Jones described his gear for me as if he were reading a grocery list: Nomex flight suit, helmet, parachute harness, .38 revolver with a source of additional ammunition, handheld radio, first aid kit, food, water, and a parachute knife located in a pouch on the airman's left leg for cutting nylon lines caught in vegetation. As an afterthought, Jones mentioned, the jungle combat boots that would probably never experience *jungle or combat* ... the bayonet that couldn't cut warm butter... and, lastly, the pointy-talky travel translator for ease of conversation with locals, should the airman drop in uninvited.

When he went to war in Laos, Jones was a full three years younger than my youngest son, who, at the time of this writing project, had only just acquired his first, serious girlfriend, and was "learning to cook for himself." At least that was the phrase my son had used when he Instagrammed me a photo of some charred meat on an even-more-charred plate. The contrast between the phrases, "cook for himself" and "additional source of ammunition", was unsettling to me, and immediately made me wonder what today's younger generation would do if it were suddenly faced with the prospect of a compulsory draft.

"*My NOS was a four-power, battery-operated, telescopic night scope,*" Jones told me. "*I had the green-tinged picture everyone has become accustomed to seeing today. This was early in the night scope development. My station was at the open door on the left side of the aircraft, just a few feet in front of the left reciprocal engine.*"

The words, "open door" caught my attention, and I immediately replied to Ron's email. "In what sense of the word, 'open', are you speaking?" I inquired. He responded, "'Open' ... as in, 'open'." Then I had the audacity to ask, "Do you mean, 'open' as in, 'throughout-the-entire-flight-open'?" He wrote, "What other kind of 'open' is there?" I said, "Right. Exactly." Later research revealed it was not uncommon for Stinger airmen to tether themselves to the inside of the fuselage and lean out the door, so as to gain a clearer view of incoming AAA. These facts, bolstered by the image of Ron Jones, three years younger than my meat-charring youth minister son, hanging from the open door of an aerial gunship, stationed just a few feet in front of its whirling engine blades, quickly attached a sort of action figure persona to Ron's character. From then on, I drew a *whip* in the top, left corner of every communiqué I received from Jones, and I privately took to calling him ... "*Indiana.*"

I also began to realize that in Russell and Indiana, I had found the "eyes" of Gunship 883. One eye used heat-seeking infrared to see into the soul of every supply-toting carcass that rambled or rolled along the Ho Chi Minh Trail, four-thousand feet below. The other spotted them with his magic war goggles. Jim's *heat* was Ron's *elephant*. Ron's *water buffalo* was Jim's sultry *blip* of red. Together, they provided valid targets for mild-mannered, vacationing Al, who, in turn, would align two reticles to indicate he had a clear shot, gain permission from Indiana or Clancy, and pull the trigger. All the while, the "young guns" kept feeding Al bullets – never firing a single shot, as the name, "gunner", might suggest. It was all as easy as washing the car. Except when some of the blips were human. Al never got used to that.

These "eyes" were critical to the success of the crew's missions, indeed to the entire interdiction campaign in 1970. History claims that allied aircraft destroyed some 4,000 trucks during the 1970–71 dry season. Almost overnight, the former cargo-planes-turned-killing-machines had become the NVA's worst nightmare, and Al's crew was the scariest of them all. Other crews were good; But Al's crew was primal. Indiana's NOS could pick up the tiniest source of light from miles away. He and Russell grew so adept at their skills, that sometimes the crew would finish their mission sooner than expected, and Al would grant their wishes to go "hunting" for anything that moved on the trail. Keeping within the rules of engagement that governed free fire zones, Indiana and Russell would see a potential target and instruct Al over the headset to fly towards it. Although there were mechanical limitations to the NOS, the crew found ways to overcome them.

"*Because of the limit of the NOS to move left and right, we had to improvise,*" Indiana wrote me. "*If Al turned directly toward the target, I would lose sight of it. So, we developed a system where we would gradually fly toward the light source with me trying to keep the target at our 10 o'clock, until we reached Al's normal firing position. Of course, the truck drivers usually drove without lights.*"

Every now and then, though, they'd get cocky and turn them on. Then it was easy for Al to hose 'em down."

Indiana said it exactly like that – "hose 'em down". No qualifiers. No apologies.

Of the ten men on the plane that night – except for maybe Lopez – the gunners were the most unzipped. Firestone told me once that he had gone to Vietnam for the adventure. *"I guess as young guys, 'risky' is what we wanted,"* he said in his email. My jaw dropped when I read this. Had we been conversing in person, I would not have been able to hide my incredulity, and Firestone would have asked me what the hell I was doing writing a book about war. Eventually, though, I grew accustomed to the drill, and a type of dance developed between the crew and me in which they would lead with nonchalant descriptions of mass devastation, and I would follow by casually pretending my head had not just exploded. Once, while reading a letter from Firestone, I found myself questioning whether I had even one brave bone in my body.

"The biggest percentage of our missions were armed recon," Firestone's letter began, "But perhaps the most satisfaction was being able to help the ground troops with their missions. I have in mind one TIC ("troops in contact") where we emptied our ammo rack, went back to refuel and reload, and then returned. The guys up front will need to verify this, but it seems we flew in our circle that night with running lights on, as other aircraft were in the area. I do remember the flak that night was pretty intense and I always thought it could have been one of the most engaging missions of the year. I need some verification as to whether that was the night we received photos of the damage we did to the enemy – I'm talking about actual photos. I remember you could count the bullet holes in their faces."

I still shake my head when I read those words,particularly after realizing Firestone was describing the same story Al had told me about the young, Aussie RTO. These were little boys in the sky protecting little boys on the ground, for heaven's sake – while back home, kids their own age were setting fire to the same flags painted on the sides of the AC–119, and I was playing with Matchbox cars. I have searched my notes from the crew many times, and have never found a shred of indignation over the anti-war sentiment that defined that era, except for the time I was bold enough to ask Al about it.

"We saw the gratitude and the smiles and the laughter of the people who had asked us to come help them," he said. "But all we saw back home was ungratefulness. We felt so ... unappreciated."

But they had a job to do, so they kept on doing it. "*Every other night*", as one of the truck hunters told me. "*And we flew whatever aircraft they assigned to us. As long as the guns were sighted in, and the holes in the floor weren't too large – hell, we'd fly a bathtub if they had asked us to.*"

CHAPTER SEVENTEEN

ACE

"You slipped into the hollow cockpit and strapped and plugged yourself into the machine. The canopy ground shut and sealed you off. Your oxygen, your very breath, you carried into the chilled vacuum, in a steel bottle."
James Salter, <u>The Hunters</u>, 1956.

It is the curse of man to *become* the thing he does. The doctor, the lawyer, the writer, the truck hunter … indeed all occupations known to mankind are subject to this curse. Even the farmer strolling in his field, scattering seeds and whistling as he goes, is aware on a subterranean level that others will measure his character by whether his wheat comes up in straight or crooked rows … full and fruitful, or shriveled with cutworms. The very thought of it affects the tune he whistles. This is why two strangers who have begun their conversation with the weather, or sports, or politics, or cars, inevitably get around to the real business of deducing just who it is they are talking to, when they ask … "So, what is it you *do*?"

The tragedy is, by becoming the thing they do, men think they are becoming somebody – while all along, they are becoming *something*.

Some say as many as five *billion* bullets were fired during the Vietnam War – or, fifty-thousand rounds per "kill". Spewed from the mouths of Colt and Carbine, Stoner and Springfield, Heckler and Koch, and Smith and Wesson, the bullets of Vietnam were a signature, of sorts, an autograph on the dotted line that read, "Men have been here … and this is what men do."

These, however, were not the only guns the US military took to Vietnam.

They also carried Enfields, and Thompsons, Garands, and Grease Guns, and guns with the word, "sniper", in their titles to signify the type of men who would be shooting them – "experts", especially skilled at killing economically. There were guns with romantic names, like the "Swedish K", the "Madsen", the "Owen Gun", and the "Sterling submachine gun". And, as if not to be outdone by these more sophisticated methods of destruction, they brought their shotguns, too – their Winchesters, Ithacas, Remingtons, and Brownings – so that when they met a man at close range, they could kill him without aiming.

But perhaps more than any other gun, the one that changed the face of war was the M16. Unlike its older brother, the M60, which fired 7.62mm shells and required two to three men to operate it in the field, the M16 was light and nimble, the prize of any boy who ever dreamed of war. The .223 caliber, 5.56mm, gas-operated, magazine-fed rifle with semi-automatic and fully automatic capabilities was not only fun to shoot – it was devastating. The large wounds inflicted by the M16 and observed by soldiers in Vietnam were so gruesome, that photographs of them remained classified into the 1980s.

Thus, with all the shooting going on in Vietnam, there was a constant vibration that worked its way into the core of men – the larger the caliber, the greater the damage to their core. Ken Firestone once described the sound of Stinger's 20s as a "roar" that enveloped a man, overwhelmed him, went down inside his belly, where it lodged, set up shop, and made a racket so deafening, the man became the gun itself ... separate, yet indistinguishable. By late-spring, the transformation of Al's men from human to weapon was nearly complete, their blistered souls red-hot with cyclical fire. Had someone asked them what line of work they were in, their answer would have been to shake their heads and say, "We know not what we do – it's far too loud in here to think."

In early May, when life had begun to spiral into monsoons and madness for the truck hunters, a certain event happened that made the crew wonder if history's greatest ironies are written in battle.

It had been a slow afternoon in the skies northeast of Ban Ban, and the men were fighting boredom. Having lost count of their missions, they had resigned themselves to the fact that this was all there was to war. The acquisition of a target. The squeeze of a trigger. The plume of red in the trees below. Then a breezy jaunt back over the fence. Familiarity had bred contempt in them, not for the things they shot, but for war itself. It was all so numbingly predictable. Then Russell spotted something unexpected on his FLIR, and contempt gave way to adrenaline.

"I've got heat at zero angels, Al," said Russell.

"Think it's a truck?" asked Al.

"That's no truck," said Jones, zeroing in on Russell's unidentified bright spot with his NOS. Al began to circle, and as he did Jones got a clearer look at the object. "What do we have here?" he murmured to himself, "Twin turbines ... fives blades..." Suddenly, it was clear to Jones. "That's an Mi–8!" he declared, and the whole crew came alive. "Russian-made ... loaded for bear ... fast as hell, in case anyone's wondering," he concluded.

"Good work, Jonesy," said Al, hailing airborne command almost before the words had left his NOS's mouth. In his heart, Al hoped the Ravens had done their job and spotted the bogey. But with the increased bombing in Laos, there seemed to be a constant shortage of FAC intel. "This is Stinger Two-One to AC," said Al, "Descending to maintain three, zero, zero, zero ... come in, AC ... over."

"Lima Charlie, Stinger Two-One ... this is ABCC ... verify assigned altitude as three, zero, zero, zero ... go ahead."

Al gathered his thoughts, considering the gravity of his next transmission, then pushed the button again. "Break- break, AC... I've got visual on a bogey ... possible terminator ... zero angels ... over."

"Stinger Two-One ... copy that possible terminator ... standby five," replied airborne command.

At the sight of Stinger, the Mi–8 took off abruptly and was now in plain view, speeding east toward Hanoi at less than three-hundred feet, barely skimming the tops of the dense jungle. It was the only enemy aircraft Al and his men had seen all year long, and it had the effect of a cat wandering past the doorway of a Doberman's doghouse.

"AC ... this is Stinger Two-One ... bogey on the move ... request to engage ... over," said Al, keeping his eye on the helicopter below. From Al's vantage point of three angels, the terminator looked like a single mosquito on a green, picnic blanket.

"Negative, Stinger Two-One!" came Airborne's immediate response, "Too many uncle birds in the area ... gotta keep it friendly ... do not engage bogey ... repeat ... do not engage bogey ... standby five."

"Bullshit!" came someone's voice from the back of the plane. "They don't want us to have any fun."

"That's enough, fellas," said Al. "AC's just doing his job. You heard him ... there's a lot of friendlies around here."

Al felt a tap on his shoulder, and he glanced to his right to see Obie covering his headset's mouthpiece. "That was no friendly," Obie whispered.

"You can never be too sure," said Al, as he watched the helicopter disappearing into the sea of trees. Inwardly, though, he suspected Obie was right. What he would have given to shoot down an enemy aircraft! And in a cargo plane at that! Al allowed himself the brief daydream of "ace" status, and his thoughts seemed to buoy his plane's hulking shape above the jungle billows.

Since planes were first equipped with weapons, history tells us perhaps ten-thousand men have achieved "ace" status in the various theatres of war. To do so, one must shoot down no less than five enemy aircraft. The first ace ever recorded was WW1 fighter pilot, Roland Garros, but his status remains in question, since many historians say he only shot down *four* planes. Unfortunately for Garros, his countryman, Adolphe Pégoud, is usually credited with being the "first ace". As an example of wartime irony, however, the stadium that hosts the French Tennis Open is named after Garros. And every time a player fires a winner past his opponent on the first serve, it is called ... an "ace". If Al had shot down the Russian helicopter, he would have had only four more to go. He was just picturing the award ceremony, when his radio suddenly crackled to life again.

"Stinger Two-One ... this is ABCC ... come in." "ABCC ... this is Stinger Two-One ... go ahead."

"Stinger Two-One ... terminator verified ... repeat ... terminator verified ... you are now cleared to hunt and destroy the enemy."

"*Yeehaw*!" cried Wilson, "That possum's on the stump!" His Missouri twang echoed through the plane's metal bowels. If there was one thing Ron Wilson enjoyed, it was a good hunting trip with friends.

Al grinned at Obie and called for full-blowers in the J85s. "Keep a sharp eye out, boys," he said to Jones and Russell. "Who-ever's flying that bird took off fast the moment he saw us. I don't suspect he'll slow down until he gets to friendlier territory."

Up the narrow river valley Al flew, scanning the trees below and keeping a wary eye on the steep terrain that rose up like shadowy monks on either side of him. At his six, the Mekong River ambled along the western frontier of Laos. In the distance, the Annamite mountains stood as border guards, keeping the Chinese culture of Vietnam from mingling with its Indianized neighbor states. Occasionally, Al caught a glimpse of his quarry far ahead of him – its twin turbines standing out from an other-wise non-distinct backdrop – but then it would dart behind an outcropping and lose itself in the endless vegetation. The stars were myriad tonight, the perfect setting for an aerial battle.

Al had never hunted a man before – at least not one that was running from him – and the feeling that came from it was a mixture of thrill and loathing. *Who am I now*? he wondered.... *A farmer*? *A father*? *A cattleman*? *A killer*? Below his plane, where the trees emptied out onto the plains, the village lights were just beginning to blink on, and Al imagined ordinary people down there, trying to live as if extraordinary violence wasn't erupting all around them. In his mind's eye, he saw a father and his daughter in their pirogue, paddling up the Nam Ou to visit relatives, past quiet eddies and stunning limestone karsts, trolling for dinner in the dim light, giving thanks for another day in which none of their loved ones had been blown to bits by war. The sound of an oxcart rumbling toward hearth and home scraped along the footpaths of Al's heart ... mingling with the hum of Stinger's power unit ... making him think of his own family far away.

"See anything, boys?" Al called through the blackout curtain.

"Nothing worth chasing," said Russell. "Just a whole lotta green," sighed Jones. "Shit," said someone.

Casting his dreams of glory to the wind, Al banked left in a wide, lateral turn, pointing Stinger toward the western border of Laos, and on to Udorn. Suddenly, he felt farther from Oklahoma than ever before, and a wave of deep loneliness cascaded over him. *I'm no ace, he thought to himself. I'm just a father of little girls.* Turning portside so that Obie wouldn't see the flush of emotion overcoming him, Al pushed the button on the interphone.

"Day is done," he said.

Except for one minor detail about his boot camp days, my father never told me what he did during the war. Apparently, there had been some sort of mix-up that landed Bill Cunningham, a man of considerable education, in a platoon of virtual idiots. Not being one to rock the boat, my father went along with the arrangement until one day his sergeant discovered him reading another grunt's mail to him. And behind that grunt was a line of six others, waiting to have their letters deciphered.

"What the hell are you doing, Cunningham?" said the sergeant to my father, who immediately snapped to attention.

"Sir, I'm helping my fellow grunts, sir," replied my father, with a crisp salute.

"Well, Private Cunningham, if you have time to read everybody's mail, perhaps you've got time to do KP duty, as well!"

"Yessir," said my father, who then proceeded to peel potatoes for the next two weeks. Eventually, he was transferred to another platoon with soldiers who could read for themselves, and there he completed his basic training before being shipped out to the Philippines, where he spent the remainder of the Pre-Korean Insurgency on a tiny island, listening to the radio.

Listening to the radio? I thought, *What kind of courage does that require? Even I can listen to the radio – and I'm only eight years old.*

I recall wondering if maybe I had misunderstood my father, and that his role as a "high speed radio operator" was not unlike that of the young, Aussie RTO who Al had encountered in the jungle. I wanted so badly for my father to be a warrior, who visited exotic places and accomplished daring feats. Most of all, I wanted him to be a hero. As it turned out, however, I had understood him perfectly. Throughout his military career my father did, in fact, sit alone in a shack on a secluded island, never under siege, never face-to-face with the enemy, never in danger of anything more than a tropical storm, or a mild sunburn, or a bad piece of mango. And while my father sat there, listening to the waves and the birds and the radio, other boys' fathers were out becoming heroes.

Much later in life, when I was a grown man and the miles between my father and me stretched across counties and states lines, I learned that to be a high-speed radio operator, one had to have mastered naval radio procedure and be able to receive messages at a minimum speed of twenty-five standard groups per minute, while sending them at a similar, blinding speed. I also learned that these messages saved the lives of countless American soldiers, and were transmitted by light signal and code.

Code!

The word leaped at me from the tall grasses of my childhood, evoking images of brave operatives hunched over straight-key Morse machines in dim bunkers, their sleeves rolled up, their faces lit by Turkish cigarettes, their thumbs and knuckles flashing left and right, saving the allies with "dits" and "dahs".

So, my father *had* been a hero, I decided. But I had simply known it too late.

As Stinger flew west and the terminator flew east, Al and his men were borne along with their miserable thoughts. Some were sad at the missed opportunity. Others were pissed because it felt good to be. But a few of them, the ones more given to the sensitive matters of life, wondered if by pursuing the enemy so cavalierly, they had crossed a terrible, unforgivable line. *Who have we become? they thought. And in what story are we now characters?* Only the setting sun was a reminder to them that tomorrow might be a better day. After all, it had to be—

It was Jim Russell's birthday.

PART FOUR

"THE RED DIRT OF HOME."

02:14 / 8 MAY / 1970

Phou Bia crouched like a witch in an alleyway, waiting for the child that dared to wander close to her. In the thin and morbid moonlight, Al could just make out the tops of trees and the gaunt, tectonic fingers that groped upward on the mountain's northeast exposure, reaching up for him and his crew.

"We gotta get thinner!" Al ordered through the interphone.

Soaked with labor, the men looked at one another and their shoulders sagged. Knowing it would take a jolt to get them moving, Jones took off his headset and laid into them. "You heard what the captain said!" he shouted, his muscles burning from the frantic purge of everything that could be thrown out of the plane. "Unless we want to give this Stinger back to the taxpayers, we better get our asses moving!"

But they had pitched everything they could find, and still their captain wanted more? What more was there to get rid of? With terrorized expressions, they glanced around the windswept cabin for anything that had eluded their eye. Jones felt a wave of guilt and helplessness wash over him. Though Lopez was the official jumpmaster on the gunner deck, he was the only co in the back of the plane, and he had done his best to lead the charge. Now that the plane was going in, Jones couldn't bring himself to make eye contact with anyone. Suddenly, Lopez noticed something; In the crew's haste to lighten the plane, he had overlooked the obvious.

"Ay, mierda!" he exclaimed, and everyone on deck turned to see the thing that Lopez was cussing. At the aft starboard corner of the gun deck, the giant launcher sat like a stubborn child, eleven-hundred pounds of flares and housing, refusing to be moved.

"Get that bitch off the ship!" someone shouted. But the box was heavy, and one man's strength was no match for it. "Help me!" Lopez replied. For a moment, the truck hunters stared at him, unaccustomed to this strange vulnerability in their flare man. Had it not been for the haunting sound that occurs when something loud and moving approaches something hard and immovable, they might have remained in that posture. But knowing they were about to become a greasy smudge on the side of a mountain, they rushed to his aid, and with a mighty heave, shoved the thing out the door. Down and down into the darkness it tumbled, until the crew heard the box smash against the rocks. The echo of their underside barely skimming the tips of Phou Bia sent a shiver up their spines.

"Fat girl overboard!" confirmed someone, and the plane erupted in cheers. Unaware of how tight his grip had been on the yoke wheel during the ascent, Al relaxed his shoulders for the first time since the ordeal began.

"How's our juice, Nash?" he inquired.

"Nose is cold, sir," said Nash. "I'll do my best to monitor engines and fuel consumption. But like I said—"

"Right," said Al, cutting off his engineer. "Way past bingo. Not to worry. Can you work your magic and keep us going?"

Nash ran his forefinger across his thin mustache, a habit he had acquired whenever problem solving. His butt was numbed from sitting on the empty ammo can behind the console. He would have given a day's pay for one of those embroidered pillows sold in the Hmong villages. "I can try to float fuel between the tanks," he replied. "That might help."

"Check fuel against ETA, and keep me posted," said Al.

"Roger," said Nash. Clancy looked up from his computer, and gave a thumbs up. With Phou Bia already several miles at their six and RTAFB still a long way off, Stinger's problem with fuel loomed larger than ever – and though nobody was admitting it, everyone was thinking it. Al and Obie's arms were near exhaustion from fighting the yoke, their legs on fire from standing on the rudder. From the moment they had gotten the plane turned around, they had been controlling its bank primarily with full left aileron, and secondarily with full left rudder. But the plane had a mind of its own, and both men knew if they let up for even a few moments, Stinger would turn clockwise around the longitudinal axis and never recover. Suddenly, a thought came to Al.

"I need a green bag," he announced.

"Say again," said O'Brien, wondering if the farm boy in Al might be taking over.

"We need to tie this off full left ... to see if I can let go of the yoke," Al explained. "I don't know what else to tie it with; Everything has gone out the door. Get me someone's green bag!"

O'Brien looked at Nash, and they both looked at Al like he was crazy. Behind the curtain, Clancy and Russell grinned at each other. "Sir," said O'Brien. "I'm pretty sure our men are all wearing their flight suits."

Laughter from the gun deck could be heard through the interphone – the kind that comes when someone knows it might be his last chance to laugh, and he doesn't want to waste it. But Al ignored it. His next transmission was meant entirely for the gunners. "Unless one of you men wants to be voluntold, I suggest someone bring me his green bag, ASAP."

Now, whether it is due to forgetfulness, or to a pact the crew made to protect the honor of the man who gave up his flight suit, the world may never know which man came forward. But Al had his green bag in less than thirty seconds, and somewhere in the rear of the plane, one young airman shivered in his underwear.

Back on the flight deck, the men set about the task of securing the yoke in the same position Al had held it in for over an hour. Their goal – though no one talked about it – was to find a way every man could make it out of the plane, should the need arise. As time and fuel drained away, the men used every knot they knew – square knots, sheep shanks, figure eights, and more – but to no avail. No matter how they approached the problem, the Nomex flight suit was no substitute for the strength of Al and Obie. Like a spirited colt, the nose of the plane would simply not be controlled by any hand but its trusted jockey. In the end, the green bag was given back to its owner, and Al and Obie struggled on against the gravitational pull of planet Earth.

About a hundred miles from Udorn, Nash told Al they were basically out of fuel, and Al faced his hardest decision of the mission. For the second time that night, he told his men to do something he wouldn't wish upon his worst enemy. "All right, men," he said. "Hit the silk. We'll meet at zero angels."

The crew put on their chutes again, and prepared to jump.

Now, there is a certain finality to the decision to jump into the Laotian jungle. Tales of torture by Pathet Lao eclipsed even those involving beasts in the wild wasteland beneath Stinger's crippled wings. Lt. Dieter Dengler's account of his escape in 1966 had made the circuit at Udorn, Phu Cat, and Phan Rang, leaving most pilots more apt to go down in flames than punch out over enemy territory. In the wake of Milacek's order, thoughts of bamboo torture and being fed alive to ants jabbed at the men's souls.

Cofer cupped the mouthpiece on his headset. "What will Al do after the rest of us have jumped?" he asked, looking around at his comrades. But none of them had an answer.

Knowing their plane like the back of their hands, the men were aware of the emergency exit in the floor of the flight deck behind the pilot's seat. Bailout through the exit involved a headfirst dive into the small tunnel that passed through Stinger's fuselage and vomited out into space. It was intended for use only if the flight deck crew did not have time to make it to the paratroop door, and it was generally viewed as a last resort to abandon ship. Years later, in quiet discussions with one another, the men agreed it was the thought of Al struggling to make it out that hole in the middle of a tailspin that brought about the vote to disobey his order.

"We talked at length of how we could get all the crewmembers out of the aircraft," said Jones. *"We just could not devise a way for Al to get out. Once the pilots released pressure on the rudder and ailerons, the aircraft would spin out of control, trapping anyone inside the gunship. As a crew, we decided we would either all bail out or all stay aboard, regardless of consequences."*

This agreement amongst the men was kept from Al until 2001, when someone shared it with him at a reunion. But he always suspected some sort of referendum had occurred in the back of the plane, because it was not like his men to disobey him. It's interesting to note, also, that their disobedience was to a higher power, further up the chain than their captain. Unbeknownst to the crew, Al and O'Brien had already received direct orders to bail out from General Brown at RTAFB. Having recently seen a Phantom splatter all over his base, Brown was damn sure not going to allow more carnage on his watch. With ten crew members on board, the carnage would be unforgivable.

As Nash continued to shift the remaining drops of fuel from tank to tank, Al and Obie set their eyes on Udorn and the very real possibility that this might be the last landing either of them ever negotiated. There was nothing left for Russell to do on the deck, so he said so long to Clancy and joined the rest of the crew in the rear. In the shadows of the gun deck, he found them snuggled against the warm power unit, like little boys hoping to get back to Mom.

"*So, there we were,*" Jones stated in one of his newsy letters, "*Half a wing gone, no more gas, M–16s scattered all over the jungle, and lighting up the sky for every NVA gunner's target practice. Certainly not our best night.*"

Nevertheless, the plane kept flying.

CHAPTER EIGHTEEN

THE RUNWAY OF UDORN AND THE SOLIDNESS OF GRACE

"No one has ever collided with the sky."

Stinger struggled on toward Udorn. There was no more talk of a bailout, and all was quiet in the back of the plane, except for the drone of the 3350's. Warmed by the power unit, the men sat with their parachutes on, knowing they would not be using them. Up on the flight deck, Nash stared at the fuel needles, pegged out all the way to empty, and not a wiggle in them.

"You just keep flying, Captain," said Nash. "I'll get you the gas."

A half mile before final, Al's heart sank. *What happened to the lights?* he thought, looking ahead to his designated runway. He glanced at the runways to the left and right of him, and could see their green threshold lights shining brightly, their red lights marking their ends. But where runway One-Seven should have been, a monstrous blackness opened wide to swallow Stinger whole.

"We're dark on one-seven," said Al to the tower. But the tower was silent. "Dark on one-seven," repeated Al. "No chance for fly-by. How copy?"

Again, nothing.

Al peered into the darkness, and tried to recall the configuration of the base. The parallel runway's blue- fringed taxiway knifed across the approach, connecting it with the apron as he remembered it ... and the red beacons were where they should be ... flashing on, flashing off ... but ahead of him there was still nothing, and all he could do was point his plane into the nothingness.

Far below, throngs of sleepy-eyed personnel gathered to watch the spectacle, many of whom had been ordered from the barracks due to the still-fresh memory of the Rhino. Those who were inclined, and even those who weren't, knelt in pockets of prayer, keeping an eye on the red-hot dot in the sky that grew larger with each passing second. Someone in the tower had made the decision to switch on the base's public-address system, and now every word Al uttered could be heard for miles around.

"Help me, God," he said, repeatedly. "Help us ... help us..."

The blackness grew nearer and nearer. Al could just make out the outlines of firetrucks and emergency vehicles speeding in the direction of the darkened runway ... their glare a jumbled substitute for the straight and true lights that should have been guiding Stinger home.

"This is Stinger-Two-One requesting clearance for final," said Al.

No response.

"How copy, control? Dead silence.

"GC?"

Nothing. This was it. They were going to land, and take their chances, and probably die. And all because there was no light.

"Copy, GC!"

Al had all but abandoned hope of communication with ground control, when a voice leaped from the gloom below. "Cleared to land on one-seven!" cried the voice.

"Roger that one-seven," replied Al. He was thinking about the strain on the landing gear at 160 knots – 40 knots faster than the normal 120 – but he was out of options. He had altitude to think about, too, and he wanted to leave enough room for the men to jump and take their chances should the engines shut down. Of course, the crew had long since decided they were landing with their captain – no matter what.

Where are those lights when I need them? thought Al.

All of a sudden, as if the darkened runway had been part of an elaborate surprise party all along, One-Seven lit up like downtown Saigon, and Al felt a surge of hope in his chest. Stinger was lined up perfectly! O'Brien held the ailerons full left, as Al pulled back on the power a little at a time.

"RPM'S 2350," said Al, settling over the approach end of the runway.

"Wilco, 2350," said Nash. "Jets idle."

"Jets idle, sir."

Realizing the right recip had been maxed out for two hours, Al held his breath as he reversed power at touchdown, and the plane screamed down the white line toward the overrun.

"Ground Control, request clearance to taxi," said Al, when they reached the overrun.

"Stinger Two One, you're clear to taxi," came the response. And then after a brief pause … "Welcome to Udorn."

As if he had been holding his breath for the last two hours, a sudden gasp of air spewed upward from Al's lungs, bursting through the interphone and over the airwaves, reaching out to the farthest corners of the Royal Thai Air Force Base and beyond. "Thank you, Lord," he whispered. And then with a raw, unfiltered shout, he repeated, "Thank you, Lord!"

Yes, thank you, thought the gawkers and the prayers who had lived through the Rhino crash. They had braced themselves for a fiery homecoming; What they got was the smoothest display of airmanship any of them had ever witnessed. "Like butter on hot toast", O'Brien would later describe it. "Truly one of the smoothest landings I've ever been a part of. And believe me, I've criticized a lot of them since then – from the back of the plane, of course."

Al looked at his watch, and it read, 0220, a little over three hours since Russell had blown out the candle on his cake in the OC.

At Stinger's normal spot on the apron, there were hundreds of airmen and staffers waiting, many of them crying, some cheering, others still praying. Having held the ailerons full left for nearly two hours, Al's forearms were too tired to power down the plane; Nash had to do it for him.

The first person on the aircraft after Stinger landed was Lt. Col. Casey, the crew's Ops Officer; He was carrying a bottle of Chivas Regal. When Lopez saw the scotch, he pitched his parachute on the floor and came running. For a while, there was a great celebration of hugs and high- fives, and what-the-hell-were-you-thinking-getting-your-ass-shot-off comments, indicative of friends who were just happy not to be scraping their comrades off the pavement. Eventually, things quieted down, and the crew began to exit. Clancy stepped off the plane first and kissed the asphalt. Nash, like a magician exiting the stage after a mystifying show, walked his weary brain straight to Life Support, where he checked in his personal equipment and headed to the bathroom. The CO's had a debrief ahead of them, and they wondered what General Brown in Saigon would have to say about their decision to stay with the plane, rather than bail out. Russell and Jones shook each other's hands ... started to walk away ... then came back to hug one another. Since Stinger Two One was obviously not going anywhere soon, the gunners had no ammunition to reload, so they wandered around with nothing to do, grinning and slapping the back of every man they met. One by one, the men departed from Stinger, until only Al and O'Brien were left on the flight deck of the faithful bird.

"Thank you, Obie," said Al to his young co-pilot. "I couldn't have done it without you." The two shook hands, and O'Brien stumbled off to the debriefing. Finally, Al ventured out into the remaining gaggle of well-wishers, and that's when he saw the damage for the first time.

"Throughout the flight, the torched recip had always been too bright for Obie to get a good look at the wing beyond," said Al in later interviews. "So, when I saw that most of it was sheared off, I could hardly believe my eyes. All the way up to the right engine ... it was just ... gone. I don't know how we flew the thing."

The last thing the crew did together that night was reconvene and decide what to do with the adrenaline that still coursed through their bodies. They joked around and embraced each other like long-lost friends, and even considered cranking shells for a fellow crew fresh off another mission, but then remembered RTAFB's rules frowned upon commissioned officers helping non-commissioned. "Besides," said O'Brien, "We all agreed our disobedience of General Brown was probably enough insurrection for the night." Eventually, their weariness caught up with them, and slowly the truck hunters disappeared to their racks, their tanks every bit as dry as Stinger's. Only Lopez resisted sleep; He stayed up until the sunrise, nursing the Chivas Regal.

After the men went their separate ways, Al found himself on the phone with General Brown in Saigon. "Damn fine piece of flying," growled the General to the Captain, "But you should have bailed out like I ordered you to."

"Yessir," said Al. It was the only thing one can say to a four-star general, especially one whose nickname is, "Scratchley". So, he said it again. "Yessir."

After his chat with the General, Al walked out on the base, laid down on the concrete, and looked at the moon. The low clouds that had been with them throughout their mission had finally lifted, and now everything was clear and warm. It was the only time of day during the monsoon season that Al really enjoyed, and tired as he was, he didn't want to waste it. He filled his lungs with thick, spring air ... felt the ground with the tips of his fingers ... looked up at the shimmering stars. To his right, a few hundred yards away, the Phantom had exploded in flames, slicing through the barracks like a reaper with his sickle, severing the lives of slumbering babes. Al thought about his crew, asleep in their beds already, and he wondered what they were thinking just before they closed their eyes tonight. Perhaps Wilson pictured Rosetta, wearing something soft and floral, beckoning him to their bedroom back in Missouri, glancing over her bare shoulder with a look that only the two of them understood. Perhaps Russell was thinking of his fiancée, Ann. And Jones of his Patricia. One thing Al knew for sure, no one ever wonders if an F–4 is going to kill them in their sleep.

It was May, and he had just been shot out of the sky, and there was still half a tour to go before he went home to the farm. He counted the months on his fingers, taking note of special dates in each of them that he would miss on account of the war. Then he wondered why he was counting. He had always been away for Fourth of July, never there to light the sparklers and watch the girls go running around the pasture like fireflies. He had missed a host of Halloweens and Thanksgivings, plus all the other holidays civilians take for granted. *I've flown the line, and missed it all, he thought. What if my family doesn't even recognize me when I get home?* If he had wanted, Al could have laid there on the concrete and let himself get good and despondent. But with resolve, he sat up, grabbed his duffel, and stood to his feet.

Don't sweat the stuff that hasn't happened yet, Al thought, stretching to get the kinks out. It was the best advice his dad had ever given him ... back when they were living together ... hunting and fishing ... father and son ... back before he drank himself to death.

At the entrance to the base, two men shared a cigarette under the shadow of the observation tower, one of them from the Thai air police, the other from USAF Security. Ostensibly motionless, a handsome German Shepherd lay at the two men's feet, its protruding tongue a harbinger of the dog day to come. Al waved to the soldiers, gave a thankful salute to the machine gun embankment in the tower, and walked out to the street.

As he stood there in the fast-approaching morning heat, all the fibers in his skin felt electric, and he reviewed the events of the evening:

He had flown a plane on one wing....

... brought it all the way home through enemy territory....

... delivered his men in one piece....

... and now they were all fast asleep, except for one of them.

It was a feat that was sure to be talked about tomorrow at the O Club. He would hardly be able to walk through the room without turning heads. For a moment, Al felt like a god – *The King of The Asian Sky*, he thought to himself – and his chest puffed out noticeably. He even considered walking back to the hotel instead of taking a cab, he felt so alive. Then he remembered his own frail voice on the interphone during approach, and the sound of the three words he had uttered across the Udorn PA came floating back to him.

Help me, God, he had said.

And God *had* helped him – had He not?

With a toot of its horn, a cab snuck up on The King of The Asian Sky, and nearly scared him half to death. By the time he tossed his duffel in the backseat and settled in next to it, the king had become a man again, and he gave the driver his baht before he could forget about it, plus an extra one for Lopez, wherever he was tonight. With a lurch, the cab pulled away from the curb, and Al settled back in his seat to watch the city of Udorn wake up.

Down the strip they flew, past Jack's Tailors, and Nick's, and the souvenir shop. Past a woman breastfeeding her child, and a man drinking a cold Singha, his first beer of the day. Past the Paradise Pool and The Champagne Bar, and the vendor cooking monkey ball soup over a dirty, open fire – the smell of the fried garlic so intoxicating that Al almost tapped the driver on his shoulder for him to stop. But he had begun to drift off in the back seat, and he knew he needed sleep more than food.

Just before the cab reached the Siri Udorn Hotel, Al saw a man darting down a side-street with a woman on his arm, and for the briefest moment the man looked back. "Hey, Mexican!" Al called, thinking the man was Lopez. "We got work to do tonight! Don't be late!" At the sound of Al's voice, the man turned away, pulled along by the woman who seemed to be in a hurry. A few more steps and they were around the corner, and Al's suspicions were never confirmed.

At the hotel, Al saw that the lobby was flooded, already several feet underwater due to the rising clongs. He and Jones had been in a rush to get to the base for last night's mission, so they had forgotten to stuff some towels under the door. There would be water snakes in his room, no doubt.

Don't sweat the stuff that hasn't happened yet, he told himself again, as he trudged up the stairs. By 0630, Al had mopped the floor, shooed a dozen pencil-thin, juvenile Puff-Faced Water Snakes out the door, and was in bed snoring, his last words of the day another whispered, "Thank you, Lord." It would be less than eighteen hours before he and his crew were out hunting trucks again....

And a very long time before he would tell Pat about the incident.

CHAPTER NINETEEN

TROPHIES IN THE BARN

They say in his later years, Muhammad Ali's trophies sat in his barn, next to photographs and paintings of himself, gathering dust and bird-shit. In the rafters above, the pigeons went on with their happy lives, cooing and copulating, oblivious to the man who once called himself, "the Greatest". So, it is with the baubles we invent to honor ourselves. They are forgotten shortly after we cross the finish line.

―――――――――――

As is often the case with the decorous side of war, Magnet Ass and the truck hunters were heralded on the tarmac for about two hours – slightly less than the sum of each man's 'fifteen minutes of fame' combined – and then they were back into the shit the following night, over the fence and shooting trucks. Subsequently, what was left of the damaged wing was sent back to Wright-Patterson AFB in Ohio for repairs, and it did not return to Udorn for another five months. Not surprisingly, when Stinger was once again battle-ready, Magnet Ass and the truck hunters volunteered to take her out for a test-flight, despite the fact every other crew viewed the plane with mistrust that bordered on superstition. A picture of Al and three crew members, kneeling atop the reconstructed wing, hangs on the wall next to his dining room table. Whenever I ate with Al and Pat, I kept one eye on that picture as he prayed before the meal, because it lent a certain solidness to grace.

"I figured if we could fly the plane on one wing, we could fly it on two," said Al, wiping his mouth with a napkin.

For a while afterwards, newspaper articles sprung up like weeds about the amazing mission, using the theme, "On a wing and a prayer", from the 1944 WWII movie, starring Dana Andrews and Don Ameche. General Nazarro, commander of the SE Asia theatre, came to shake the crew's hands and snap a few photographs with them. By and large, however, the significance of the event sank back into the quagmire of Vietnam fairly quickly, and things returned to business as usual. If it hadn't been for news of the mission reaching the United States via the "Stars and Stripes", Al might have shielded Pat from its horror all the way to the end of his tour. As it turned out, he waited until after their furlough in Hawaii to tell her about the Mackay mission, and only then because he realized the news was about to break in the S and S. Al just didn't want Pat to worry.

As for Ron Jones, he was ready to get back to truck hunting.

"*I thought that was the end of the incident,*" Jones told me. "*Then one day, someone mentioned to me that I should put the crew in for some kind of award, since I was the Awards and Dec officer for our Detachment. Curious, I opened the A & D manual and found a possible match in the Mackay trophy. I inquired up the chain of command and got the okay. So, I applied.*"

The next year, Jones was notified that the crew was one of the finalists for the 1970 Mackay Trophy. A couple of months later, while Jones was camping in the backwoods of Michigan with his former B–52 crew, someone from Kincheloe AFB drove out to congratulate him and inform him about the award. It was the last thing Jones expected on a camping trip. "I couldn't have been more shocked if Bigfoot had shown up at our campfire," said Jones.

Suddenly, the men were heroes again.

"*My wife and I were to fly to Washington DC for the award ceremony, and the SAC Division Commander himself released his aircraft to take us to Andrews,*" said Jones. "*But an hour after takeoff, something happened to the aircraft and we had to return to Kincheloe.*"

As it turns out, Kincheloe is roughly fifteen miles from the end of the earth, and few aircraft come and go there. Since the Division Commander's aircraft could not be repaired for several days, Ron and his wife, (also named, "Pat"), were told there was no way they could be transported to DC in time for the ceremony. It was a huge disappointment for them.

As luck would have it, a c-37 flew into Kincheloe unexpectedly and offered the Joneses a ride to Andrews by way of Kansas.

"*We arrived in time for the ceremony,*" said Jones, "*But we were way late compared to the rest of the crew.*"

"*Upon landing, Pat and I climbed out of the aircraft and stood next to the ramp wondering what to do next. There was no one to meet us, and the tower had no idea why we were there. So, there we stood, Pat four months pregnant, and me in my Class A's, carrying our bags. Eventually, a vehicle that looked like a bread truck came by, with wooden planks for benches on each side. It was going from aircraft to aircraft, picking up crewmembers and taking them to Base Ops. I decided my wife and I might as well climb aboard, and I figured we could straighten out the situation once we reached a land line.*"

On board the truck, Jones saw several o-6 and o-5 field grade officers, all in their green bags and all wondering where the pregnant woman was headed. They had gone to two or three other aircraft, filling up the vehicle with additional crew members, when all of a sudden, a major in Class A's stuck his head inside the door and asked if there was a Captain Ron Jones on board.

"Yessir," said Jones.

"Your limousine is here and ready to go," said the major.

"*Pat and I looked at each other with wide eyes,*" said Jones, "*And I'm sure that made our story look all the more mysterious to everyone else in the truck. Then we climbed out and the major took our baggage to the limousine, opened the door for us, and drove off to the* BOQ. *I distinctly remember watching numerous heads all gawking out of the bread truck with a look on their faces that said, 'Who in hell was that Captain'?*"

As part of the advertisement for the Mackay Trophy ceremony, an FYI letter had been sent to Senator Henry Jackson, (D-WA), Chair of the Armed Forces Committee. In turn, Jackson sent a request to the Air Force Senate Liaison office, asking if any of Al's crewmembers were from the state of Washington. Only Jones fit that description, and soon he was given a lesson in the power and influence held by the head of the Armed Forces Committee. Whisked away from the schedule set for the rest of the crew, Jones and his wife were quickly escorted to Jackson's senate floor office, where they chatted casually for a half-hour or so with the senator.

"I still have a picture of that event," Jones told me. *"It was an uncomfortable situation for a Captain in a world filled with generals and high-ranking dignitaries. But I did feel momentarily important."*

After their time with the senator, the Joneses were reunited with the crew, and off they went to the Pentagon, where they all became thoroughly lost in the maze of hallways. Eventually, almost as a consolation prize compared to the rest of the day, the crew and their families convened for the Mackay ceremony, where they met the Air Force Chief of Staff, General Jack Ryan, and Secretary of the Air Force, Dr. Robert Seamans, and finally got a look at the trophy that would forever commemorate their miraculous mission over the Plain of Jars.

"The first thing I noticed were the angels," said Al, fighting back tears as he recounted for me his initial glimpse of the Mackay. "There were four of them stationed around the top of the trophy, each holding up a small replica of one of those ... you know, those pusher-type biplanes. I had known all along it was God who held us up that night. I could feel Him taking care of Obie and me, taking care of the whole crew. It was all I could do to keep from breaking down, right there in the ceremony."

The Mackay Trophy is the oldest award intended exclusively for flying officers of the United States Air Force. It was established in 1912 by Mr. Clarence H. Mackay, a wealthy industrialist, philanthropist, communications pioneer and aviation enthusiast. Awarded annually for the "most meritorious flight of the year", the $30,000, silver trophy stands three-feet tall and is mounted on a polished mahogany base that bears an array of silver shields, on which the names and dates of those awarded the trophy are engraved – names like "Hap" Arnold, Eddie Rickenbacker, and Chuck Yeager, the first human being to fly faster than the speed of sound. Interestingly, as the selection committee sifts through each year's nominees, first consideration is always given to *individual* pilots, rather than to whole crews. When I read this last tidbit about the trophy, I realized all the more what a rare honor it was for Al and the boys to be selected as winners. They were America at her best, a brotherhood of men from all walks of life, united against incredible odds – a "flying America" if ever there was one.

After the ceremony and the picture-taking that followed it, Magnet Ass and the truck hunters made a beeline with their wives to the O Club to celebrate, where they were surprised to find less than a hero's welcome.

"*I'm sawww-rry*," said the hostess at the entrance to the club. Her accent screamed Brooklyn. "Unless every member in your *pawww-ty* is a commissioned officer, we can't allow all ten-a-yous in the club."

"But we're all part of the same crew," said Magnet Ass. "Can't you make an exception?"

"Them's the rules," said the hostess. "I don't make 'em."

Undaunted by the coolness at the OC, Al asked Nash, who was the highest-ranking, non-commissioned officer in the crew, if he could work his magic with the NCO club.

"I've got you covered, Captain," said Nash, and he marched right down to the NCO club and asked if all ten men would be allowed to celebrate collectively. They were admitted immediately, and they drank, and laughed, and told stories, and ate good food long into the night – a fitting end to their eventful year at Udorn.

It would be another thirty years before the crew would gather together in one room.

And by then, one of them would be in the ground.

Perhaps two.

The next day, the Joneses returned to Kincheloe, and that was the last anyone mentioned of Ron's involvement in the Mackay mission ... except for one other time.

"*About the time I retired as a Lt. Colonel, a sergeant found an article in an NCO training manual that connected me to the Mackay, and he and his buddies came and asked me about it,*" Jones told me in an email. "*For the slightest moment, I felt young and famous again. Other than that, I never discussed it with anybody. Most people have never even heard of the Mackay. It's just a trophy that sits on a shelf in Washington DC, and my name happens to be on it.*"

When we started the project back in September, I wanted Al to be the hero of the story, I almost *needed* him to be. Certainly, the *book* needed him to be. Or so I thought.

But the longer I knew Al, the more I began to question Man's habit of studying his neighbor through a keyhole, and forming opinions about the narrow things he sees. I even wondered if it was a bit odd to cull three hours from a man's life and write a book about it forty-five years later. Deep in my heart, I suspected the real greatness to Magnet Ass had nothing to do with those three hours. But if it wasn't the Mackay Mission that made Al great ... what was it? The question haunted me, and I knew if I couldn't answer it, I could never in good faith publish the book.

Learning about the Mackay trophy from Jones made me remember something Magnet Ass told me in the dead of winter. We were standing on his porch one evening – and when I say, "we" were standing, I mean that I was standing and *Al* was clinging with all of his might to his walker. The air was bitter as hell, and only a few, lonely china berries still clung to their branches. I heard one land on the hood of my car, and immediately I remembered my childhood. Above Al's house, Orion's sword hung, magnificent and menacing.

"I don't care so much for the word, 'hero'," said Al, brushing a wisp of hair from his forehead and nearly losing his balance. "I'm not the hero of this story – God's the hero."

"Of course, he is," I said. "Nobody with a brain in his head would think a man could fly a plane straight with one wing blown off."

Al turned toward me, and in spite of the devil cow, he fixed his eyes on mine. "Do you believe God held my plane up?" he asked.

"Well, sure I do," I replied.

Truth is, the question had caught me off guard, and I had answered it with the first flippant thing that came to mind. Somehow, Al knew there was no soul to my answer.

He took hold of my arm, and his grip was relentless. "Do you *really* believe it?" he asked.

I flinched at Al's touch, because his fingers were hard and cold as a stone. But he didn't seem to notice.

What's with this line of questioning? I thought. My mind reeled backwards to ancient disappointments related to God. Had I not asked Him with all my heart to heal my father, when he was dying of lung cancer? Had I not made a similar request regarding my mother's excruciating back pain? Both times deafening silence had been God's answer. My father had passed away when I was still young, and my mother was left with her pain pills. Now ... with Al's beseeching eyes locked on mine, it was my turn to give an answer, and I could no longer hide from the question that came volleying back at me from heaven.

Do you believe?

I blinked at the cold wind that suddenly swept in from the northwest. And again, my resistance to it was strong. *What the hell kind of question was that?* I thought. *I've been a Christian since I was eighteen – of course I believe! What more do you want?* Then I realized the "you" in my thoughts wasn't the old man standing next to me on the porch, squeezing the fire out of my arm. It was the "You" high above me, the "You" all around me, the "You" who made the black sky and the blue, and every bird that flapped or fell from it. And the You was wanting an answer, one way or the other. "I need to know for sure," said Al.

"I ... I don't know for sure," I stammered.

"You *have* to *know*, Will!" Al exclaimed, tightening his hold on my arm. "Or I'll find someone else to write the book!"

He coughed violently, and a fleck of dark red saliva appeared at the corner of his mouth. Something in his vice-like grip told me it was all right to be certain.

"Okay!" I said suddenly. "I believe God held your plane up!"

It felt like an enormous confession to me – along the lines of Luther nailing his Disputation on the Power of Indulgences to the front door of his church – and, if I'm going to be honest, I expected Al to at least recognize my statement with a pat on the back, or a small genuflection. But he just looked at me with those insanely blue eyes of his, and said....

"You still don't get it, boy."

And he went inside and took a nap.

CHAPTER TWENTY

LIGHT

"I began by telling the president that there was a cancer growing on the presidency, and that if the cancer was not removed, the president himself would be killed by it."
John Dean

Several times during my research I suspected Ed Lopez had passed away. But each time I told others of my suspicions, they dismissed them with wholesale confidence, or, as it turns out, abject denial.

"There are tens of thousands of *Ed Lopez's* in this world," Wilhemenia Nash told me one day on the phone, when I relayed my doubts he was still alive. "Maybe we just need to keep looking until we find him. Besides, who are we to say Ed is gone when there's no evidence to prove it?"

"I understand, Wilhemenia," I replied, "But records show there were only *three* US airmen by that name in Southeast Asia during 1970. And two of those are buried in Arlington."

"That leaves one," said Wilhemenia.

Curse the woman's sense of math! "I've been unable to reach that one," I admitted. "Unfortunately, the Air Force has lost track of him, too."

For a moment, it was quiet on the other end of the phone, and I listened to my own heartbeat.

"Well," said Wilhemenia at last, "A man's not dead until his name's on the stone."

She had a very good point.

When firmer intel reached me that Adolfo "Ed" Lopez, Jr. had, in fact, passed away on Christmas day, 2012, I was strangely relieved, because I no longer had to suspend my belief. Perhaps the saddest part of this news was that my view of Ed Lopez had been limited largely to his inebriated excursions through the streets of Udorn, and his sporadic discharge of incendiaries across the Laotian landscape. Like a drunk uncle flicking Black Cats at a Fourth of July picnic, I saw the flare-man in this less-than-flattering light, and I was sorry I knew so little else of him.

"Surely there's something more you can tell me about Ed," I asked Al on my last visit to his house in Waukomis.

Al took a sip of water and thought for a moment. By now, his pneumonia had become a way of life for him, coming and going with the consistency of the mail. In her chair by the picture window, Pat had positioned herself for support. She was cooking stuffing in the oven, and I could smell its bewitching goodness from across the room.

"Ed was a quiet man," said Al. "Everybody liked him. He did his job. There's not much more to say than that."

"*Quiet's* not much to go on," I said, snarkily.

Al looked at me, and for the second time in our relationship his eyes conveyed reprimand. "The man had a speech impediment, son," said Al.

For a moment, I felt the smallness an enlisted man must feel in the presence of a general. Like a punch to my gut, I remembered Al telling me of Ed's speech problem way back in our early correspondences, but that bit of information had gotten buried long ago. How could I have missed it? Of *course*, the man was quiet. I'd be quiet, too, if I had lived with stuttering all my life. I might even get rip-roaring drunk occasionally to forget about it. Suddenly, I realized that a few meager months of research had made me a know-it-all, and my face turned bright red with the acknowledgment.

"Sorry, sir," I said.

"Stop calling me 'sir'," said Al."

"Yessir."

"Stop it! That's an order!"

"I need someone to try my stuffing," said Pat, jumping up from her chair and heading towards the oven. Somehow, she had sensed the "yessir game" had grown septic between us and, as always, she rushed to save the day for those she loved.

After dutifully sampling several of the dishes Pat was creating, Magnet Ass and I lapsed into thunderous silence again – each of us wondering what the other was thinking. It was not like Al to be sharp with his men, and it occurred to me I must have needed it more than I realized. How arrogant it was for a third-party observant, forty-seven years removed from the story, to act as if he knew a single thing about the men who actually lived it. The reason I didn't know Lopez was because I didn't *want* to know Lopez. I wanted a caricature of him to serve the purposes of my book, and the book was never mine in the first place. Lord knows I had tried for it not to be.

I looked at Al, and I saw he was looking back at me – his head cocked painfully from the devil-cow that had gotten him down.

"I'm sorry," I said.

"Me, too," said Al, and his smile told me I was still on his crew.

"Is there more I need to know about Ed?" I asked, timidly.

"Probably not," said Al. His eyes were blank, and he was tired of trying to recall things.

I was desperate for information. "Maybe something about the flares, or the responsibilities Lopez had as the 10?"

At that, Al's eyebrows raised, and his recollection seemed to be kicking into gear.

"Some people thought Stinger's illuminator was a waste of government dollars," he said. "And they may have been right. But war's a funny thing. Sometimes you have to be right in the middle of it, before you admit 'plan A' doesn't make sense."

"I have no idea what you're talking about, Al," I said, sick of acting as if I did.

"We never used the illuminator to hunt trucks," Al said, plainly.

"Never?" I said, shocked at the revelation.

Al shook his head. "Nope – not once. It had a white mode that would've gotten us shot out of the sky the first time we switched it on. The infrared filter wasn't much use either. The enemy could have followed its beam right back up to the plane.

"So ... it *was* a waste then," I said.

"That depends on your point of view," said Al.

He was dreaming with his eyes open again, scrolling back to a time when his body did whatever he commanded it to do. He shook his head slightly, and an amused look animated his face.

"I *do* recall one time when Ed used the white mode on his illuminator. We were coming back to Udorn from an early mission. We had killed six trucks, so it was a pretty good night all in all. Anyway ... Ed starts shouting through the interphone like a little kid, 'Can we do a spirit mission, boss?' And I immediately think to myself, that's a pretty good idea."

"A spirit mission was something the pilots did to celebrate an especially good night over the fence," said Pat, happier now that her men were talking.

"Like an NFL end zone dance," I inferred.

"Exactly," said Al. "We had just come back from the PDJ, and, like I said, we had killed six trucks, so we were feeling pretty good about ourselves. Just before final, I get the call from Lopez, and he's wondering if we can buzz the movies and give the fellas the business." Al looked at me inquisitively. "Are you old enough to remember drive-in theatres?"

"I remember them," I said.

"Well, we had something like that – except you sat in chairs instead of cars," said Al. "Sometimes the men who weren't scheduled for a mission that night would gather for a beer and a movie. It made for some of the gentler memories of the war."

I imagined the airmen relaxing in the warm, Thai evening – their shirts unbuttoned, their cold bottles of Beerlao sweating under the pre-monsoon moon.

"So, I get Ground Control on the line," said Al, "And I request a 'flyby', and they seem happy to comply."

"The flyby is like a salute," offered Pat.

Al chuckled. "Or, in this case, a bug in the bottom of a soda can. You're happy right up until the moment you discover it."

"Do you think they knew what you were up to?" I asked.

"Who?" asked Al. "GC?"

"Right."

"Oh, I'm sure of it," said Al. "We were all looking for ways to forget about the war whenever we could. Even the men at Control needed a break from time to time."

Pat shifted in her chair. "Tell the story," she said, impatiently.

Al leaned back in his chair, and for a moment he looked fifty years younger to me, free of cancer, his whole life stretching out in front of him. Every man becomes a boy again when he's at the rudder of a good tale.

"So, there we are," he said, "Royal Thai spread out beneath us like a blanket of lights. Right in the middle of that blanket is this huge patch of glowing blue – and I know the men are yucking it up down there. We always had good stuff to watch. Planet of The Apes ... The Great Escape ... we were usually a couple of years behind in the movies available on the base, but we made do with what we had. As it turns out, the guys were watching an old Steve McQueen movie, called *Bullitt*."

The phone on Pat's desk rang and she chose to ignore it....

Anyway," said Al, "I bring Stinger in low and slow, just like the fighter pilots – but much slower. The Phantoms were always doing spirit missions above the movies, showing off, standing on their burners and making so much ruckus, nobody could hear a word the actors were saying on the screen. If there was one thing I wanted this spirit mission to accomplish, it was to outdo the Phantoms."

"F-4s" muttered Pat, "You couldn't live with 'em, and you couldn't live without 'em."

"So, there's Lopez ..." said Al, "Sitting in the back of the plane with his finger on the switch, chomping at the bit to ruin the party for everybody down below. By that time, the men recognize exactly what's going to happen, but there's nothing they can do about it. Right when Stinger's over the movie theatre, Lopez flips the switch on the illuminator and ... BAM! I'm telling you, boy, the whole base lights up brighter than Einstein. And Steve McQueen disappears from the screen like a ghost."

At that, Pat clapped her hands, and I heard a little squeal emit from her throat.

"Ed must have kept his light on the men for at least a minute or two, before I flew away and circled back around for a landing," said Al, triumphantly. "Anyway, I'm sure our little stunt was unappreciated, but heck, when you kill six trucks, you gotta tell someone about it. If you ask me, it was the best spirit mission anyone ever pulled at Udorn. And we couldn't have done it without Ed Lopez. It was his idea."

Al looked out the window and smiled at the birds on his feeder. "I miss that Mexican," he added. Then he coughed, and the little boy retreated back into the frail body of its grown-up host.

"That's a good story, shug," said Pat. "I think Will should put it in his book," she decreed.

Most of the words written in Al's book grew out of sadness. By definition, war is "killing people and breaking things". There is nothing cheerful about it. Cancer is sad, too. I can still feel the hot presence of tears on my face, as I stood at my father's grave in 1991. His cancer was a different kind than Al's, but it had the same dismal trademarks. No doubt, there are people who will read this book who are dealing with their own sad circumstances.

The death of a career....
The suicide of a son or daughter....
The disintegration of a marriage....
The insane division of abnormal cells in one's body....

Sometimes the sad and the bad and the mad things in our lives catch us unaware, and we are unprepared for the missions into which they hurl us. We find ourselves in a tailspin. We cry out for help.

Mayday! Mayday! Mayday! But no one comes to our rescue. And we wonder – how did this happen to me? How did I not see this coming? How will I ever recover ... or be joyful again ... or get back home?

If Al showed me anything, it was that *all* flight needs to be celebrated. We can bitch and moan about the missions we find ourselves on, or we can accept them as they come to us and make the most of them. Other Captains might have refused to take on a man like Lopez. They might have argued his penchant for booze made him a menace to their crew, and an unstable candidate for launching burning shit out of a plane. But Magnet Ass had a way of seeing the best in his fellow man, and bringing it to light. In the end, he knew the strong need the weak almost as much as the weak need the strong.

Much later in the project, I found those old notes from Al about Ed Lopez's speech impediment, as well as a letter from Jim Russell that corroborated the details:

"*On truck hunting missions, Lopez's primary responsibility was to monitor AAA behind the aircraft and provide appropriate warnings, so that Al could bank left or right. Lopez had a speech impediment, but we could always tell how close the AAA was by the pitch of his voice.*"

When I asked Al about Jim's assessment, his face lit up with recall.

"I remember a time over Route 6 when we were getting hammered with 37's," said Al. "Like Russell told you in his letter, Lopez's job was to spot for artillery fire and to tell me how to get away from it. He was supposed to say, 'Triple A ... bank right, or bank left' ... and I would have time to react. It was a pretty good system, and it had worked well on a lot of missions. Anyway, on this particular night, Lopez is hanging out the starboard aft cargo door, spotting for tracers. All of a sudden, I hear him stuttering. 'Trip – trip – trip – *there she goes!*' Luckily, it didn't hit us, because I never had a chance to maneuver."

"What'd you tell him?" I asked.

"I told him he needed to be a little quicker next time," replied Al.

"That's it? That's all you said?"

"Well, sure."

"But ... couldn't Ed's stutter have gotten you all killed?" I pressed.

Al looked at me as if I had just stumbled over my own feet, and a great, white light from heaven was now illuminating the spot where I lay sprawled out on the ground.

"The fact we flew in a trash can every night could've gotten us killed," said Al.

He had a way of making the obvious indisputable.

Later that day, after Pat had listened to the phone message she ignored during the illuminator story, she called me aside in the kitchen and, with an ashen complexion, told me Mayo had found another spot on Al's pancreas.

To be completely honest, I don't know whether Lopez is dead or not. One source has him punching out on 12/25/12. Another source, (which literally came to me while I was writing this chapter), says he's still alive and kicking. So, I've finally decided how I'm going to chronicle the remaining days of Ed Lopez until told otherwise. Here it is in its entirety. Lord, forgive me if I've somehow got it wrong.

After the Vietnam War, Staff Sergeant Adolfo "Ed" Lopez, Jr., oldest member of the truck hunters, took his French wife, Marcelle, and their two boys, and headed back to Mexicali, Mexico, where he sold all his possessions, said 'goodbye' to his parents, and moved his family to La Jolla de Mismaloya, just south of the resort town, Puerto Vallarta. There, he acquired a fishing boat, a small battery-operated generator, and a 1.5 million candlepower illuminator that was smuggled out of Saigon by a chiseling, little war vet, and had been gathering dust on a barroom shelf since 1975.

The light and the generator cost Ed thirty pesos and a bottle of tequila. The boat was free, because it had a hole in its starboard side, just beneath the gunnels.

Ed is 81-years-old now. But he and his sons still fish every night, and sell their catch by day to a taco shack situated just south of the expensive resort that bears the town's name. Sometimes, by the light of the moon, Ed anchors offshore near the famous home where John Huston once filmed, "Night of The Iguana". He listens for the soft "*clink*" of the anchor on the rocks beneath his boat, then drags it leeward until it catches and holds. He starts the generator. He turns on the illuminator and aims it at the water. He opens three cold beers – one for himself, and one for each of his sons. And he waits for the fish to rise to the light.

If the moon is right, (and it always is), Ed Lopez will think back over the decades to another night, an ocean away and a lifetime ago. He will see Mother Moon, pale and pumpkin, scolding her boys for not wearing their parachutes. He will smell the searing shells as they sizzle past his vessel. *Dear God ... there was a lovely side to Nam*, he will think. And he will smile, because he knows no harm can befall him. Not as long as Magnet Ass is at the wheel, and Marcelle is back at home, waiting to make love to him in the morning.

And that's how I will think of Adolfo "Ed" Lopez, Jr. until his name is on the stone. If none of this is true, it should be. Besides....

It's how my father would have told the story.

CHAPTER TWENTY-ONE

THE DEVIL COW

"When I was sick and lay a-bed, I had two pillows at my head, And all my toys beside me lay, To keep me happy all the day. And sometimes for an hour or so, I watched my leaden soldiers go, With different uniforms and drills, Among the bedclothes, through the hills."
    Robert Louis Stevenson, (1850–1894)
    "The Land of Counterpane"

When I walked into Al's room at Greenbrier, he was propped against a rampart of pillows, his legs drawn up nearly to his chest, staring out the window at a junco that was pecking in the grass. Around his ghastly frame, the covers fell in creases, creating steppes, and valleys, and a broad battlefield of linen, reminding me of a poem I had read in a book as a child, but had long since tucked away in the back of my mind. I had never seen Al in a horizontal position, and it was so unnerving that I almost felt as if it were *I* who was lying prostrate in a bed, and *Al* bringing comfort to me.

"Hello, cub scout," said Magnet Ass.

"Hello," said I, pulling up a chair to his side. Al had never been in assisted-living before, but when he came down with pneumonia this time, it was worse than ever, and Pat wondered if she could still give him the care he needed. Deep down, she suspected she couldn't, but it was hard to give up the role to which she had become accustomed. For the last seven years, she had been Al's fellow warrior against cancer, his co-pilot, flying back and forth from Mayo, over hills and valleys and dark, dreary plains, as bleak as any found in Laos. So, when Al's doctor ordered him to Greenbrier Village for physical therapy, Pat suddenly felt a great sense of loss, and it was one of the saddest days of her marriage. As always, though, she dug down into her storehouse of resolve, convincing herself that Al would rebound one more time, for she knew he was a fighter. At Greenbrier, she spent the first thirty-six hours of Al's convalescence, praying by his side, spooning chicken soup to him, and politely giving orders to the long-suffering staff, until at last she had worn herself out and surrendered her vigil. As I stood there now, looking at her fallen pilot, Pat was back in Waukomis, propped up in her own bed, trying to recover. It was so strange seeing one apart from the other. AM without PM."

Al shivered, and I saw that one of his bare feet had wriggled out from under the blanket. I gave a little tug on the landscape, no doubt disrupting battalions of tin soldiers arrayed in rows and hidden in the flanks of Al's fast receding memory. But he seemed to appreciate it, because he flashed a smile in my direction.

"Here's a story for you," he said, as if he had been lying there thinking about it for hours, waiting for me to come and absorb it.

"You've done enough, Al," I said.

"I'll be the judge of that," he replied.

So, I sat down in the chair for one last tale. And this is how Magnet Ass told it.

By 1975, memories of the war had been wadded up, jammed into the duffel bag of national conscience, and no one gave a warm bucket of spit anymore about Vietnam. Thus, when the NVA roared over Saigon like an uncontained fire, the fall of the French-laced capital fizzled next to the blaze of our country's own pending birthday. We were, after all, almost two-hundred years old.

Proud. Strong. Safe among our own.

After his stint overseas, Al served quietly in various ways – as a pilot to a general, a flight instructor and examiner, an operational officer, and even as the TTS Squadron Commander at

Altus AFB, the favorite of all his jobs in the Air Force. His career took him and his family all over the country – from Oklahoma, to Georgia, to California, to Ohio, and back to Oklahoma again. In total, Al gave thirteen more years of service after Vietnam. But eventually, he traded his wings for a tractor and went back to farming, where he and Pat disappeared into the dust of the earth.

In the late winter of 2008 – on a morning where the mercury read, "*twenty-one*", but the thirty-mile-per-hour wind left one's face feeling like a piece of meat abandoned on the bottom shelf of hell's freezer and forgotten – Al and Pat went out to hunt for newborn calves, and to tag the ones born overnight. It was 7 o'clock in the morning, and the forty or so heifers waiting to be hauled to sale that afternoon huddled against the fencerow with their wide-eyed offspring.

"This'll be easy as pie," said Al to Pat, as they drove their pickup across the frost-bitten field. He had been tagging calves since he was a kid, and there was no reason to believe this time would be any different. Had he been listening to his 68-yr-old body, he might have heard something otherwise. "Brace yourself, old friend. This is really going to hurt."

Even the Loggerhead Shrikes sensed a disturbance in the morning's hush. Where the south-wandering barbed wire met the corner and meandered west, an adult male looked up from his breakfast as Al drove by. Beneath the bird's terrible, little talons, a Blanchard cricket frog – rock hard from a week of impalement – was slowly being pecked into oblivion. To his left, spread out like a sumptuous larder, two finches and a skink stared at the scene through frozen eyeballs, skewered on barbs of their own, drying under the lonely sky.

Al stopped the truck, got out, and stretched his legs. He was old now, and the war was rarely on his mind anymore. But something was different this morning ... something in the air maybe ... or the way the sunlight bounced off the barbed wire, reawakening a memory of perimeters around encampments far below Stinger's belly. Al coughed, and the Shrike abandoned his breakfast and flew away.

"Calf's over here," said Al, spotting the wobbly-legged creature on the other side of the pickup.

"Sweet, little '0815'," crooned Pat, as she opened her tag kit, removed a tag for this year's fifteenth spring calf, scribbled the four-digit number on one side with a black marker, and slipped its male and female ends onto the applicator. She shuddered at the wind whistling through the open window, and she handed the loaded applicator to Al. "Bless his sweet, little, frozen heart."

With numb fingers, Al took the tool from Pat and strode toward the calf. To his left, surveying the operation surreptitiously, was the calf's mother, a creature Pat would later describe as, "historically gentle". As Al drew closer, the cow's downcast eyes made him remember afternoons in the Udorn marketplace ... passing pretty Asian women on the sidewalks ... their glances never rising above his trouser cuffs ... their lips pressed thin to conceal all hints of approval or disapproval. But Al was certain they were looking at him then, just as he was certain the cow was looking at him now.

"Easy, girl," whispered Al to the calf's mother, her own two tags dangling in the wind, one bearing her identification number, the other bearing the name of the bull she came from, so as not to breed her back to her father.

"She wouldn't hurt a fly," whispered Pat, from her warmer vantage point in the truck. As he had done so many times before, Al approached the little Hereford, stroked his hand along the calf's neck, slipped the applicator over the upper edge of his ear, and punched the tag through the membrane.

The calf let out a cry.

Now, it is a shocking thing when the *unexpected* springs from the expected. This is the plane that crashes through the high-rise on a lazy Tuesday morning. Or the man who shoots the songwriter, then sits down at the crime scene to read a bit of *Catcher in the Rye*. Or the war that erupts in a honeymoon destination and lasts for two clotted decades. Thus, when the calf's mother lowered her head and charged Al, he did not see the maniacal rising from the maternal. She covered the ten yards that sepa-

rated man from beast in less than a second, tossing him four feet
in the air, and battering him against the truck.

"Shug!" cried Pat. The impact rocked the vehicle sideways.
For a moment Al's face and the cow's were framed together in
the window, close enough for Pat to note every detail of her husband's surprised grimace and the cow's bulging, brown eyes.
Then Al disappeared from Pat's view, and the cow retreated as
suddenly as she had attacked.

When Pat realized the animal wasn't going to charge again,
she scrambled out of the truck on the driver's side – because
the passenger door was so banged up – and she hurried to help
Al. "Heeyah!" she shouted, scattering the cow and her calf with
blinding fury. Away they ran with the herd. Bells ringing. Brown
rumps bumping along the barbed wire. Beneath the truck, Pat
found her husband, where he had rolled to avoid being stomped
to death. He was coiled in pain.

"I don't know what got into her," wheezed Al, holding his
ribs and inching his way out from under the truck. Just before
he cleared the running boards, he glanced back and spied the
applicator lying in the dirt, and was reaching for it when he felt
Pat's grip on his arm.

"Leave it!" she ordered, the thought of a dead, stomped pilot
on her hands more than she could bear. "Get in the truck, NOW!"
she added. "We're done for the day!"

"Now, Pat...," wheezed Al, "We've got forty heifers to haul to
sale this morning. If we don't stop fooling around, we're going to
miss our window." Al paused, as if considering his own foolishness, and he hoisted himself up to a sitting position, the frigid
touch of the quarter-panel no balm to his cow-beaten body. He felt
a piercing pain in his side, and he knew Pat was right. "Call John,
and have him meet us here at the field. He'll know what to do."

Neighbor John was five miles away, eating pancakes at his
home, when he received Pat's call. The panic in her voice sent
him out the door, wiping syrup from his mouth, collar up against
the cold. Ten minutes later, he was at the field helping Al into
the pickup. Against their wishes, Al drove himself to the emer-

gency room, twenty-one miles away – while Pat and John went to load heifers.

Later, Pat went to the hospital to visit her pilot. She wrote in her diary:

"He has broken ribs and cracked ones, too. Plus an injured area below his neck and shoulder blades. He is in a lot of pain."

In the late evening, daughter Diane took Pat to Enid to get the pickup, and she brought Al home to convalesce. Throughout Al's recovery, John and Pat took over the chores, feeding the cattle, tagging the babies, mending the fences, chopping the ice. They carried on this way for seven weeks, while Alan got better.

On March 2, 2008, Al woke unable to breathe, and with a searing sensation in his neck and shoulder. "It's like a hot cattle-iron," Al told the doctor at the ER in Enid. After a thorough examination, the doctor said the cow was to blame for Al's shortness of breath, and that it all should subside within a matter of days. The doctor was right about the shortness of breath – Al was breathing like a champ before the end of that week. But the pain in his neck and shoulder never did go away.

By January of '09, the pain was so great, Al went through surgery, and then excruciating weeks of physical therapy. Eventually, his mobility improved. But the pain still lurked, deep down in the hollows of his body ... like a dozen VC, all crammed into a single spider hole ... waiting to spring upon the unsuspecting and run them through with a bayonet. Waiting. Waiting. Week after week. Month after month.

Just waiting.

––––––––––––––––––––

In May of 2010, Al was diagnosed with cancer, and he and Pat sold every animal they owned, and neither of them ever tagged another calf or cow again. No doubt, some of their neighbors – those who held war in contempt, or harbored jealousy toward the farm-boy-turned-hero – maintained the devil cow had had the last word on Magnet Ass. But I refused to believe that. And I doubled my efforts to prove the cow was nothing but a four-legged anomaly, into which Al had stumbled accidently. But nothing more than that. She couldn't have been. I could not bear the thought of something so insignificant dealing such a blow to someone so towering in spirit. Al had survived Vietnam ... had his wing shot off a half-mile above the earth ... delivered nine men safely back home to their loved ones ... won a trophy with his name on it, now housed in the world's most prestigious museum. Al had to be bigger than the devil cow. He had to be!

But the truth was undeniable.

The stupid, stumbling, cud-chewing bag of leather had broken Magnet Ass with a single toss of her head. And that was the long and short of it.

In June, when my manuscript was nearly in the hands of my editor, I forced myself to engage again with the hundreds of bits of information I had accumulated during my long research, looking for a thread that might tie some of the loose ends together. In a cabinet, next to my writing chair where I had done ten months of servitude, mistakenly shoved way back into the shadowy recesses, I found two letters from Al's daughters, the only correspondence I ever received from Christine and Diane Milacek. They contained paragraph after paragraph of admiration for their parents, tales of hard work on the farm, family camping trips in a Volkswagen Beetle, humorous anecdotes about liver and Brussel sprouts – a meal Pat believed was "good for farmers" and should be served once a week. And though the letters were two distinct accounts, written by daughters as different in soul and temperament as their parents were from one another, one topic remained consistent in their writing. They spoke of faith in God as if it were a planeload of brave, young airmen – a flying citadel against unexpected evil everywhere. Perhaps, Christine Milacek's words were most dear to me:

"When hearing about my father's cancer, I was extremely upset. Something inside me was very calming, though. I knew with our family's deep faith in God, he would be okay."

These were the treasured words that had eluded me – and when I found them, I could finally see the truck hunters in their broader glory. We are all truck hunters of sorts, doing our best to interdict the thought-bastards that sneak into the country of our minds uninvited, traveling along the synapses undetected, setting up their reigns of terror unopposed. Yes ... somehow, Al and Pat's faith was *exactly* like this flying citadel, rooting out the cruel subversives with the precision of Aesculapius, sending them packing with a *heeyaw*!—as if they were a cow gone mad. It was an effective faith, every bit as effective as Stinger herself.

And they had given it to their children.

I looked at the clock above Al's bed, and its interminable ticking made my heart sink. With each tick, the race to finish Al's story before his body crashed and disintegrated seemed more futile than ever. The cow story had been a strange one to finish with, but I immediately sensed its importance, for it took me back to a quote I had heard in a college literature class and logged away. Something by Thucydides. Something sad. Something sweeping. What was it? Then it came to me. "Wars spring from unseen and generally insignificant causes, the first outbreak being often but an explosion of anger."

And so, I stood there with the father of scientific history at my side, staring down at the father of two little girls now grown and gone. Suddenly, I didn't want to be at Greenbrier. I looked at the door, then back at Al. I felt glued to the spot. My legs unwilling to move. I knew I would not be making a conventional exit. I felt myself rising up toward the ceiling. Up and up. Then through the roof. Out into the cold, damp air, with the juncos. Below me, I could still see the man in his bed. Simple. Paltry. Meaningless and less than meaningless. Tick. Tick. Tick. Tick. I reached out to him with little boy fingers – or perhaps I was reaching out to my own father. I'll try to come visit again, I thought. Maybe I said it out loud, I'm not sure. All I was certain of was that I still had thousands of words to write. And many more I wished I could say out loud to Al.

He was sleeping when I sailed away into the Oklahoma sky.

CHAPTER TWENTY-TWO

FLYING SOLO

"You feeling okay, pal?" I asked the next day, as Pat and I hovered over Al's bed at Greenbrier. It was the only time I called him anything but "sir" or "Al", and I'm glad I did it. I didn't want to drive away without him knowing I had crossed over the line between memoirist and friend.

Al grinned as he pondered my question. "If I was any better, I'd have to be twins," he said.

I had to think about that one for a moment, and while I was thinking, Pat produced a huge wedge of pie from her purse, wrapped in cellophane for my trip home. "I never knew Nixon's wife died of cancer," said Pat, handing me the pie. To pass the time, she and I had been talking about the startling parallels between Al's life and that of Richard Milhouse Nixon. Each man had been born in a little, white house his father built. Each loved a woman named, Pat ... produced two lovely daughters ... served his country faithfully ... and had a life deeply affected by cancer. But that's where the similarities ended.

"They say Patricia Nixon died ten months before Richard," I replied. "Some say her cancer broke his heart and put him in the grave. Did you know Nixon signed the National Cancer Act of 1971?"

"Well, I'll be," said Pat.

"You learn something every day," said Magnet Ass.

A thick silence settled between us, and I kicked at the gold, shag carpet that had outlived several fashion cycles at Green-brier Village.

Al snatched a rattling breath of air, and I could see the effects of his pneumonia still clinging to him. The death of his youngest brother had come as quite a shock to him, particularly since he was the baby in the family.

"He was only sixty-five," said Al, picking at a bit of fuzz on the blankets that were gathered around his ankles. "Never sick a day in his life ... never took a pill ... hard to figure ... hard to figure."

"How did it happen?" I asked, surprised at my willingness to wade into another person's pain, and with no treatment plan whatsoever.

"Heart attack," said Pat. "He was just fine ... and then he went upstairs to work on his computer, and he stayed there longer than normal. After a while, his wife got concerned and went up to check on him. She found him on the bed, curled up like a little child. He was already gone by then."

Aware that Al's brother, Carl, had also passed away, I waded further in. "So ... you're the last brother left," I said, looking at Al.

"Last man in my family," he replied.

"Will you try to make the funeral?" I asked.

Al hesitated. "I don't know about that," he said, glancing up at Pat.

Pat folded her arms. "Colorado's an awful long drive," she said.

"I could take him with me," I offered. "I promise to bring him back."

Magnet Ass looked at Pat, his eyes wide with eagerness, like a pilot who hasn't soloed in years. I could tell she wanted to say 'yes' to my preposterous idea. But she knew the road trip's luster would fade by Goodland, and I'd be left with an old man on my hands. "I'm sorry," she apologized. "It's just that Alan's so weak, and—"

"It's okay, Pat," said Al. "We don't have to explain things to Will. I've got no business flying off half-cocked to Colorado. My life's here with you. Besides, we have a whole apple pie to tackle – minus a chunk for the Cub Scout," he added, looking at me with vibrant scorn for taking such a big piece.

We chatted for a while longer, and then Pat disappeared from the room for a moment to speak with the ladies at the nurse's station about his medicine, leaving the Cub Scout and the Colonel alone together. It was the only extended time in our relationship where no words were spoken, but it wasn't awkward. It was more like a rest on a sheet of music, where neither of us played anything. His eyes were blue and inviting, and when Magnet Ass took hold of my hand, I believe a bit of galvanized matter left his fingertips and traveled up my arm, lodging in that place we call, "heart", but, in reality, is more like a "generator". I could have sat there for centuries, plugged into the finest life I ever witnessed, but eventually Pat returned, saying it was time for her to put Al's drops in. So, we hugged, and I walked out of Greenbrier and got in my Buick, and headed off on Wood Road....

... *chunkety-chunkety-chunkety-chunk.*

Where 412 intersects with I-35 and heads north through the Flint Hills, I pulled my car over on the side of the road, and turned off the engine. It was dusk and I stared at the eastern sky.

I've always thought it funny how much is going on right behind a person's back, while he is ooo-ing and awww-ing over a sunset. Who's to say Haley's Comet hasn't shot across the *eastern* sky a thousand times in our lives, and each time we happened to be looking west? We are a people enamored with endings. The *end* of the day ... the *end* of the movie ... the *end* zone dance, which is often more glorified than the touchdown. Preachers preach about t*he end*. Motivational speakers tell us to *begin with the end in mind*. A writer becomes so target-fixated on the *end* of his story, he forgets to enjoy the characters in it. Sometimes, like a complete idiot, that writer loses all sense of decency, and he asks a question like, "Are you afraid your husband's going to die?" And then the lovely angel to whom he has posed the idiotic question is forced to think about the stuff that hasn't happened yet, rather than being allowed to live in the now.

What a fool I was. What a fool I *am*.

As I sat there, refusing to look west in my rearview mirror, it occurred to me another monumental ending had come to pass just a month before Magnet Ass got his wing shot off. It was April of 1970 when Paul McCartney left the Beatles, ending their reign over the music of the Sixties. Somehow the world had continued to turn without them. And Cofer had continued singing in the choir, until at last, he sang his final note and flew off into the wild blue. There is power in songs. Life in the tears they coax from our breasts. More loveliness than we know what to do with.

"You can't die, Al," I whispered. "It's not a book yet ... it's not a book!"

And then my own tears came like a great sea tide. Fat, and falling, and full of salt. Tears for the soldiers and their moms. Tears for the little boys whose dads never saw them do great things. Tears I wished had fallen at Bill Cunningham's grave. Tears that never were and never will be.

"Don't die, Al!" I cried.

But I knew he would.

We all do.

In the east, where the blue sky of the day was merging into the black sky of the morrow, there was a thin line of light remaining. I found if I squinted through the saltwater at that line, I could make out all the colors of the rainbow. There was gold near the bottom of the line, buoying up the lesser colors. Above it, coral and melon, magenta, sienna, burnt umber, and iron. Narrower and narrower the line of light grew, until at last, it faded into the color of a crow's wing, and night fell over Waukomis.

It's a crushing task living on Planet Earth, suspended between nothingness and eternity. We make things harder on ourselves by wanting what we don't have, and hating what is ours in abundance. We scratch and claw for safety and significance. We worry about the stuff that hasn't happened yet. We imagine that between the black sky and the blue, a moment exists wherein if a man could fly eastward fast enough, the sun would hang perpetually on the horizon, never sinking – so we fly like crazy to make the sun stay put. And we never stop to think that a never-sinking sun will also never rise.

After blubbering there in the blackness for a while, something happened in my chest. Something free and lifting. Something like a bird must feel when its blood quills finally mature, and it knows it's ready to fly. I dried my tears and started the ignition. The engine purred to life, and I smiled at the sound of its power. The yoke felt comfortable in my hands, almost second nature. As if I had been doing it all my life, I looked at my instruments and began to go through my run-up checklist.

Parking brake on. Check.
Wing flaps set for takeoff. Check.
Flight controls operable. Check.
Trim tabs good to go. Check.
Altimeter ... heading indicator ... fuel selector....
Check. Check.
Check.

With a great thumping in my thorax, I put my vessel in drive and slowly inched onto the tarmac. Ahead was the onramp. Pulling up on the right aileron, I rolled into the clover leaf that led to I-35 and I set my flight path north, with the prevailing wind at my back and full blowers burning red as Mars. It would be a beautiful night over the Flint Hills, and my only regret was that I hadn't kidnapped Magnet Ass when Pat stepped out to the nurse's station. In a way, though, he was with me. I could see him clear as day in the right-hand seat, his neck young and fluid again, his gaze hard-fixed on me. To hell with the devil cow!

"It's a pity more people don't fly," I heard him say, as he rolled down his window.

I looked through the windshield and up into the sky, and seeing it was a mixture of its usual black and blue, I replied, "People are just afraid." Then I paused, painfully aware he was still staring at me, and shocked that the confession I was about to make had taken root in my soul without my consent.

"I was afraid, too, until I met you, sir," I said. But if Magnet Ass heard me, he didn't show it. He was leaning back against the cool seat leather, his wisp of hair flapping crazily in the wind like an Ace's scarf, his mind already far out over the Flint Hills, his trust in God successfully cranked into the chamber of another airman.

"Stop sirrin' me," he whispered. And then with a faint smile, he added, "We're bingo, boy. Let's go home."

EPILOGUE

One bitter night in February – while visiting my mom in hospice – I drove out to our farm in Piedmont, with a piece of chalk and a will to make things right. At the entrance to the Mathewson Cemetery, I discovered the caretaker had placed a padlock on the gate, and for a moment, it looked as if my mission might be aborted. Undeterred, I parked my car on the red shoulder of Richland Road, and I hopped the fence. The night was cold and coagulated. Beneath my feet, the last stand of winter Bermuda crunched noisily, as I hurried to the center of the cemetery, where a single Native Cedar stood watch over my father's grave, alone against the punishing wind. With quivering fingers, I removed the piece of chalk from my pocket, and knelt down next to the stone. Because of a generous moon, the three-word epitaph was easy to decipher.

"He was kind," it read, exactly as I had prescribed it to my mother, so many years ago. I had always felt proud of those words – that is, until I realized what isn't said about the dead is often more important than what is. Meeting Al had helped me see more clearly now. My father wasn't inaccessible. And he wasn't a coward either. From the moment he announced his cancer on Christmas morning of 1990, to the afternoon he passed away in his own bed, Dad never complained once – not even when the rust-colored spit came up with every cough, stealing his dignity, and startling him each time as if it was the first.

I gazed at the words on the stone and stretched my hand in their direction, timidly.

"Those boys on the TV are going to be okay," the stone seemed to be whispering to me. "It's you I'm concerned about, though. How you doing, son?"

"Not great, Dad. I could use a job."

The sound of my own voice brought me back to reality. With resolve, I drew the chalk raspingly across the third word in the epitaph, and I wiped my tears with the back of my hand. Then, as if each letter was an act of defiance, I wrote the one word I had never used to describe my father – or, for that matter, myself – in a blank space, at the bottom of the stone. When I was done writing, I stood up and threw the piece of chalk as far as I could outside the perimeter of Mathewson Cemetery. Then I walked to the fence, hopped it again, and drove away.

Somewhere in the night, a 500-year rain washed over the state of Oklahoma, leaving prehistoric puddles from Altus to Alva, postponing high school baseball practices with diluvial efficiency, erasing my nocturnal vandalism. And though the words on Dad's gravestone once again read as they were meant to read – the things that weren't said of him are true of me today.

"He was B-R-A-V-E."

And so, on February 23rd, 2017, at 6:55 AM, Colonel Al Milacek died of esophageal cancer. On the day of his funeral, the schools in Waukomis were closed in his honor, and a couple of young pilots arranged for a fly-over at the precise moment we were saying goodbye to his body at another cemetery, an hour north of my father's. His story was not a book yet. But I suppose it was for the best. Sometimes the most significant tales are the ones that are never completely told.

Or understood.

96313318R00169

Made in the USA
Lexington, KY
19 August 2018